Unreal Engine Game Development Blueprints

Discover all the secrets of Unreal Engine and create seven fully functional games with the help of step-by-step instructions

Nicola Valcasara

PUBLISHING

BIRMINGHAM - MUMBAI

Unreal Engine Game Development Blueprints

First published: December 2015

Production reference: 1181215

Published by Packt Publishing Ltd.
Livery Place
35 Livery Street
Birmingham B3 2PB, UK.

ISBN 978-1-78439-777-7

www.packtpub.com

Credits

Author
Nicola Valcasara

Reviewer
Martin Pernica

Commissioning Editor
Edward Bowkett

Acquisition Editor
Shaon Basu

Content Development Editor
Adrian Raposo

Technical Editor
Suwarna Patil

Copy Editor
Vibha Shukla

Project Coordinator
Sanchita Mandal

Proofreader
Safis Editing

Indexer
Mariammal Chettiyar

Graphics
Disha Haria

Production Coordinator
Arvindkumar Gupta

Cover Work
Arvindkumar Gupta

About the Author

Nicola Valcasara is a freelance game developer and cofounder of Deuxality Games Ltd. He is an expert programmer, specializing in mobile development, with a strong passion for games and technology. He started to work in the game industry in 2012, after winning the first prize at the Microsoft Rapid2D competition for young developers.

He has also been a reviewer of *Unreal Engine Android Game Development*, *Packt Publishing*.

My first thanks goes to my friends. Darroch, for your omnipresent optimism and for the great artist that you are, Pelo, for being my tester and a valid reviewer of the book content, Mene, for your bike and genuine friendship, and thank you all to be always there to support me with my choices.

A thank you to my family, a safe haven where I find peace in the bad periods of my life. Thank you, mum, even if you don't approve my career, you are always in my life with your reassuring presence.

About the Reviewer

Martin Pernica is a game developer with a focus on rendering and physics. He started programming on old PCs very young age, and after this, he started working mainly as a web developer for companies. After some years of web development, Martin switched to the game development industry and started his own game studio. He is also teaching his own courses in the local university about mobile, web, and game development. He always tries to look under the hood of problems and challenges, and then solve and optimize them, which is his passion.

www.PacktPub.com

Support files, eBooks, discount offers, and more

For support files and downloads related to your book, please visit www.PacktPub.com.

Did you know that Packt offers eBook versions of every book published, with PDF and ePub files available? You can upgrade to the eBook version at www.PacktPub.com and as a print book customer, you are entitled to a discount on the eBook copy. Get in touch with us at service@packtpub.com for more details.

At www.PacktPub.com, you can also read a collection of free technical articles, sign up for a range of free newsletters and receive exclusive discounts and offers on Packt books and eBooks.

https://www2.packtpub.com/books/subscription/packtlib

Do you need instant solutions to your IT questions? PacktLib is Packt's online digital book library. Here, you can search, access, and read Packt's entire library of books.

Why subscribe?
- Fully searchable across every book published by Packt
- Copy and paste, print, and bookmark content
- On demand and accessible via a web browser

Free access for Packt account holders

If you have an account with Packt at www.PacktPub.com, you can use this to access PacktLib today and view 9 entirely free books. Simply use your login credentials for immediate access.

Table of Contents

Preface

This book will help you learn how to develop wonderful games using Unreal Engine 4 and its Blueprint Visual Scripting.

Discover all the secrets of this engine and create seven fully functional games with step-by-step instructions. In this book, you will learn the secrets of Blueprint; from the single node to the most complex function. Whether you are a beginner or an expert programmer, this guide will introduce you to this world and show you the infinite possibilities that this engine can offer by developing seven exciting and fully functional games.

What this book covers

Chapter 1, *Getting Started with Unreal Blueprints*, introduces you to the Unreal Engine editor and Blueprint graph. We will create the first project on both Unreal Engine and Visual Studio 2013.

Chapter 2, *Tic-Tac-Toe*, covers a simple game: a player versus player, classic board game. You will learn how to the create a Blueprint graph with nodes and wires.

Chapter 3, *C++ Code – PAC-MAN*, explains the creation of a classic coin-up game only using the C++ code. You will learn how to communicate between Visual Studio and UE4 in this chapter.

Chapter 4, *UFO Run - Play with the Environment Effects*, explains the particle effect system and user interface tools by creating an action game, starting from a template offered by the engine.

Chapter 5, *Top-Down Shooter*, helps you to play with animations and create an artificial intelligence by customizing the assets that are offered by the marketplace.

Chapter 6, *A Platform Maze*, explains how to use Matinee to create short cinematic clips or move objects around a level. Use the physics to handle ragdolls and destructible objects.

Chapter 7, *An Open World Survival Game*, creates huge worlds with the terrain manipulation tools that are offered by the engine, populate them with object using the brush tools, and give them a life by creating an inventory system using the knowledge learned during the book.

What you need for this book

You will require the following software:

- Unreal Engine 4 (at least version 4.8)
- Visual Studio 2013

A knowledge of basic C++ is recommended; however, not required. Some generic knowledge of the game programming terminology could be useful; however, not necessary.

Who this book is for

This book is ideal for intermediate-level developers who know how to use Unreal Engine and want to go through a series of projects that will further develop their expertise. A working knowledge of C++ is a must.

Conventions

In this book, you will find a number of text styles that distinguish between different kinds of information. Here are some examples of these styles and an explanation of their meaning.

Code words in text, database table names, folder names, filenames, file extensions, pathnames, dummy URLs, user input, and Twitter handles are shown as follows: "We can include other contexts through the use of the `include` directive".

A block of code is set as follows:

```
#pragma once

#include "GameFramework/Actor.h"
#include "Collectable.generated.h"

UCLASS()
class PACMAN_API ACollectable : public AActor
{
  GENERATED_BODY()

public:
  // Sets default values for this actor's properties
  ACollectable();

  // Called when the game starts or when spawned
  virtual void BeginPlay() override;

  // Called every frame
  virtual void Tick( float DeltaSeconds ) override;
};
```

New terms and **important words** are shown in bold. Words that you see on the screen, for example, in menus or dialog boxes, appear in the text like this: "Click on the **Blueprints** button in the **Level Editor** toolbar."

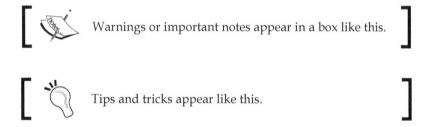

> Warnings or important notes appear in a box like this.

> Tips and tricks appear like this.

Reader feedback

Feedback from our readers is always welcome. Let us know what you think about this book—what you liked or disliked. Reader feedback is important for us as it helps us develop titles that you will really get the most out of.

To send us general feedback, simply e-mail feedback@packtpub.com, and mention the book's title in the subject of your message.

If there is a topic that you have expertise in and you are interested in either writing or contributing to a book, see our author guide at www.packtpub.com/authors.

Customer support

Now that you are the proud owner of a Packt book, we have a number of things to help you to get the most from your purchase.

Downloading the example code

You can download the example code files from your account at http://www.packtpub.com for all the Packt Publishing books you have purchased. If you purchased this book elsewhere, you can visit http://www.packtpub.com/support and register to have the files e-mailed directly to you.

Downloading the color images of this book

We also provide you with a PDF file that has color images of the screenshots/diagrams used in this book. The color images will help you better understand the changes in the output. You can download this file from https://www.packtpub.com/sites/default/files/downloads/7777OT_ColoredImages.pdf.

Errata

Although we have taken every care to ensure the accuracy of our content, mistakes do happen. If you find a mistake in one of our books—maybe a mistake in the text or the code—we would be grateful if you could report this to us. By doing so, you can save other readers from frustration and help us improve subsequent versions of this book. If you find any errata, please report them by visiting http://www.packtpub.com/submit-errata, selecting your book, clicking on the **Errata Submission Form** link, and entering the details of your errata. Once your errata are verified, your submission will be accepted and the errata will be uploaded to our website or added to any list of existing errata under the Errata section of that title.

To view the previously submitted errata, go to https://www.packtpub.com/books/content/support and enter the name of the book in the search field. The required information will appear under the **Errata** section.

Piracy

Piracy of copyrighted material on the Internet is an ongoing problem across all media. At Packt, we take the protection of our copyright and licenses very seriously. If you come across any illegal copies of our works in any form on the Internet, please provide us with the location address or website name immediately so that we can pursue a remedy.

Please contact us at `copyright@packtpub.com` with a link to the suspected pirated material.

We appreciate your help in protecting our authors and our ability to bring you valuable content.

Questions

If you have a problem with any aspect of this book, you can contact us at `questions@packtpub.com`, and we will do our best to address the problem.

1
Getting Started with Unreal Blueprints

Welcome! If you have arrived here, it is because you want to look at Blueprints in depth and learn all its secrets, from the simplest node to the most complex code extension. This is an introductory chapter. Here, you will take your first steps in Blueprint, you will create your first project, and start with the editor, learning its interfaces and its tools.

In this chapter, we will cover the following:

- What is Blueprint?
- Different types of data, nodes and Blueprint
- Knowing the environment
- Debugging your Blueprints
- Creating a visual studio solution

What is Blueprint?

Blueprint is a high level, visual scripting system that provides an intuitive, node-based interface that can be used to create any type of script events in the Unreal editor. The tools that are provided can be used by level designers, artists, and any non-programmer person, to quickly create and iterate gameplay (or even create entire games) without ever needing to write a line of the code:

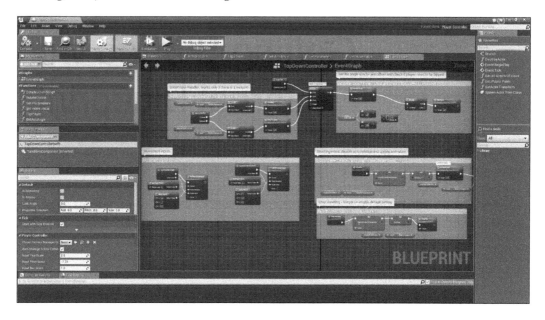

For those of you coming from UE3, Blueprint is the evolution of **Kismet**. It inherits most of the strong keys of the Kismet system, adding the full range of concepts and tools that are generally only available to programmers.

Through the use of Blueprints, anyone can virtually prototype, implement, or modify any gameplay element. Here, we are going to discover how to create most of them. The following is a list of common uses that are covered by this guide:

- **Games**: Sets up game rules and tweaks gameplay conditions
- **Players**: Creates variants with different meshes and materials, or allows character customization
- **Cameras**: Changes the camera dynamically during play
- **Inputs**: Handles the inputs that are passed by the player
- **Items**: Includes weapons, pickups, triggers, and so on
- **Environment**: Creates randomized props or procedurally generated items

In order to understand Blueprint, we first need to understand its structure. The following image is an extremely simplistic graph that shows where Blueprint is collocated in a game and who are its parent and child:

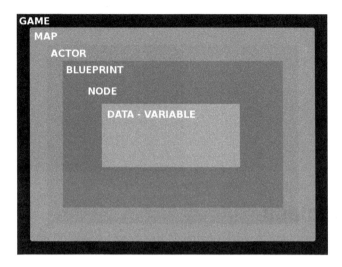

Each of these elements can have multiple children and each element has its different type and behavior.

Types of Blueprints

There are four main types of Blueprint, each one has a specific purpose and is useful in a specific situation. We will learn how to choose the correct one while studying the examples of this guide; however, in the meantime, let's take a look at them in order to understand their differences.

Level Blueprints

A Level Blueprint is a specialized type of Blueprint that, as the name suggests, acts as a level-wide event graph. A level Blueprint is created by default for each of your levels and can be edited only in the **Level Blueprint** Editor. This is the only type that cannot be created and there is only one Level Blueprint for each level.

In this Blueprint file we handle the level flow: we can control events, **Matinee**, and sequences of actions in the form of **Function Calls** or **Flow Control operations**.

To open the Level Blueprint for the purpose of editing, click on the **Blueprints** button in the **Level Editor** toolbar and select **Open Level Blueprint**, as follows:

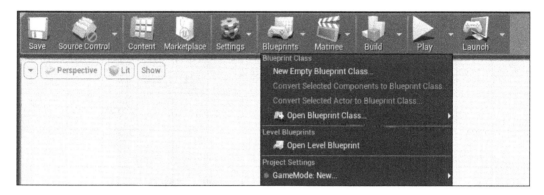

Blueprint class

A Blueprint class, simply called Blueprint, is the most used type and you will become familiar with it during this guide. This type allows the content creator to easily add functionality on top of any existing gameplay classes. A Blueprint class extends a parent (either a code parent or another Blueprint class) and can be edited with a visual editor. Any Blueprint class that is created in the editor can be found in **Content Browser** and can be added to the map as an instance, like any other type of **Actor**.

The following are the most common **Parent Classes** that are used when creating a new Blueprint:

- **Actor**: It is an object that can be placed or spawned in the world
- **Pawn**: It is an Actor that can be *possessed* and it receives input from a Controller (which can be a user or an Artificial Intelligence)
- **Character**: It is a Pawn that includes the ability to walk, run, jump, and so on
- **PlayerController**: It is an Actor that is responsible for controlling a Pawn
- **Game Mode**: It defines the game rules, scores, and any aspect of a game type

Data-Only Blueprint

Data-only Blueprints are basically Blueprint classes without the node graph. They contain all the properties and components that are inherited from its parent and allow the user to tweak properties or set items with variations without needing to find these properties in a big node graph.

A data-only Blueprint doesn't allow you to add new elements; however, it can be converted in a Blueprint class with just one click, if required:

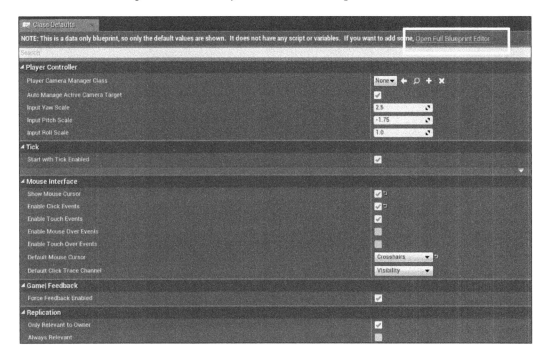

Blueprint Interface

A Blueprint Interface is similar to an interface in general programming. It allows different types of object to share a common information setup. It is a collection of one or more functions (declarations only, no implementations) that can be added to other Blueprints. A Blueprint Interface needs to be added to a Blueprint class in order to work, and a Blueprint class that has implemented an interface can have and use all of its functions.

A Blueprint Interface can be made in the editor; however, it has limitations as it cannot do the following:

- Add new variables
- Edit graphs
- Add components

A good example to understand an interface is that a player, a tree, and a concrete wall are three completely different objects but all of them can receive a projectile shot by a weapon. Instead of creating a different function for all of them, an interface can help us by creating a function called `onReceiveDamage` that is shared (however, implemented differently) by all of them.

Blueprint Macro Library

A Blueprint Macro Library is a container that holds a collection of Macros or graphs that can be placed as nodes in other Blueprints. They are very handy as they can store the commonly used sequences of nodes with inputs and outputs for execution and data transfer.

Knowing the environment

Let's take a look at **Unreal Engine 4** and its editor. I am assuming that you have already installed the engine and visual studio 2013 on your machine; therefore, I will skip the process of registering, downloading, and installing the engine. If this is not the case, you can go to the epic website (`www.unrealengine.com`), sign up for free and get your copy by following their instructions with a couple of easy steps.

Creating a project

Open the Unreal Engine Launcher. Under the **Library** section, choose the version of the engine that you prefer, and launch it, as follows:

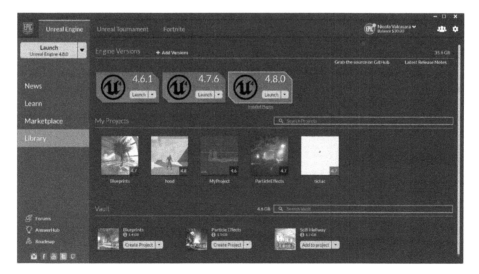

The **Unreal Project** browser will open. By default, you will see the **Projects** screen. Here, you can see your projects and the samples that you downloaded from the **Marketplace**. For our purpose, we want to create a brand new and empty project. Under the **New Project** section, you can choose between the **Blueprint** or **C++** projects in a list of built-in templates:

Due to the nature of Blueprint, the code and Blueprint live happily together. These choices are different in only one way: the C++ project will also create the visual studio solution for your project but each of those choices will generate the same Uproject and the needed files to launch the editor.

Due to this harmony between Blueprint and code, if you choose to create a project from the **Blueprint** section you can, at any time, generate its **C++** project: the engine will create the Visual Studio solution as soon as you add your first code class from the editor (**File | Add Code to Project**).

Choose a **Blank** Blueprint project, name it and choose a **location** (the default is `C://Users/Your Name/Documents/Unreal Projects/`). Before creating the project you can also set three main aspects of it: the general graphic quality, the device target (mobile, pc, console), and if you want to you can include the Unreal Engine **Starter Content** in it (the **Starter Content** contains some useful general purpose assets such as primitive meshes, particle effects, materials, and so on).

For our purpose, we can leave those settings as is and click **Create Project**.

Creating your first Blueprint class

Welcome to the Unreal Engine 4 editor. You will now see the example map opened and ready for your input in front of you. We are not creating anything fancy right now: we will only explore the user interface of Blueprint and start to learn the basic commands and shortcuts in Blueprint.

There are two ways to create a Blueprint class: from **Content Browser** or from the top tool bar. The toolbar Blueprint button gives you quick access to the existing modifiable Blueprint classes and you can access to the Level Blueprint only from here. Be aware that from here you can only create the Blueprint class. If you want to create, for example, **Blueprint Macro Library**, you need to use the **Add New** button from the **Content Browser**:

The **Add New** button and its equivalent mouse command (right-click in the **Content Browser)**, will open a pop-up menu with all the assets that you can create in the engine, as follows:

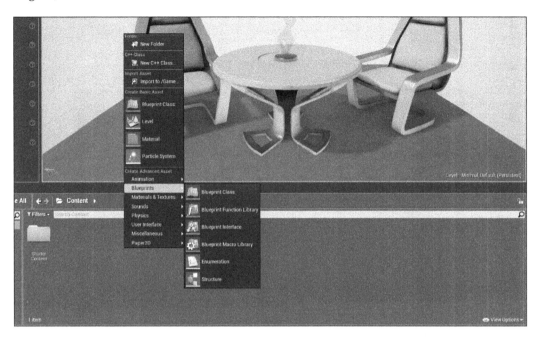

Most of the asset needed for you projects can be created in the editor. We are now focusing on Blueprint; however, it is worth specifying what we can create from this menu and what needs to be created with an external software:

Can be created in Unreal Editor:	Needs to be created using an external software:
Game Levels	Static Meshes
Materials	Skeletal Meshes
Particle Systems	Skeletal Animations
Cinematic Sequences	Textures
Blueprint Scripts	Sounds (WAVs)
AI Navigation Meshes	IES Light Profiles
Pre-calculated Light Maps	Nvidia APEX files (APB and APX)
Level Lights	

During studying the examples written in this book, we will see some of them, such as particle systems, navigation meshes, and materials, and some external assets, such as meshes and textures.

About the Static Meshes, it is possible to create them in the editor using the **Binary Space Partitioning** (BSP) brushes; however, it is a tedious process and worth only when talking about simple shapes such as walls or stairs. A dedicated software such as the freeware **Blender** or the more famous **3ds Max** or **Maya** can surely do a better job in less time.

Navigate to **Add New | Blueprints | Blueprint Class**, as follows:

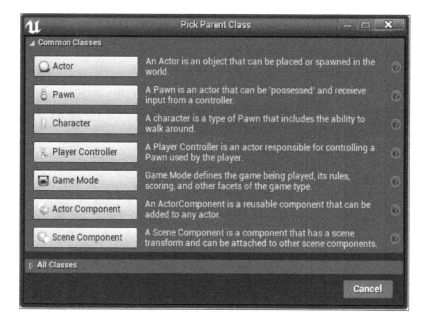

Here, we will choose the **Parent Class** of our Blueprint script. The editor shows us the **Common Classes** (we already saw them when previously talking about Blueprint classes); however, the list of parents that we can use is potentially unlimited. If you click on **All Classes**, in the left-hand side corner at the bottom, you can see a very long list containing all the objects that are available at that moment as a parent for your Blueprint.

Click on **Actor** and call it **BP_Introduction**.

 It is very important, even for a small project, to name your assets/scripts in a smart manner from the very beginning using a suffix in order to recognize and immediately find the required file even between hundreds of files.

Double-click on the **BP_Introduction** file to open it and we will finally arrive at our Blueprint Editor:

As you can see from the preceding image, the Blueprint Editor is divided into several panels. Each panel is independent; this means that they can be moved, resized, deleted, and duplicated in order to have a workspace that fits your choice.

Let's take a closer look at all of these sections in the following:

Menu bar

Menu Bar has the following options:

- **File**: You can manage your Blueprint files from here. You can save and import other assets in the session, and manage source control. There is also a section dedicated to Blueprint, where you can compile, refresh, and compare your Blueprint revision in source control.

- **Edit**: This is a typical edit menu. It can undo, redo, and modify history. You can also search for something in your Blueprint or change the editor settings and preferences.

- **Asset**: Go here to open **Content Browser** or to check the references viewer of any of your assets.

- **View**: View preferences can be set by this menu. Change the pin visibility or set the zoom.

- **Debug**: Here, you can set the brake points and the watches for your Blueprint. We will go through the Blueprint debugging later in this chapter.

- **Window**: If you accidentally close one of these tabs or you want to open another tab, you can do this going in this menu. All the Blueprint Editor specific tabs are contained. It is also possible to save or load a custom layout here.

- **Help**: You can find useful information about Blueprint here or directly through the epic forum and Wiki.

Toolbar

The toolbar is displayed at the left-hand side top of the Blueprint Editor. Its buttons provide easy access to the common commands that are needed when editing Blueprints. This is a dynamic bar, which means that it provides different buttons, depending on which mode is active and which Blueprint type you are currently editing, as follows:

- **Compile**: Every time you modify the script and want to run it, you need to compile. This button changes, depending on the state of your script. It shows if there is an error or a warning and if the script need to be recompiled.

- **Save**: It saves the current Blueprint.

- **Find in CB**: It shows **Content Brower** and highlights the selected Blueprint.

- **Search**: It finds references to functions, events, variables, or pins in the current script.

- **Class Settings**: It opens the Blueprint properties **Details** panel. These settings usually belong to the parent class of Blueprint. You can add Blueprint Interfaces to the Blueprint class here.

- **Class Defaults**: It shows the default properties in the detail panel. Here, you can change the default properties of the new instances of this class.

- **Simulation**: It starts the game in simulation mode.

- **Play / Stop / Pause**: It manages the execution of the game in the selected environment such as mobile, standalone, and custom viewport.

- **Possess/Eject**: It switches from **Simulate** in editor to play in editor mode.

- **Debug Filter**: If you have two or more instances of this class in the game, you can choose which one to debug here.

Viewport

In **Viewport**, you can view and manipulate your Blueprint's components:

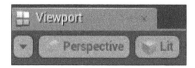

By default, you have a three-dimensional perspective view of your object. You can manipulate the settings of the Viewport using the buttons on the top-left corner. The first button allows you to switch between **Perspective** and the **orthographic** view, the second one sets how you see the object if it is **Lit** (rendered with light), **Unlit** (rendered without light) or in simple **Wireframe** instead.

The right-hand top series of buttons gives you some useful tools in order to manipulate your object:

- **Select and translate / rotate / scale object**: If one of these is selected, the corresponding three axis images appear on the pivot point of the object and you are allowed to move, rotate, or scale the object in one or all its axis.
- **Toggle Coordinate System**: This button toggles the coordinate system between world and the local (object-related) system.
- **Surface snapping**: This button toggles surface snapping, it enables an object to snap in a surface when possible.
- **Snap to the grid**: This button toggles whenever the object snap to the grid or not.
- **Snap size**: This button sets the accuracy of the snapping.
- **Rotation snapping**: This button toggles the snap through a rotation grid.
- **Rotation size**: This button sets the rotation-snap angle.
- **Scale snapping**: This button toggles snapping object through a scale grid.
- **Scale size**: This button sets the scale snap value.
- **Camera Speed**: This button sets the speed of the camera when it is moving in the viewport with values between 1 to 8.

Component panel

In the **Components** panel, you can find all the components of your Blueprint that are shown in a hierarchy form. A component is a piece of functionality that can be added to an Actor. Components cannot exist by themselves; however, when added to an Actor, the Actor will have access to the component and use the functionality provided by it:

In this panel, you can add/remove and manage your components. Each component has its own specific purpose and combining them allows you to create almost anything that you need.

CapsuleComponent, for example, provides collision geometry to the Actor. **MovementComponent** controls the movement, **AudioComponent** enables the Actor to emit sound, and so on.

Components added in the component list can also be assigned to instance variables, providing them access in the graphs editor.

In order to add a component to Blueprint, you can click on the **Add Component** button and select the component from its menu, as shown in the following image:

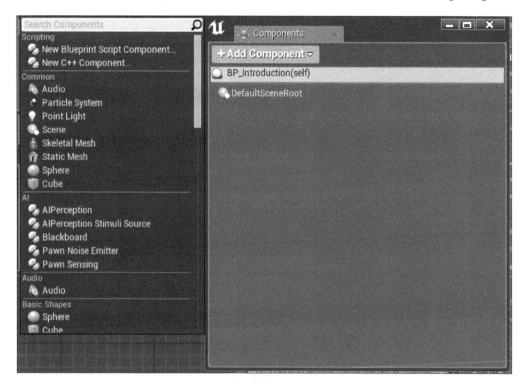

Components can also be added by dragging and dropping them from **Content Browser** in the **Components** panel.

Each component is placed at the location of the instance by default. However, they can be transformed, rotated, and scaled if necessary in either the **Details** panel or the Viewport, as we saw earlier.

Detail panel

The **Details** panel contains information, utilities, and functions that are specific to the current selection in the Viewport or the content panel.

It contains all the editable properties of the selected object (such as the **Transform** parameters to move, rotate, and scale it):

At the very top, you find the search filter. This allows you to quickly find the property that you need (very handy when you have a long list of properties).

The **Property Matrix** button will open the **Property Matrix** grid. It is a special tool that allows easy bulk editing and value comparison for a large number of objects or Actors. It displays a configurable set of properties for a collection of objects as columns in a table view that can be sorted on any column. The **Property Matrix** grid also provides a standard property editor that displays all the properties for the current selection set in the table view.

The display filter icon allows you to filter the properties according to your need.

Some properties have three buttons. They allow you to open the selected property in **Content Browser**, attach the property from the selected one in **Content Browser**, or revert the property to default:

My Blueprint panel

The My Blueprint panel shows all the **Graphs**, **Functions**, **Macros**, **Variables**, and **Event Dispatchers** contained in your Blueprint, including component instance variables that are added in the component list or variables that are created by promoting a value to a variable in the graph editor.

By default, your Blueprint contains one **EventGraph** and one **ConstructionScript** for your **Functions** but you can add any **Graph**, **Variable**, or function you might need by the **Add New** button:

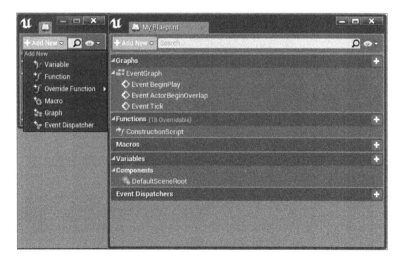

Graph editor

The graph editor panel is the heart of the Blueprint system. It is here that you will create your network of nodes and thanks to their wires, your game lives:

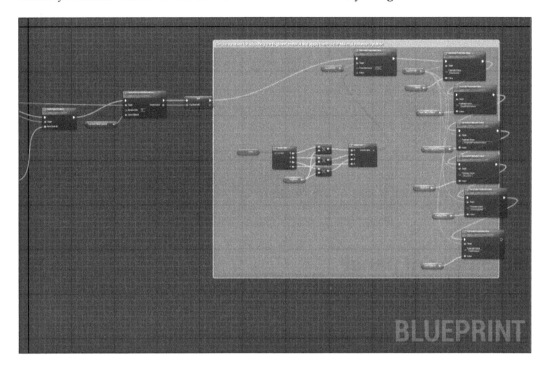

First of all, this table gives you some handy shortcuts for your movements in the graph.

 A smart usage of these shortcuts can save a lot of time when developing your projects. Try to memorize this table and always use the shortcuts when possible.

Control	Action
Right-click + Drag	Pans the graph
Mouse Scroll	Zooms the graph
Right-click	Opens context menu
Click on node	Selects the node
Click + Drag in the empty space	Selects the nodes in the marquee select box
Ctrl + Click + Drag in the empty space	Toggles selection of the nodes in the marquee select box

Control	Action
Shift + Click + Drag in the empty space	Adds the nodes in the marquee select box to the current selection
Click + Drag on node	Moves node
Click + Drag from pin to pin	Wires the pins together
Ctrl + Click + Drag from pin to pin	Moves the wires from the origin pin to the destination pin
Click + Drag from pin to the empty space	Brings up the context menu, showing only relevant nodes. Wires the original pin to a compatible pin on the created node
Click + Drag + C on the empty space	Adds a comment box containing the selected nodes

To add a new node to the graph, you can use the two methods explained in the table (right-click on the empty space or drag any pin from an existing node) and you can also drag and drop any asset from **Content Browser** to the graph editor. It will automatically add the corresponding node to the graph, as follows:

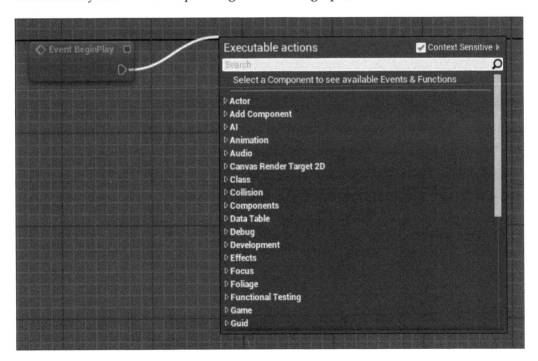

You can also drag and drop any **Variables** from the **My Blueprint** panel to the graph in order to automatically add its correspondent **getter** or **setter** (by selecting the desired node from the pop-up window that appears or by holding *control* for a **getter** or *Alt* for a **setter**) as shown in the following image:

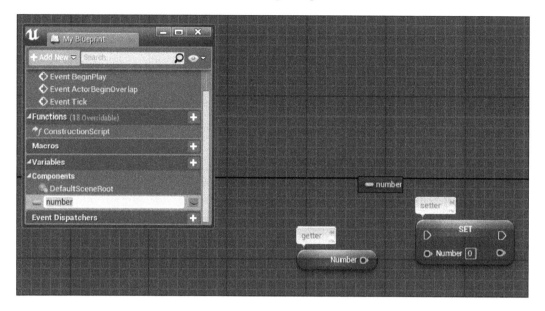

You can find the same behavior seen in the Blueprint graph editor exhibited in the **Construction Script Editor** and in the **Macros Graph Editor**.

Let's now check the graph editor in deep: which variables are accepted and what are the nodes and pins that we just introduced.

Types of variables and data

Under Unreal, there are different types of variables: typical data types, such as **Boolean**, **Integer**, **Float**, and so on, and more complex reference types, such as objects, Actors, and custom classes. Each type has a unique color for easy identification, as shown in the following table:

Variable type	Color	Example	Description
Boolean	Red		Boolean represents true/false data.

Variable type	Color	Example	Description
Byte	Dark Green		Numbers from 0 to 255. This is the smallest data type in terms of spaces; only 1 byte of memory.
Integer	Cyan		Integer values (number without decimals). Ranges from -32,768 to 32,767. Used to store values such as ammo, lives, and collected items.
Float	Light Green		Float values (numbers with decimals). More accurate than integers as it has a precision of seven digits and is used, for example, to store the radius of a sphere, or the damage taken by an enemy, or any value that should contain decimal numbers.
Name	Violet		Name is the lightweight system for using string. It is case-insensitive and cannot be manipulated. Similar to the byte, it is the smallest data type when talking about text and is used to store keywords and indices.

Variable type	Color	Example	Description
String	Magenta		String is the only string class that allows manipulation. It is more expensive than the other two text data; however, strings can be searched, modified, and compared against other strings.
Text	Pink		Text represents a display string. It is used to store object descriptions, times, numbers, and any formatted text. It is typically used in a table for the localization system and cannot be manipulated.
Vector	Yellow		Vector contains an array of three float values and is typically used to store positions on three-dimensional space (XYZ) or color information (RGB).
Rotator	Purple		This is similar to Vector, it stores an array of three float values that contains the rotation of an object in a three-dimensional space (in the order: Roll, Pitch, and Yaw).
Transform	Orange		Transform combines translation, rotation, and scale of a three-dimensional object.

Apart from these default data types, there are tons of other custom data types and we will see how to create our custom ones further in this book. These types can be regrouped in five categories, as follows:

- **Structure**: Struct (value) types. A structure is a container of custom variables. It is used to group related variables in a single entity in order to simplify data combining and data management.

- **References to objects or Actors**: As the name suggests, these data types are references of any object/actor in the game. They are useful when we want to communicate between two different Blueprint classes.

- **References to interfaces**: They are the same as object pointers; however, they are referred to as interfaces objects.

- **References to classes**: Similar to object references, this type of variable contains references to a class. The main difference is that this type points to the default class, while the object reference points to a single instance of this particular class in the game.

- **Enumeration**: An enumerator is basically a byte variable that, instead of numbers, has a human-readable list of names. It can be used to store any kind of object state or type (Game States, tree types, weapon types, player states, and so on).

Nodes

A node is an object that can perform a unique function, such as variable holder, event, math calculation, flow control operation, and so on. However, the way in which nodes are created and used is common to all nodes. This helps the user during the process of the graph creation.

A node has a common layout that we can find in any kind of node that we create, as follows:

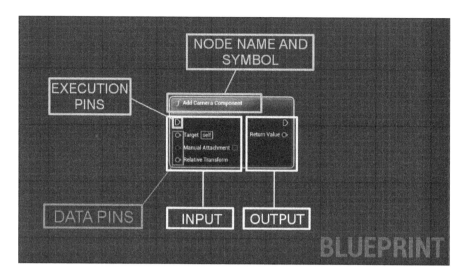

In the preceding image, we can notice the following: on the top we find his name and a symbol. Name, symbol, and color are self-explanatory and help the user to identify the node's behavior quickly, even if it is the first time that he is using it. In the preceding image, *f* means function, typically with a blue background, and the title suggests that this node is a function that will **Add Camera Component** to a target when called.

On the left-hand side of the node, we find the **INPUT** pins, and on the right-hand side, we find the **OUTPUT** pins. We can find nodes with only input (or output) pins; however, their position is unequivocal, as follows:

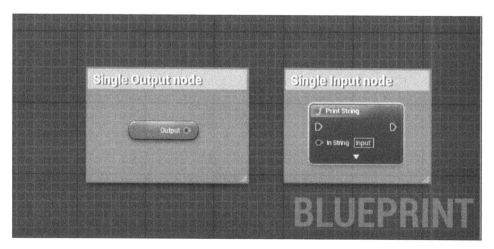

Pins

There are two main types of pins, execution pins and data pins, as follows:

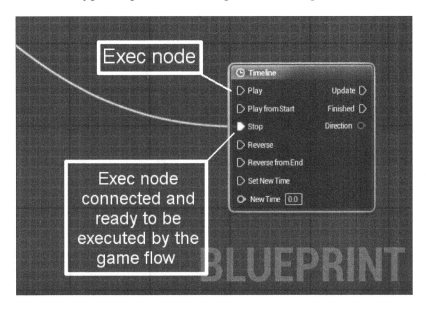

Execution pins are used to connect nodes together in order to create a flow of execution. A node is executed when its input execution pin is activated by another node. Once execution of the node completes, it activates its output execution pin to continue the flow of execution. Usually, there is only a single input and output execution pin (as functions only have one entry point and one exit point); however, other types of nodes can have multiple input or output execution pins, allowing different behavior depending on which pin is activated. For example, **Timeline** has multiple input execution pins to call **Play**, **Stop**, **Reverse**, and so on, and multiple output pins in order to call a custom function each time when each time loop is finished.

Data pins are used to put the data in a node or receive data from a node. Data pins are type-specific and can be wired to variables or other data pins of the same type. Unreal helps us to recognize the different types of variable, not only with the name, but also with its color. Their color is unique and common in all the tools of Unreal, not only in Blueprint. As execution pins, data pins are also displayed as an outline when not wired to anything and solid when wired.

Blueprint debugging

When developing your Blueprints, you will soon find that at times something is not working as you expected. To diagnose these problems, Unreal Engine 4 gives you a powerful debugger system that allows you to see your Blueprint script flow in real time, as follows:

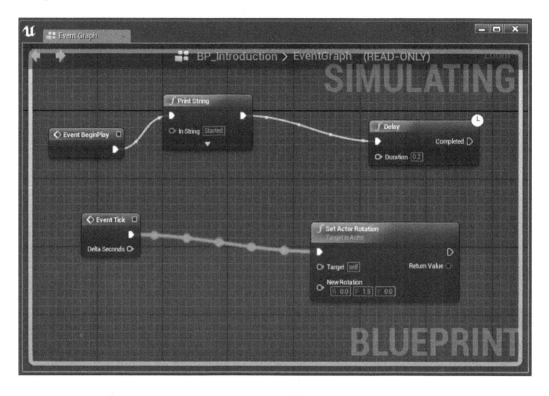

When you play or simulate in the editor, you can see the pulsating active wires as your script gets executed in your graph editor.

The debugger system is attached to the first instance of your Blueprint class that the editor finds in your level (alphabetic order) as soon as you play or simulate your game. If you have more than one instance and you want to specify which one to debug, you can select it from the toolbar.

You can set a Breakpoint in a node: when added you can play your game and when the simulation reaches that node, the game will pause and jump to that node in your graph so that you can step through your script to see where the issues are occurring.

To add a Breakpoint to your Blueprint, right-click on any execution node and choose **Add breakpoint**. You can also toggle the Breakpoint of a selected node by pressing *F9*:

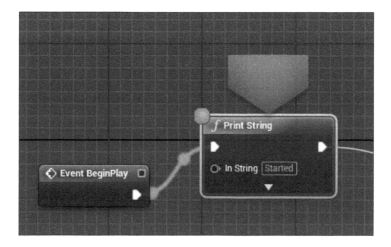

When a Breakpoint has been added to a node, a red circle will appear in the left-hand top corner of the node. This means that, as soon as the gameplay reaches that node, the game will pause and focus on this node.

Another debugging feature is Watch Values. You can set any variable in your Blueprint to be able to see any variation of it in real time while the game is running. This is an important tool that helps you to find any logical error due to wrong calculations and human mistakes.

To set a value to be watched, right-click on a variable in your graph and select **Watch this value**. A floating text bubble will appear above of the variable, showing the value of this variable being changed while the game is executed, as follows:

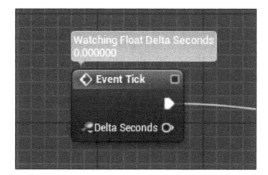

Blueprint debugger tab

From the **Window** tab, in the menu bar, you can open **Blueprint Debugger**. This panel shows all the watched variables or Breakpoint assigned. You can add multiple Blueprint debugger tabs by holding *Shift* and clicking on **Actor** in your scene:

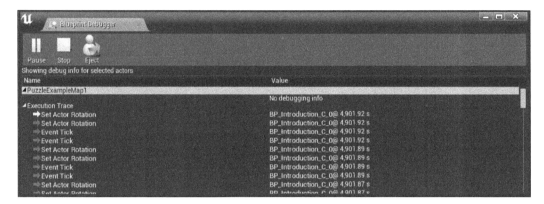

The lower section of the debugger is called **Execution Trace**, this will become populated as soon as you play or simulate in the editor and show all the executed commands in the order in which they were issued (the top one as the most recent).

Compiler result

The last panel in the debug section is the compiler result. This will show all the compiler errors or warnings that occur when compiled with your script. Each line contains a message about the issue and a direct link to the node that causes the problem.

Visual Studio

You learned how to use the **Unreal Engine 4** (**UE4**) editor and the basics of Blueprints. Now is time to go through the core of the engine. Code! Let's take a look at Visual Studio and get ready to comprehend lines of code together while we create our Blueprint scripts. In the examples provided in this book, you will often see different approaches to the same simulation. The goal of this guide is to teach you to not only be able to decide when Blueprint is useful, but also be able to write some lines of code.

Creating the project solution

We created our project as a Blueprint empty project, now we need to create our Visual Studio solution for it. Open your project folder through Explorer. You should have a situation similar to the following screenshot:

Unreal Engine provides you a C++ wizard that helps you in this process. Locate `.uproject` (usually the name of your `project.uproject`). Right-click on **Generate Visual Studio project files**. The `UnrealBuildTool` file should start and you should see your folder slightly changed at the end of the process, as follows:

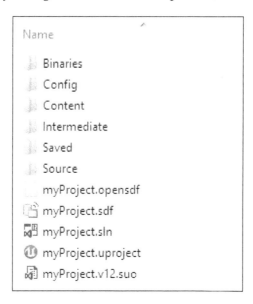

If this solution doesn't work, you can generate the project solution directly from the editor. Under the menu bar, navigate to **File | Generate Visual Studio Project**. If it still doesn't work, remember that the engine will generate a project solution as soon as you add a C++ class to the project in case there isn't any Visual Studio project.

Let's have a brief look at these folders, as shown in the following:

- `Binaries`: It contains executable or other files that are created during compiling.
- `Config`: Configuration files are used to set values that control engine and game default behavior.
- `Content`: It holds all the content of the game, including asset packages and maps.
- `Intermediate`: It contains temporary files that are generated during the building of the engine or game.
- `Saved`: It contains autosaves, configuration (same `*.ini` of `Config` folder) files, and log files. Here, you can find crash logs, hardware information, and swarm options and data.
- `Source`: It contains all the source files for the game divided in to object class definitions (`.h` files) and object class implementation (`.cpp` files).

Now, we can open the project solution by double-clicking the `.sln` file or under **File | Open Visual Studio Project** through the editor:

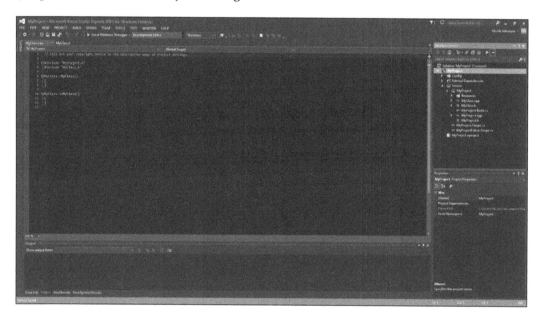

One of the problem of UE3 was that whenever you wrote or modified your unrealScripts to test and see your modifications in the engine, you were obligated to restart the editor, losing a certain amount of time due to closing and opening it a hundred times during the development.

On UE4, this is not needed anymore. You can compile your script directly within the editor, and each modification you make on both side (Code or Engine) is automatically updated.

Add a new class from the editor

To add a new class from the editor, we can navigate to **File | New C++ Class...** from the menu bar. A pop-up window similar to the Blueprint one will appear where the editor will ask you to choose the parent class.

 Notice that here you can choose to *not* have a parent for your class, which is different from the Blueprint class, where it *needed* to have a parent class.

When you choose a parent, you need to specify a name for it and its path (keep all your code under the Source folder). The C++ wizard will add a header and a C++ file for you and, when finished, will ask you whether you want to immediately edit that file:

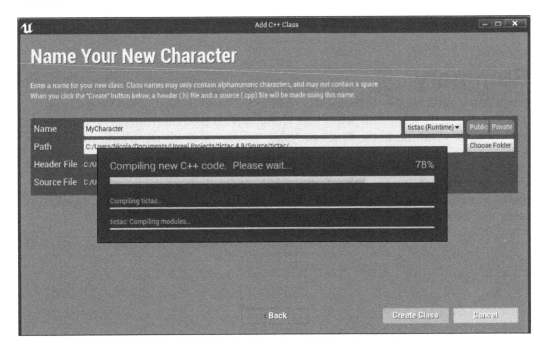

For any other parent class that you choose, except *none*, the wizard will add the most used functions for you on the new class together with the constructor. By default, you will find your class ready to be implemented with the `BeginPlay` function and the `Tick` functions:

Now that you know how to create your classes, you are ready to write your own code. We will see what to write and how to debug from Visual Studio in detail in the next chapters.

Summary

Now, you should be able to create a project in UE4 and its Visual Studio solution. You know exactly what Blueprint is and how to read the Blueprint classes written by someone else or found in the Epic examples. You are able to create your own classes and start experimenting with nodes and wires.

In the next chapter, we are going to use what we studied here to create our first game. We will also see how different Blueprint classes communicate among each other and how to use BPS Brushes to create simple environments.

2

Tic-Tac-Toe

In this chapter, we are going to create our first game starting from an UE4 template and using Blueprint classes. As a first project, we will create a tic-tac-toe clone. This simple project allows you to focus only on the logic of Blueprints, without being worried about level design, graphic or any other aspect of game developing. We will need some basic meshes by the way, and for our purpose we are going to use the BSP brushes.

In this chapter, we will cover the following:

- BSP brushes
- Direct Blueprint class communication
- Static Meshes via Blueprint
- Variable array
- Blueprint Macro
- Text render via Blueprint
- Custom events

What do we need?

Anyone knows how tic-tac-toe works: it is a 1vs1 game that is played in a 3 x 3 grid, where the goal is to create a sequence of three symbols of the same type in a horizontal, vertical, or diagonal row. The game is turn-based, where each player can place his symbol (typically O or X) anywhere in the grid.

This game has a huge history and many people have written books and programs talking about it. We will be a part of them, discovering how even the simplest game can be complicated when talking about computer games.

In order to create this game, we need the following:

- A static camera that is always pointing to the grid
- A 3 x 3 grid that is made by nine individual square Static Mesh
- Two Symbols: O and X
- A user interface showing which player can make his move and the state of the game
- A game logic: a controller for the grid state and a turn handler

Preparing the game

Finally, we arrive at creating our first game! Open the launcher, select the latest version of the engine and start a new project. We are going to use the **Puzzle** template under the **Blueprint** section. Call it **TicTacToe**, leave the other settings, such as **Desktop/Console**, **Maximum Quality** and **With Starter Content**, as default and click **Create Project**:

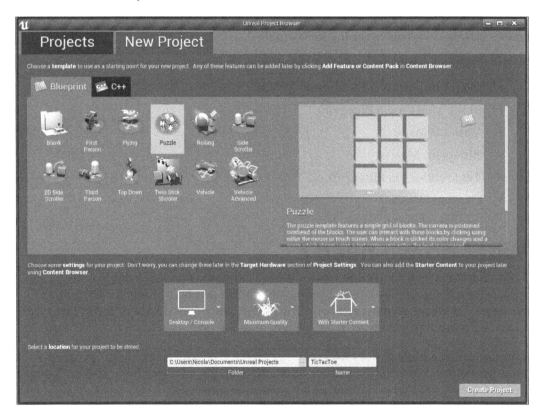

This is a simple template showing how the engine can be used for a puzzle game. If you click on play form the toolbar, a 3 x 3 grid (exactly what we need!) will show up, and you can interact with the pieces of the grid by clicking on them; they will change color and there is a rudimental UI showing you a counter of the pieces that are touched:

Click on the `PuzzleBP` folder in the **Content Browser**. Let's see what this template offers us. You should be able to recognize some of those elements as we discussed them in the previous chapter.

- **Blueprints**. This is the core of the game. It contains four Blueprint classes:
    - **PuzzleBlock**: This is the single block of the grid. It handles the touch events inherit themselves and contains the Static Mesh of the block.
    - **BuzzleBlock Grid**: This handles the events about the game grid. In this class, the grid is created as soon as the game is launched and the score is updated here.
    - **PuzzleGame Mode**: This is the **Game Mode** data only Blueprint class. As seen in the introduction chapter, here we can set the default classes for this game.

- ○ **PuzzlePlayer Controller**: This is similar to the game mode and is the player controller class. Here, you can set the default settings of your player controller (the object that is directly controlled by the player). Here, you can control the player inputs, set its camera manager, and in a more complex game example, set a default life, equipment, spells, and so on.

- **Maps**: Here, we can store our maps. As you can imagine now, there is only the puzzle template map.

- **Meshes**: Here, the meshes and materials needed for this template are stored. At the moment, in this folder you can find there is the **Cube Material**, a **Cube Mesh** (for the floor) and the **PuzzleBlock** grid Mesh (with rounded edges).

- **Tutorial**: You can find some useful dynamic tutorial files here. You can double-click on them and a pop-up window will guide you through the template. Feel free to watch or delete those files as we don't need them in our game.

Clean the unnecessary items and scripts

The files contained in this template are perfect for our purpose; however, we need to clean them a little bit before adding our nodes and wires.

Open **PuzzleBlock** and go to its **Event Graph**:

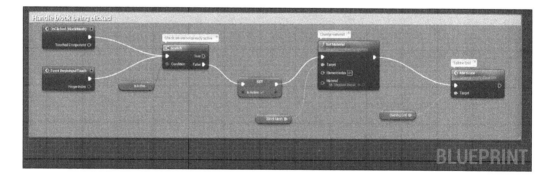

You can see that this graph is pretty simple. As soon as this object is clicked or touched, use a **Branch** node to compare a variable (**Is Active**). If true, then do nothing; if false, then set **Is Active** to **True** with a **SET** node (in this way, we will avoid firing the followed events every time the player clicks on this block again) and change the material of **BlockMesh** using a **Set Material** node. At the end, add the score calling a custom event, **Add Score**, in the Grid class.

We can remove everything after the **SET** node. Also, remove the comment box. You will now have a situation similar to the following:

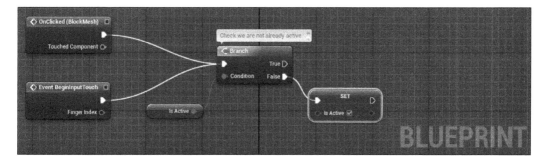

Compile, save, and close it. Now open the **PuzzleBlockGrid** class and go to its event graph.

The editor automatically saves after every 10 minutes. You can modify the frequency of it under **Edit** | **Editor Preferences** and the **General** section under **Loading & Saving**.

Here, it is unnecessary; however, get used to compiling your class every time you make any modifications. Otherwise, you will be unable to see these modifications when you play or simulate your game.

Things are starting to get interesting now. You can see two different sections: a spawn blocks section and a score handler section. The score section contains the custom event that we saw on the block class: it takes the score integer variable and adds one using an Addition node. When done, it uses a **Set Text(String)** node. This last node uses a string variable that you can find on the viewport as target and the result of a **BuildString(int)** node that combines the word score with the **Score** variable as the value, as we cannot use integers in a string before converting it:

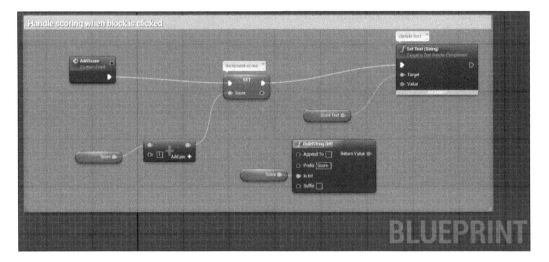

Select everything from this section and delete it. Also delete the **Score** variable from **My Blueprint** window. You will notice that there is also a **Score Text** variable that cannot be deleted from this window. This is because it is a reference of a render text component. You can go to the **Components** window and delete **Score Text** from there.

Let's take a look at the spawn blocks section. Don't be afraid of all these Xs and %s, this section basically takes the size of the grid and creates a corresponding series of PuzzleBlock.

In detail, as soon as the game starts, it launches a **ForLoop** node that takes the number of blocks that need to be created (calculated from the size variable of the grid with a simple multiplication node) as input. Each loop spawns a PuzzleBlock with the **SpawnActor** node that has a position calculated by the script and a reference of the PuzzleBlock script as input.

 Notice how the **SpawnActor** node automatically adds an input node for the grid reference as soon as we set our custom to class Actor.

The position is calculated by mathematical operations:

- X coordinate: *(Index % Size) * Block Spacing*
- Y coordinate: *(Index / Size) * Block Spacing*

 For those of you who don't know what % (or mod) means, it is the modulo operation. It finds the reminder after the division of a number by another. In our case, we are using it to calculate the column number of our grid. The size of the grid doesn't matter. For this calculation, the result of *Index % Size* is always an integer number between 0 and the size value. For example, *6 % 3 = 0, 7 % 3 = 1, 8 % 3 = 2*, and *9 % 3 = 0*.

We can leave this code as it is. However, we know the exact size of our grid so let's simplify this script: Remove the **Size** variable nodes and the first section of the script, as shown in the following:

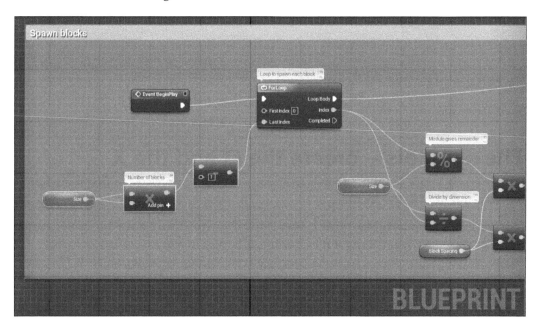

Now, on the **LastIndex** field of the **ForLoop** node, put *8 (Size*Size) -1* and on the modulo and division node write 3. We can now safely remove the variable size from the MyBlueprint window.

We are done with this script for the moment. If you followed the instructions correctly, you will have a situation as shown in the following:

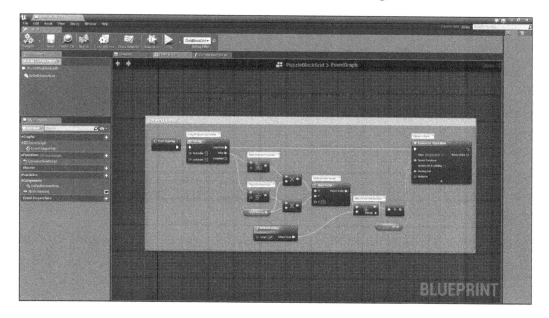

Save, close and return to the main window.

The symbols – create the O and the X

We are going to use the BPS brushes to create our two symbols. Let's first see what they are and how to use them.

BSP brush is a wonderful tool that is useful to create quick and basic mesh-like walls, floors or stairs; however, even if it is theoretically possible to create any complex shape with these brushes, I would strongly advice you to use external tools that can do this job better and use the built-in engine tool only for rudimental shapes or quick testing purposes.

This tool can be found in the **Modes** panel in the top left corner of the main window:

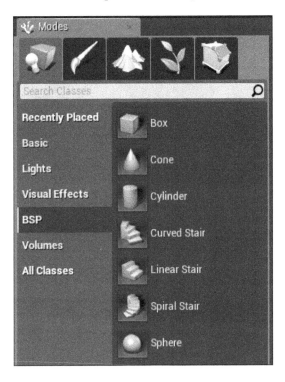

From there, you can simple drag and drop the selected shape in the viewport and, once added, modify its parameters, such as transform (a group of parameters that contains position, rotation, and scale of an object), aspect, material, behaviors, and so on.

We will work directly in the main scene; therefore, even if it is possible to work with everything in position, I prefer to have a clean space in order to move around my object easily without being worried about touching something that I don't want to (and avoid having some objects that cover the view of my object while working on it).

On the right-hand top of the editor, you can see **World Outliner**. Here, you can see all the objects contained in your level. You can organize in folders or groups and with the help of the eye icon to the left of each item, you can toggle their visibility. Let's close the eyes of what we don't need:

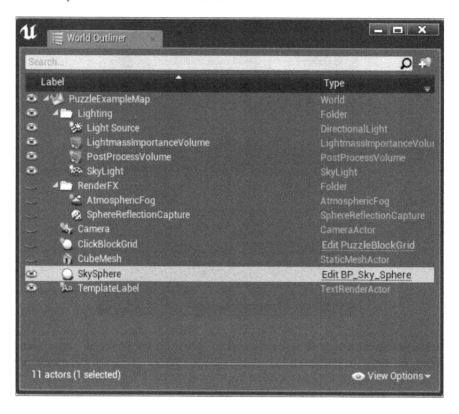

From the BPS panel, drag and drop a cube in your viewport. Once added, you have access to its properties, located in the **Details** panel. From there, set its location to the center of the scene (0,0,0) and its dimension as **X**=230, **Y**=30 and **Z** =30 in the **Brush Settings** section. If you want, you can drag and drop a cube mesh from the content browser at the bottom of your brush as a reference for its dimensions. We want an **X** not a **+**; therefore, set the **Z** rotation of your brush to 45 degrees:

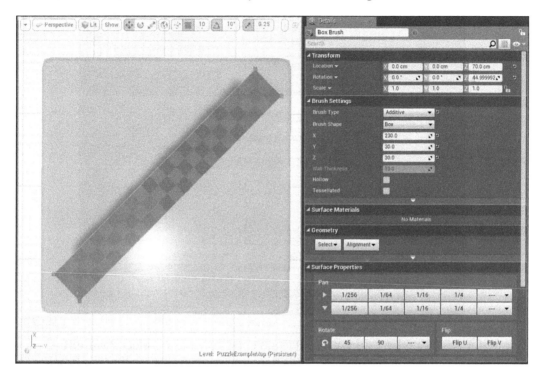

To create the other bar of our **X**, use *Ctrl + W* to duplicate it (or right-click and **Edit | Duplicate**) with the selected brush. And set its transform again to be 0,0,0 and the rotation to -45 degree.

Now, we have our wonderful **X** but it is still a simple brush. We need to convert this creation in a Mesh to order for it to be manipulated by our scripts. Select both of the sections of the **X** and click on **Create Static Mesh** in the **Details** panel under the **Brush Settings**. If you don't see it, click on the **Advanced** options at the bottom of the brush section (it's the small arrow at end of the brush section. The advanced options are hidden by default):

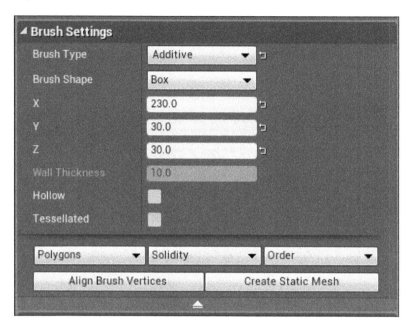

The editor will ask where do you want to save the new mesh, select **PuzzleBP | Meshes** and call it **SM_Symbol_X**. After this process, you can see that the brushes are gone and your symbol is now labelled as single **Static Mesh** actor. You can now remove it from your scene. We will use them dynamically in our Blueprint.

For the O, the process is similar. Drag and drop a **Cylinder** BPS at the scene and move it to 0. You will immediately notice that it is actually not a cylinder; it is more of a hexagon. This is due to the sides of this shape that are set by default to 8. Change it to 32 and you will immediately notice that the brush becomes more rounded and nice. Resize it to a height of 30 and radius of 100 in order to fit it in our block:

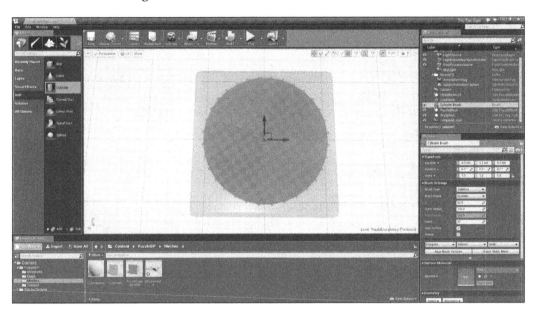

Now, let's drill a hole in our shape. Duplicate the circle, reposition it to 0 and set the brush type to **Substractive** under the **Brush Settings**. The mesh disappears. This is because the two brushes have the same size. Set the radius to 70 and you will finally see our O symbol.

Select the two brushes and create a Static Mesh as we did for **X**, and call it **SM_Symbol_O**:

Creating a new material for the symbols

You can see that the two created symbols have a gray squared pattern on them. This is because there is no material applied. We are now going to create our custom materials: two simple plain color materials will be enough for our game.

Go to the **Content Browser** and create a new folder in our **PuzzleBP** folder and call it **Materials**. In order to add a new material, click on **Add New | Material** (or **Add New | Materials** and **Textures | Material** with the selected new folder if this option is unavailable for the default choices).

Call it **M_Symbol_Red** and double-click on it to open the editor:

This section will not be explained in detail as it works in a similar manner to Blueprint. It has a grid-based interface where you can add any node, available on the **Palette** panel, to the **Materials** node (it is in the centre of the screen). You can see a live preview on the top left of the screen and through the toolbar you have some tools to debug and statistics about your material.

The main difference with a Blueprint class is that instead of starting from a node and developing further indefinitely, here every node is added before the main node. In the **Details** panel, you will notice how many possibilities that node can offer.

Here is one example of a realistic water material:

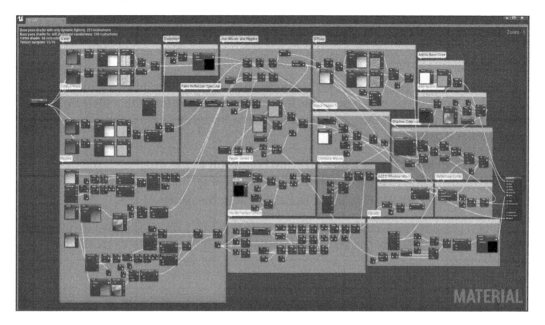

In order to add a color, we use a **Constant3Vector** node. Right click on the empty space in the **Grid** panel. You can easily find the node that you want by typing it in the input field:

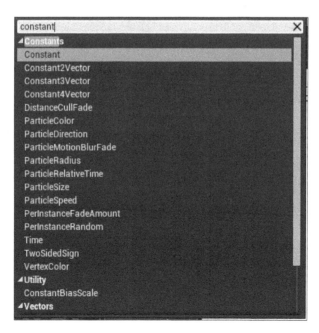

From that node, you can pick any color that you want by double-clicking on the colored square or from the **Details** panel. Choose a nice red from the color picker panel that appears and click **OK** when you are happy with your choice. You can even write your hexadecimal color code or pick a color from any of the pixels that you have in your window with the eye dropper.

Connect the output pin of this node to the **Base Color**. You can now see that the sphere has become red in the preview. We want a glossy color with a little bit of reflection. In order to do that, we need to remove **Roughness** from the surface and set it so that it is little bit **Metallic**.

Add a constant node, set its value to 0, and connect it to the roughness pin. It immediately starts to glow. Now, in order to make it shinier, add another Constant node, set its value to 0.1, and connect it to the **Metallic** pin.

These two parameters accept values between 0 and 1 (0 = no effect and 1 = full effect) and when set are used by the algorithm of the main material node to create the desired effect.

The end result should be something as follows:

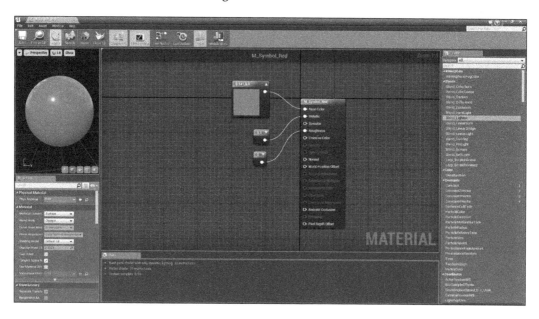

Save and duplicate it in order to create the black material. Call it `M_Symbol_Black`, and the only parameter that you need to change is the **Base Color** to a plain black (Hexadecimal code 00000000).

In order to assign these materials to our symbols, double-click on one of them and under the level of details (**Details** panel | **LOD0**) section, assign our material to the material 0 field by dragging and dropping it from the **Content Browser** or by clicking on the menu on the right-hand side of the preview:

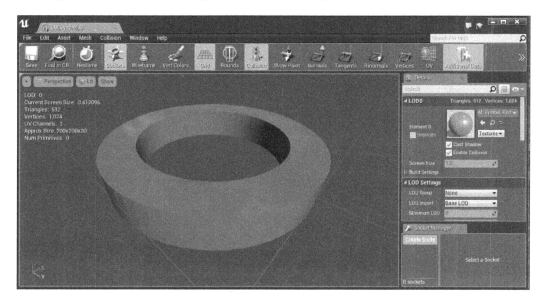

Now that we have our two symbols and the code is clean, we are ready to implement our logic in the Blueprint classes.

Writing our Blueprints

Now, we need to add some logic to this project. In order to achieve the tic-tac-toe mechanics and develop speaking, we need to do the following:

- Handle a turn-based mechanic
- Know when someone wins
- Show the state of the game
- Store a winning counter for each player
- Handle the restart

Turn-based mechanics

Open **PuzzleBlock** and **PuzzleBlockGrid** Blueprints as we are going to frequently switch between them.

First of all, we need to know which player has to move: the X or the O. In order to achieve this, also since this is a two-player game, we can use a simple **Boolean** variable that is stored on the **PuzzleBlock** grid class and grant it accessibility through the single block class.

Go to the grid class and add a new variable, call it IsX, and give its type as **Boolean**. From now, for our convenience, player 1 is always X and player 2 is O. Add **Tooltip** from the **Details** panel such as is player 1 and leave the other parameters as default:

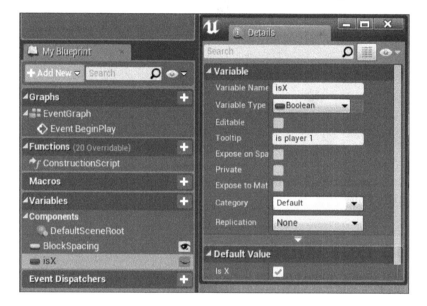

Now, in order to check which player is playing from our block class, we use a direct Blueprint communication. If you go to the block class, you will notice that we have a variable called **Owning Grid**. This is an object reference to our grid. From there, we can access any variable or function that is stored on our grid.

To access the **Is X** variable, drag the **Owning Grid** variable in the **Event Graph** and click get. This is the getter that points to our grid class. To find the IsX variable, pull out the output node of the getter and search it in the popup window that appears as soon as you release the mouse button. You can see that the wizard shows you two options: the getter and the setter; choose the **getter**.

We can now use this variable in a **Branch** node. This node accepts a **Boolean** variable as input and has two execution pins for both of its conditions. Connect the input execution pin to the last node of our existent script and the variable pin on our **Is X** variable. We are now ready to add the correct symbol to our block:

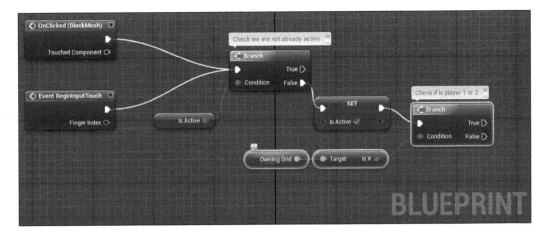

Set Static Mesh via Blueprint

To dynamically add the symbol on our Actor, we can use the set **Static Mesh** node that refers to an existing empty **Static Mesh Component** previously positioned inside the block object. This empty **Static Mesh** will act as placeholder for our symbol and store a position that is based on the block location.

 Note that this is a good solution for this case; however, it is not the best one when talking about bigger projects. Each component, even if it is empty, uses memory and it should be added and used only when needed.

On our block class, under the **Components** panel, with the **DummyRoot** component that is selected, navigate to **Add Component | Static Mesh** and call it **Placeholder**. Use the viewport window to move it a little above the block mesh (my transform location is 0,0,70) and make sure that it has none on the **Static Mesh** properties under the **Details** panel:

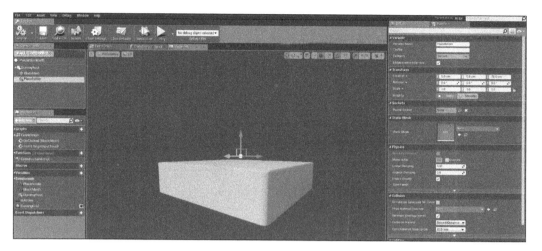

Create a getter of **Placeholder** in **Event Graph**, as we did for the **Owning Grid**, and create two **Set Static Mesh** nodes. Connect the **Placeholder** reference at the target input pin of both of them and under the **New Mesh** field, set our O and X symbol.

Now, we can connect the **True** pin of our last **Branch** node to the X mesh node and the **False** pin to the O node:

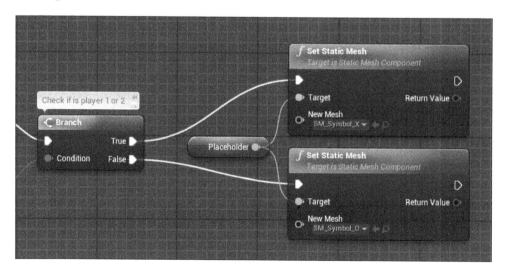

If you compile and play the game now, you will be able to see our symbols spawning as soon as we click on the grid. However, as you may notice, they are all the same symbol. This is because the game doesn't know that this game is turn-based and at this moment the players are always seen as player 1 (due to **Is X** variable).

Fix this issue is easy: We need to connect the **Is X** variable with a **NOT** node as soon as we spawn our mesh:

Connect the **SET** execution node of this piece to both the set mesh nodes and if you try to run it now, you will see that each time you click on a PuzzleBlock, the symbol spawned changes.

Working with arrays

In order to check when a player wins, we need to have an array of all the blocks and their state. We can use that array to iterate through its elements in order to find out if there is a winner.

In Blueprint, any type of variable can be promoted to be an array. On the right-hand side of the **Variable** type of the **Details** panel, there is a little button that, if clicked, creates an array of the selected type.

In our **Grid** class, create a new variable and call it `BlockArray`, as Type for this variable search our **PuzzleBlock** under the object reference section and select it. Now click on the **Array** button and you will notice that the variable has a different icon now and is ready to be populated. To achieve this, we can use the return value of the **SpawnActor** node of our spawn block section.

Drag the output execute pin of that node and search add item to array. We will use our array variable as an input array and connect its **Return Value** as item:

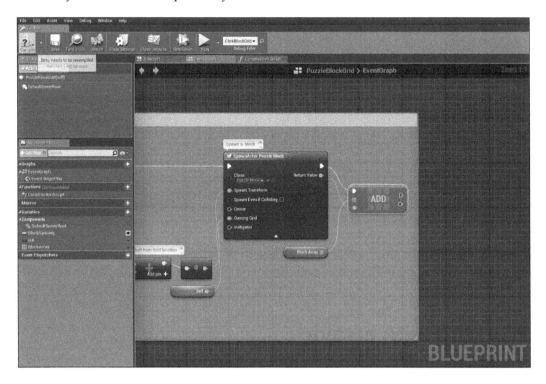

Now, we need to store a variable that indicates the state of the block. We use a byte variable for that. A block can have three statuses: 0 = none, 1 = player1 and 2 = player2. This variable will be used when we check the array and will help the code to quickly identify which player owns that block.

On the block class, add a new variable of type byte and call it `BlockState`. Give it a default value, 0, and add a couple of setter that points to this new variable on our **EventGraph** before setting our static Meshes. Obviously, set it to 1 for player 1 and 2 for player 2.

Creating a macro

To find the winner, we need to iterate through all the possible winning combinations (3 rows + 3 columns + 2 diagonals) and check whether the selected combination has the same state. If it has the same state (and not a null state) we have a winner.

To make our life easier and keep the **EventGraph** clean, we will write a couple of macros.

A macro, as we saw in the first chapter, is a collection of nodes compiled in a single individual unit that can be called anywhere (however, only in its parent Blueprint class if it is not in a Macro Library) like any other node.

We will create two macros. The first one will compare a block state with a byte variable and return true if is the same and false if otherwise. We need to make this comparison 24 times on our next macro and have every required node regrouped in a single node helps a lot.

The second macro takes a byte input (the player number), compares all the combinations, and returns true if there is a winning combination and false if otherwise.

Let's create the first macro. Go to the **My Blueprint** panel of the **Grid** class and add a new macro by clicking the **+** button. Call it isOwner and open it:

We immediately notice that there are input and output nodes ready and, on the **Details** panel, a section where we can add our input and output pins. Add two inputs: the first one is of type integer called BlockIndex and the second one is called **Player**. About the output, create a **Boolean** variable and call it IsOwner.

Now, we need to add a **GetArray** node in order to find the indexed block: set the reference of our **Block Array** variable as array, and our nearly created **Block Index** variable as an index. From that node, we can now get its **Block State** variable and compare it with the macro **Player** variable. Add an equal (byte) node, connect the two input pins with the corresponding variable and finally close the macro connecting the last pin to the output node:

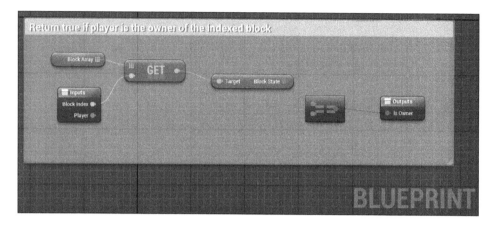

Save, close, and create a new macro. Call it `CheckIfWin` and open it. Now, we only need an input of type byte called **Player** and an output of type Boolean called **Win**.

The idea of this node is that if the player is the owner of all of the blocks that compose any of the eight combinations, it will return true, and false if otherwise.

Connect the input node to the three **isOwner** macros and give them the value of the first column as block index: 0, 1, and 2. Connect all the output pins to an And (Boolean) node (you need to click on the Add pin in order to have the three required input pins). This node returns true if all of the input values are true.

As the last step, connect the result to or (Boolean) and the result of this node to the output node of the macro. An **OR** node will return true if one or more of the inputs is true:

Now, this is the index table of our array that represents our grid. Try to create the other seven combinations on your own (in the preceding picture, I've already added the other seven combination on the or node):

2	5	8
1	4	7
0	3	6

The result is an amazing amount of wires and repetitive nodes, it could be improved using functions and other optimizations; however, it is fine for our purpose:

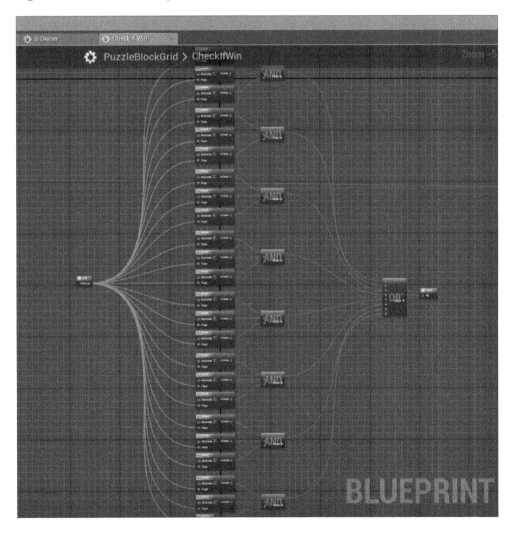

UI using text render

We have a winning handler; however, so far, we have nothing that can show the **game state** to the player. There are different ways to implement a **UI**, the most used and completely under Unreal is surely the **Unreal Motion Graphics** (**UMG**) and its widget Blueprint. We will see this wonderful tool in the next chapter.

For now, let's create our UI using **TextRenderer** components in our Blueprint class. We don't need the buttons, animations, or any complex UI at the moment; therefore, for a quick and easy implementation, some text components that are handled by our Blueprint class are perfect.

The UI that we will create is composed by the following:

- **A game state**: This text will show the different states of a game, when a player is winning, and which one of the players has to make a move.

- **Two win counters**: This text will show the cumulative number of winnings by the players.

- **Two tooltips**: This is just a static text showing that to which player does the score belongs.

Go on the Viewport Window of our grid Blueprint and, under the components panel, add five `TextRenderer` components as the child of the `DefaultSceneRoot`.

A `TextRenderer`, like any other component, can be moved in the viewport and referenced in Blueprint. Under the **Details** panel, you can find the **Text** section. Here, you can set text, font, size, and alignment similar to a normal text label. All these properties can be manipulated in Blueprint and we will use the **Text** property to show the score and game state.

The default properties that you need to set are as follows:

- **Text Renderer 1**:
  - **Variable Name**: `TextPlayer1Tooltip`
  - **Location**: `-600,400,0`
  - **Text**: `Player 1`
  - **Text render Color**: `Black`
  - **World Size**: `72`

- **Text Renderer 2**:
  - ○ **Variable Name**: `TextPlayer2Tooltip`
  - ○ **Location**: `-600,-1000,0`
  - ○ **Rotation**: `0,90,0`
  - ○ **Text**: `Player 1`
  - ○ **Text render Color**: `Red`
  - ○ **World Size**: `72`

- **Text Renderer 3**:
  - ○ **Variable Name**: `TextPlayer1Wins`
  - ○ **Location**: `-600,400,0`
  - ○ **Text**: `"0"`
  - ○ **Text render Color**: `Black`
  - ○ **World Size**: `144`

- **Text Renderer 4**:
  - ○ **Variable Name**: `TextPlayer2Wins`
  - ○ **Location**: `-600,-1000,0`
  - ○ **Text**: `"0"`
  - ○ **Text render Color**: `Red`
  - ○ **World Size**: `144`

- **Text Renderer 5**:
  - ○ **Variable Name**: `TextGameState`
  - ○ **Location**: `230,-300,0`
  - ○ **Text:** `Game State`
  - ○ **World Size**: `48`

All of them have a horizontal alignment center and are rotated by 90 degrees on the Y axis.

The final result should be something similar to the following:

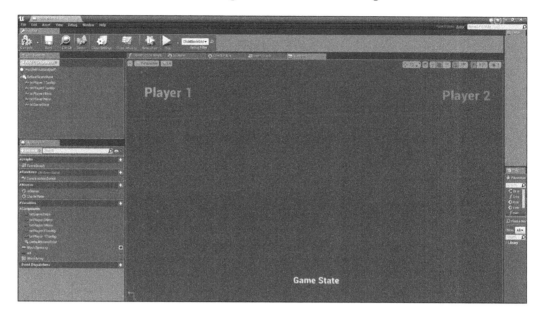

If you run the game, you should see these text fitting perfectly around the grid. Let's go back to the code and give these texts some dynamism.

Custom events

We have our macro to check whether someone is winning and we have our text that can show it. Now, the problem is when to check whether someone wins and how to use that macro properly?

The idea is to call the checkIfWin macro after every move from the Block script and refresh the Game State Text Render, based on the result of the macro.

To call our macro, we use custom event. A custom event has the same property of any other Event node, with the main difference being that we can add our input pins as we did for the macros. It can be called anywhere in the Blueprint class owner and, thanks to a reference, form anywhere in other classes.

On our Grid class, right-click on **EventGraph** and search for the custom node. Add it and call it OnMoveEnds. As you notice, the events usually start with **On...** (OnClick, OnTouch, and so on), this is because an event is usually raised when something specific happens in the game. In our case, we want to raise it on a player movement end. Under the Input section, add an Input pin of the byte type and call it player. Notice how this pin is an Output pin on the node that is already created.

Why? That is because an event needs to have a **Caller** and a **Handler** in order to work. The following example may help you: think of the custom event as a bridge that connects two roads that have a start and an end, and think of a truck as the game flow of our game, and the road as our wires. When the truck reaches a bridge, it carries its content from one side of the road to the other, maintaining its information from the start to the end point, and for a brief period of time, without touching the ground.

This is basically what a custom event does; it connect two nodes without using wires, carrying information needed at the arrival node during the crossing:

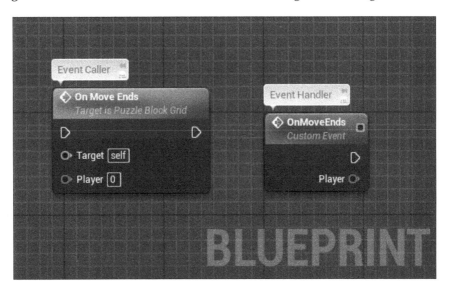

Now implement what we want the event to handle. The idea is to check whether the output player is the winner. If it is, stop the game, show who wins, and update the score. If not, keep playing and show who needs to move.

First, connect the event to a Branch node and the player with our **CheckIfWin** custom macro. The result of the macro will be the **Branch** input:

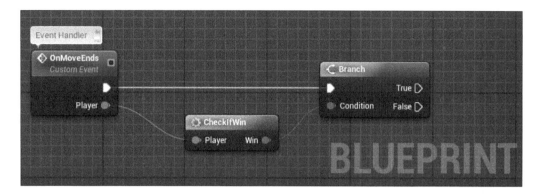

Now, we have the starting point of our custom event; we need to call it in order to activate it. Go to the block class and extend the execute node of the last Set Node. You will find the **On Move Ends** event.

Add it and put the grid reference as **Target** and our **Block State** variable as the player. Now, the event is called for every end of a movement as we wanted:

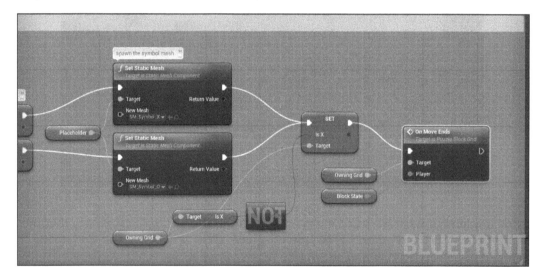

Format text

Now, we need to dynamically modify text renderer. In order to do this, we use a node called Format Text. This special node allows us to format a text with as many input nodes as we want, adding them in between a string in the order that we prefer.

It uses pointers that are surrounded by the {} delimiters in order to build the text and it returns a clean custom text that is built with our inputs.

Add a format text on our grid graph and, on the format field, write **player {player} wins!** Notice how the node automatically adds the input node player for us:

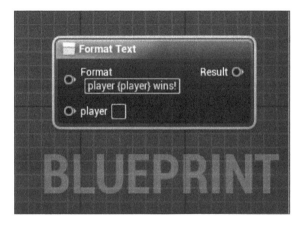

As its player input, we will convert the byte value of the player variable with a text one and use the result of this node as **Value** input for a **Set Text** node.

Extend the true output pin of **Branch** and add a **Set Text** that refers to our **Text Game State** component, connect the correct pins, and now we can finally see, if we test it, when and which player wins!

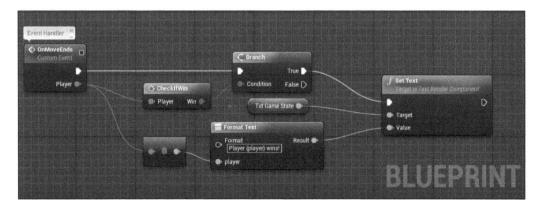

Now, we need to handle the false condition of the branch, or practically speaking, when no one wins and the game state needs to show who needs to move.

We have multiple possibilities to achieve that. We need to think in a more general way and, if we do that, we discover that is not only here that we need to show which player needs to move, but also at the very beginning of the game. If not, the players will start the game and won't know whose turn it is to move.

A custom event will be something that perfectly fits our needs. Create another custom event called `OnRefreshMoveText` and use that event to set the two states: **player 1 moves** or **player 2 moves**.

The steps of the game win state are the same. The main difference is that we use the **Is X** variable instead of the player state to find out who needs to move:

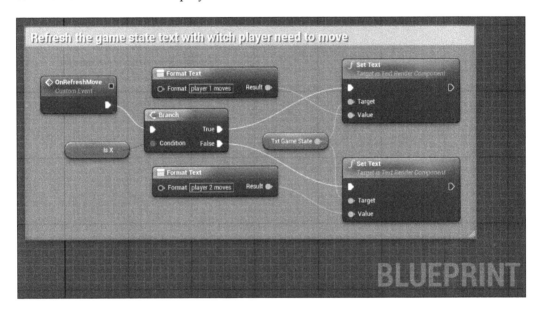

Now, we call this event in two places in our code; on the **OnMoveEnds** event, connected to the **False** exec pin of **Branch** and after the creation of our block array, at the end of the spawn blocks section:

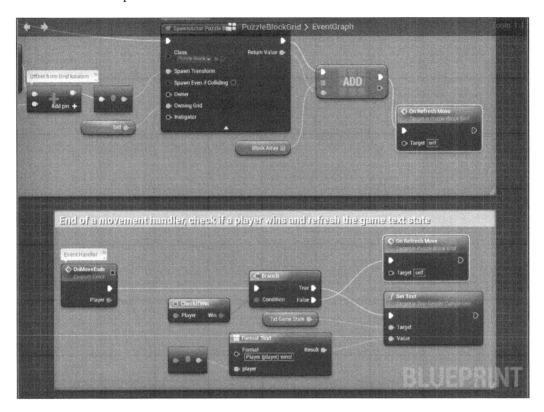

Score

We need to handle the score now. We can use **OnMoveEnds** to refresh it but first of all we need two integer variables that store the two players winning.

On the grid class, add two variables and call them `Player1Score` and `Player2Score` and be sure their default value is set to `0`.

Now the idea is that when a player wins, check whether the player is 1 or 2, add 1 to the corresponding score and refresh its textRend鏈rer.

Connect **Branch** to the **Set Text** (**TextGameState**) node. As a condition, we will evaluate the player variable of the event with an equal (byte) node. Add it to the player output variable and connect its output at the input of the last **Branch** that we created:

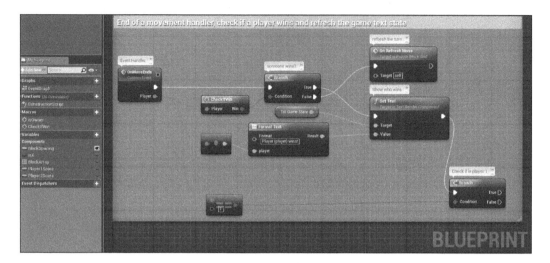

Now, for each result of the branch node, we need to get the player score variable, add 1 to its value, convert the integer value to a string, and set the string value to a set Text node that refers its corresponding **TextPlayerScore** value:

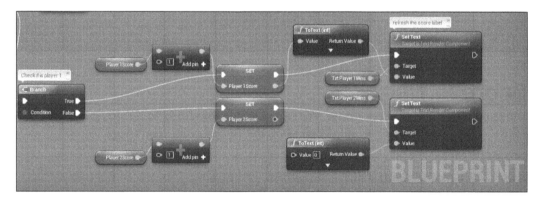

Game flow

If you test the game, you will immediately notice that, at the moment, you can see the player who has to move, and which player wins. However, as soon as someone wins, you are still able to click on the grid, and there is no way to start a new match.

We need to create our game flow that can handle the restart in order to have a fully potential game.

First, we need a method that cleans our symbols from our array and make them touchable again. As the only moment where a match needs to restart is when someone wins, we can attach our restart code when the score refreshes.

The restart in this case is simple: for each element in the block array, set **IsActive** to false, remove the mesh symbol, and set the **BlockState** variable to 0.

First, create a custom event in the block class and call it OnRestart. In this event, connect the needed nodes in order to handle the single block reset state:

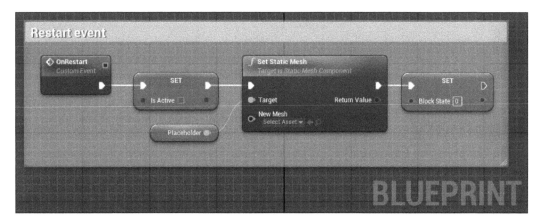

Secondly, on the grid class, create a **ForEachLoop** node. Set the target as the grid reference array and on the output execution pin of the loop body, call the `OnRestart` method with the array element as the target. With the **ForLoop** node, we will call the `OnRestart` method for each of the elements that is contained on the array. Now, connect both of the **Set Text** final nodes of our score to the input **Exec** pin:

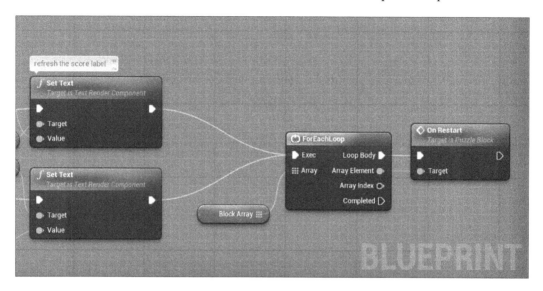

Summary

In this chapter, you have created a fully functional pvp game based on tic-tac-toe mechanics. At the moment, the game is playable and handles all the basics of the game; however, there is a lot of improvement that we can implement in our code.

With the information given to you in this chapter, try to write your own code that improves the game that you just created. There are plenty of choices and it depends on you. Here's some suggestions of what you can do with the elements that you have:

- Improve the **CheckIfWin** macro. This macro can be done with only nine calls to the **isOwner** macro.

- Handle the draw. Yes, it could happen that no one wins the match as no other moves are possible. Implement this on the **CheckIfWin** macro.

 Use a variable to store the number of blocks clicked on the grid. If a match reaches the max number of blocks, it means that no other moves are possible.

- Wait for a player input before cleaning the grid. A player will like to see how he loses or wins the match.

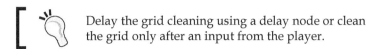 Delay the grid cleaning using a delay node or clean the grid only after an input from the player.

- Create a macro that handles the game state text. We used a lot of Set text nodes on our grid class, try to create a macro that unifies the win condition and the turn string.

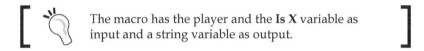 The macro has the player and the **Is X** variable as input and a string variable as output.

- Create two buttons using the block mesh and our symbols in order to let the player choose the symbol to start the game with.

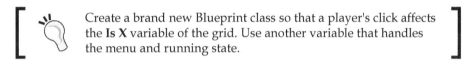 Create a brand new Blueprint class so that a player's click affects the **Is X** variable of the grid. Use another variable that handles the menu and running state.

In the next chapter, we will get our hands dirty with some code. We will improve this game by adding a basic AI and changing the UI with a much better Widget Blueprint UI system, and we will see how to communicate between code and Blueprint.

3
C++ Code – PAC-MAN

In this chapter, you are going learn how to write a code in UE4. Blueprint, as we saw in the previous chapters, is a wonderful tool that allows you to manage almost everything that you need for your project. Almost, yes, as even the most complex and complete tools have their limits and, at the moment, writing a code remains the only way to produce games with 100% freedom for exactly what, where, and how you want it.

In this chapter, we will cover the following:

- Creating a class
- Compiling and debugging a code
- Communicating between Blueprint and code
- Discussing navigation Meshes
- Discussing simple artificial intelligence
- Discussing collision type and preset
- Discussing player input

UE4 is different from its precursor UE3 that used its own scripting language (**UnrealScript**). UE4 allows you to write your code in native C++. This should be easy for those of you who already know this language and will make life easier for those of you who are starting to learn the programming languages.

This chapter will focus primarily on the code. It requires a basic knowledge of C++. Don't worry if you are not a programmer, the main focus of this book is to teach you how to use Blueprint correctly, not how to program. Feel free to move ahead with the book if you find yourself lost in this chapter, we won't talk about C++ in the future chapters.

Preparing the game

As a game for this project, we are going to recreate the famous PAC-MAN. This is a simple game that can introduce us to some important behaviors in a game: collisions, movements, collectables, and enemies!

PAC-MAN, for those of you who don't know this game, is probably the most famous arcade game of all time. Released on 1980 and developed by Namco, it is recognized as being the longest running video game franchises from the golden age of arcade video games:

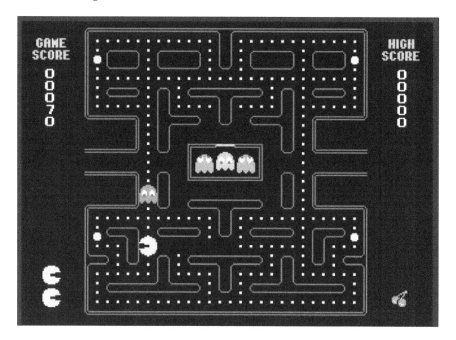

The game is quite simple: the player guides PAC-MAN through a maze, eating the dots along his path. When all the the dots are eaten, PAC-MAN is taken to the next stage. There are four threats that roam the maze trying to catch PAC-MAN. If an enemy comes in contact with PAC-MAN, PAC-MAN dies and the player loses a life, only to respawn after a brief period of time on his respawn point. Enemies can be eaten by PAC-MAN, thanks to some power-ups that are positioned around the map.

We are going to create this game in 3D, using basic shapes from the editor and a top-down view camera.

Let's check what we need as the assets for this game:

- **PAC-MAN character**: A yellow sphere
- **Enemies**: Four colored cylinders
- **Maze**: A collection of walls built using BSP brushes
- **Dots**: Little yellow spheres
- **Power ups**: Little red spheres
- **Materials**: Five plain color material (yellow, red, blue, pink, orange) and a transparent blue material that is used when the enemies are vulnerable and can be destroyed by PAC-MAN

Creating the project

None of the templates of UE4 can help us here. Therefore, through the launcher, create a new empty C++ basic project, call it `PacMan` and click on **Create Project** as follows:

You have now opened a Visual Studio project and the Unreal Editor in the default scene with the chairs. Let's create a new level by navigating to **File | New Level**, choose the default scene (the one with a plane and the light) and save it as Level1.umap.

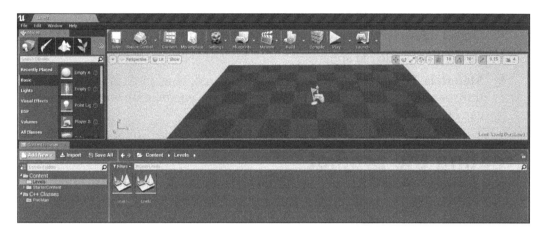

To keep everything in order, my advice is to create a folder section in the root of **Content Browser** and call the assets Levels, Materials, Blueprints, and so on, and move all the correct assets there.

The original PAC-MAN was built with 255 levels. Of course, we are going to build just the first one, not all of those levels:

 When you create your maps, you probably want to open one of them by default when you open the editor. You can set the default map by navigating to **Edit | Project Settings** and changing the **Default Maps** under the **Maps&Modes** section.

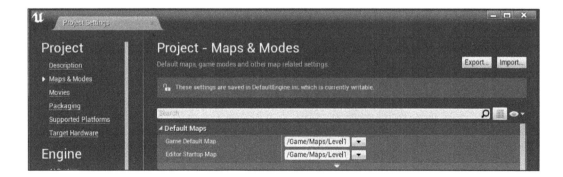

Now, create the four materials in the exact same way as we did in the previous chapter.

As mentioned earlier, the colors that we need are yellow, pink, orange, red, and blue. Call them as follows:

- `M_PacMan_Yellow`
- `M_Enemy_Blue`
- `M_Enemy_Red`
- `M_Enemy_Orange`
- `M_Enemy_Pink`

Transparent materials

The transparent material for the vulnerable enemies is quite easy. In the **Material** section of the **Details** panel, change **Blend Mode** to **Translucent**. You will immediately notice that the preview changes and the **Opacity** channel is now available. Connect a constant node to it and set it to **0.25**. The higher this value is, the less transparent the material becomes:

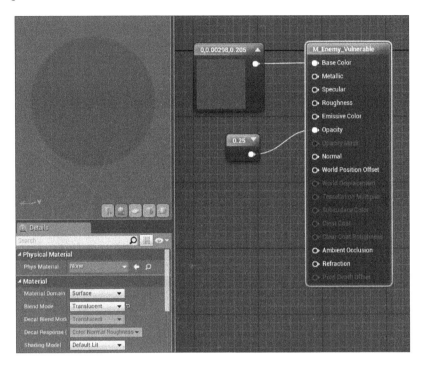

The maze

For the maze, we again use the BSP brushes. It is a tedious process as we need to draw all the single walls one by one; however, with my suggestions, you will surely find it easier.

If you still don't want to waste your time designing the maze, you can download the level from here: (www.nicolavalcasara.it/packt). Here, you can find the .umap file with the maze that we are going to create.

Before starting to mess around with BSP, it is always good practice to write down some rules about what you are going to create. In this case, as the maze is based on a square grid, we set a single square side to be 100 u (units) and walls to be of 100 u height x 10 u width.

There are no special rules about the maze design. We only need to remember to set an enemy spawn point (usually in the middle of the map) and design a maze without exit points.

The original PAN-MAN, as you can see from the previous image, uses a square grid of 10 x 10 cells (simplifying only with the walkable zones). For this level we are going to copy the same layout, keeping the camera fixed on top of the maze.

The following image shows you a smart way to design your levels. Print a square grid, keeping in mind the rules that we discussed earlier, and draw your maze with a pencil. When you are ready, just translate what you drew in the editor:

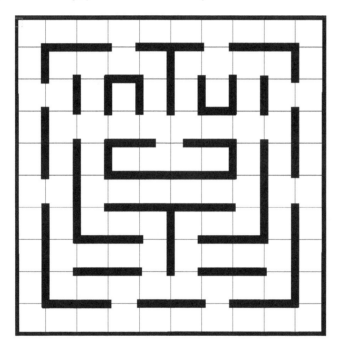

 Never underestimate math! A nice pre-calculated level that is designed using set rules is an easier and faster way to draw than a level that is drawn by hand with objects positioned by eyes. Try to notice how this rule is applied in any game that you play, even the most recent ones. Above all, our brains will immediately notice if something is not symmetrical, giving us the signal that something is wrong.

Designing the maze

Open the Level Editor that we created earlier and switch the viewport to show all the four views (top, left, front, and perspective) using the **maximize or restore this viewport** button on the top right-hand corner of it.

[If you want, you can use only one of them or switch between them using the *Alt + G, H, J* or *K* shortcut.]

I prefer this setting when I need to place new objects. The four viewports together provide no room for mistakes or misplaced objects:

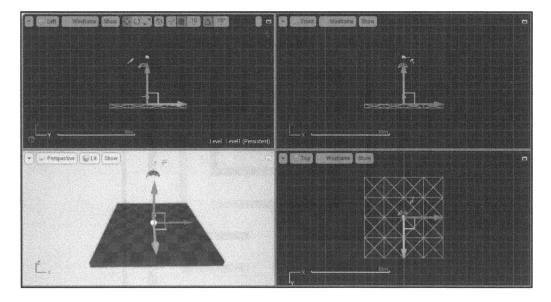

The floor of the maze needs to be, as said, 10 x 10 cells of 100 u each. Let's measure how big the default plane is in order to check whether we can use it.

To measure anything in the editor, you can use middle mouse button + drag on each of the top, front, or left viewport windows. This immediately gives you a number (in unreal units) denoting the exact distance between these two points.

As you can notice, the square is 1,000 x 1,000 u and it is exactly what we need for the maze. Nice. We can immediately start to build our walls.

Make sure that the plane is at 0 on the *z* coordinate and add a cube BSP brush on top of it. Let's start at the borders. Set the dimension of the brush to **X**:10, **Y**:1,000, and **Z**:10. The location will be -500 for **X**, 0 for **Y**, and half of this height for **Z** (50):

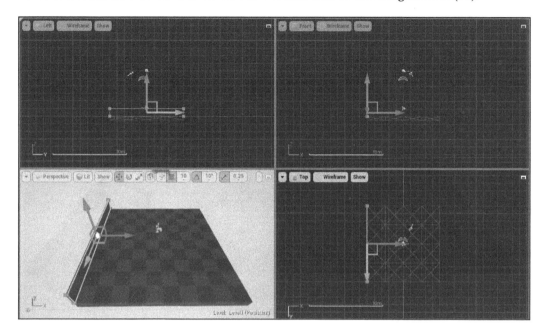

Now, instead of creating new cubes for each piece of wall, we can duplicate what we just did and move it to the correct place. In order to duplicate an object, select and drag the object around while pressing *Alt*.

Only change **X** of the duplicated wall to 500, all the other properties remain the same.

Now, duplicate the wall twice, rotate them by 90 degrees on the *z* axis and position them on the other sides of the perimeter of the plane. Now, we have a nice plane that is surrounded by perfectly positioned walls:

You should be able to replicate all the walls by yourself, just remember that the cell section is 100 units and the wall is 10 u thick. The final result should be something like the following image:

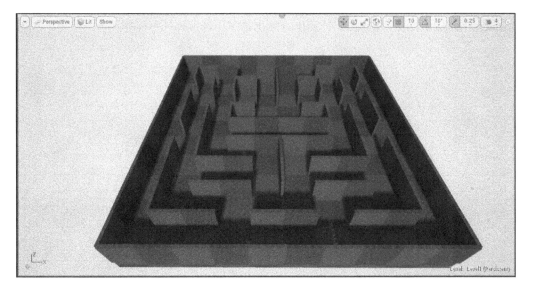

Nice; however, it is quite dull to see all those gray outlines everywhere. This is because we have not applied any material yet. Applying material on a BPS brush is not as straightforward as it was when we applied the Static Mesh in the previous chapter. The editor doesn't view BSP as a single object, but rather as a collection of surfaces. A cube, as you know, has six different surfaces. Following the rules of the editor, we can have six different materials for each section of wall; however, this is not exactly what we want.

You will then wonder: why not convert the whole maze to a single giant **Static Mesh**, as we did for the tic-tac-toe symbols? In this way, we can apply a single material for the whole object all at once.

This is not a bad idea, yet, it is not a good solution either. If you remember, I recommended avoiding the BPS brushes in order to create your **Static Mesh**. There are issues with this method (especially, lighting ones) and Epic is still working on finding a good solution. At the moment, leave BSP as it is, without conversions.

Applying a material to multiple surfaces

Even if it sounds like a simple operation, selecting multiple surfaces is not so straightforward. When talking about BPS brushes, there are two different types of selection:

- Brush selection
- Surface selection

A brush selection occurs when you click on the vertex of a brush, or select it from the world outliner, or when you select more than one brush with the multiple selection from viewport. This enables the transform and the **Brush Settings** in the **Details** panel:

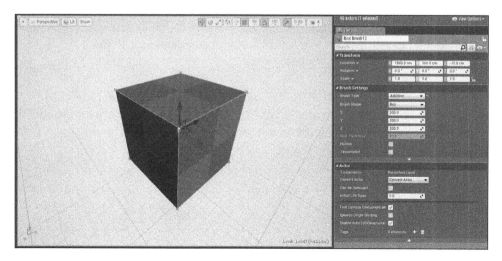

On the other hand, a surface selection appears by directly clicking on the surface of the brush. This enables the **Surface Material** and the **Geometry** section to appear in the **Details** panel:

 You can select more than one surface together using *Ctrl* + left–click; however, be careful as it is easy to miss clicking a surface and lose the selection.

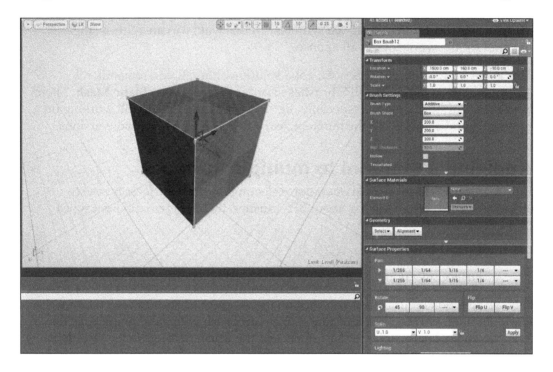

 To select all the surfaces of our maze, we can select all the surfaces by hand by clicking them or use **Gemeotry Select Tool**.

Select one wall and, on the **Details** panel, navigate to **Select | Select matching materials**. In this way, all the surfaces that are without a material are automatically selected and ready to be modified together.

Drag and drop a material from **Content Browser** in **Element 0** if it is **Surface Materials**, or directly click on the **Material** itself to show the menu. If you added **Starter Content** when creating the project, you can find some interesting wall materials, if not, just create a material on your own and add it. I used M_Basic_Wall and M_Basic_Floor for this, and the result is as shown in the following:

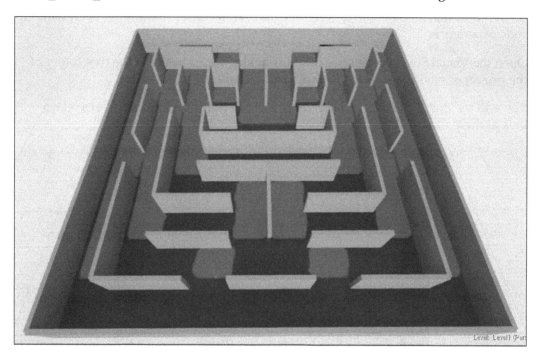

Better, isn't it? However, there is still something that is unfinished in this maze. If you notice, all the corners show a little overlap. You can leave this as it is or, if you want everything to be perfect, just add 10 (the thickness of the wall that causes this ugly result) to all the vertical or horizontal walls.

Unfortunately, this will cause another issue. In some parts of the maze, some of the walls will have a distance of only 95 u instead of 100 u. However, we can live with this.

The code

We are done with the editor, for now. It is time to open our Visual Studio project and add the logic of the game.

C++ code in UE4 is called assisted C++, meaning that there are a lot of features and conventions that help people to write fully working classes in minutes, even without code experience.

Open the Visual Studio project by double-clicking the `.sln` file in the root folder of the project or navigate to **File | Open Visual Studio** from the editor.

You will see that some files are already present in **Solution Explorer**. Let's take a look at these files:

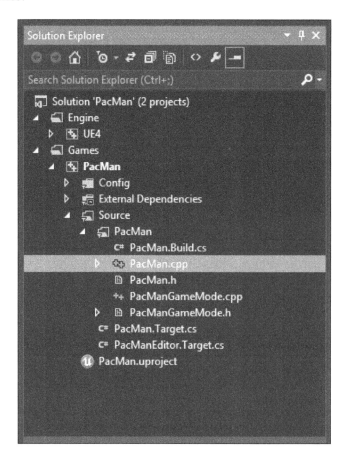

First, you will notice that there are two projects in your solution. The first one is the whole engine source code. You will usually never touch it as it is easy to make a mistake owing to the complexity of the engine, and you should not change anything in it unless you are an expert. Also, there is a whole company that is updating that code frequently, improving it at least once a month.

The second project is our game. The root folder is Games. Typically, it just contains our game project and you should be able to create a whole new solution project for each game that you are making. However, if you want, this is where you can add new game projects.

In this folder, you will find the following:

- Config: All the .ini files go here. The .ini files are program configuration files that are used to set values for properties that will be initialized when the project is loaded. Configuration is determined by key-value pairs that are arranged in sections. One or more values can be associated with a given key. Here are stored by default the editor, engine and game preferences are stored by default.

- External Dependencies: This folder is added by Visual Studio. It contains the headers of the classes that are detected to be in use at some point in the code. Do not modify anything in this folder.

- Source: This is the root folder of the code of the game. This is the folder where all the headers and the classes that we create will go.

- YourProject.UProject: This is the descriptor file of the project. It contains information such as the file version, engine version, name, and so on. It is automatically updated and there is usually no need to modify it manually.

The Source folder, as you can see, already contains some of the classes, as follows:

- PacMan.Build.cs: This class is created by **UnrealBuildTool** (**UBT**), the tool that manages the process of building the engine source code across the numerous possible build configurations. This class controls how the engine is built, including options to define module dependencies, additional libraries, included paths, and so on. If you open it, you can see which modules are used by default in our game (Core, Engine, InputCore, and CoreUObject) and the online module and the **Slate UI** under comment.

- PacMan: This is the entry point of the application, this is the first class that will be seen when you build the project and from here you set the needed game modules and the engine itself. It is very rare that this file will need any modifications as compared with the engine or the .cs files.

- `PacManGameMode`: This is the game mode class. This is the only class that is also visible on the editor at the moment.

- `PacMan.Target.cs` and `PacManEditor.target.cs`: Like `build.cs`, these two files are used to determine how to build the project, specifically, the game and the editor respectively. You can see from the **Solution** configuration, that there are two choices for each build setting: `Debug/Debug editor`, `Development/Development Editor` and so on.

Class Wizard

Let's create our first class using the engine Wizard. Navigate to **File | New C++ Class...**.A window appears that is very similar to the ones that appear when we add a new Blueprint class and choose the parent of our class. Let's select **Actor** and click **Next**.

Call it **Collectable** (yes, this will be the dot that the PAC-MAN needs to eat) and click on **Public**. Notice how the Wizard will autofill the correct paths for us, adding the **Public** and **Private** subfolders for our header and cpp files:

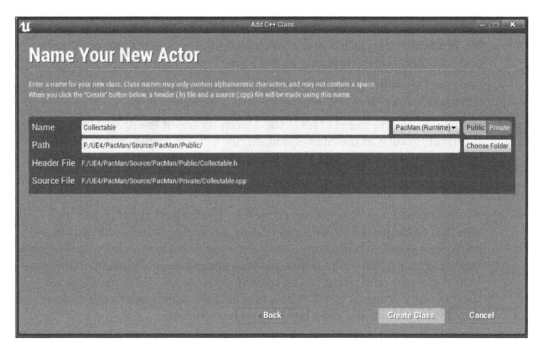

 A public class is the class that can be accessed by different modules, while a private class can be accessed only in the module that we select in the Wizard window.

As there is only one module (PAC-MAN) and we will be using it in this game, it doesn't really matter what we choose and we would have all the classes in the root folder; however, it is a good practice to subdivide headers and code in a well-organized manner with a subfolder like Unreal recommends.

Click on **Create Class** and go back to Visual Studio. Notice how the two files are created and already have some functions implemented.

Check the header to see what the editor has added for us, as shown in the following:

```
#pragma once

#include "GameFramework/Actor.h"
#include "Collectable.generated.h"

UCLASS()
class PACMAN_API ACollectable : public AActor
{
  GENERATED_BODY()

public:
  // Sets default values for this actor's properties
  ACollectable();

  // Called when the game starts or when spawned
  virtual void BeginPlay() override;

  // Called every frame
  virtual void Tick( float DeltaSeconds ) override;
};
```

Downloading the example code

You can download the example code files from your account at http://www.packtpub.com for all the Packt Publishing books you have purchased. If you purchased this book elsewhere, you can visit http://www.packtpub.com/support and register to have the files e-mailed directly to you.

You will immediately see two lines in which our parent is referred: the inclusion of the Actor header and the ACollectable class that extends AActor.

UCLASS() is the special keyword that allows us to see and handle this class in the editor.

The syntax for any new class in UE4 is as follows:

```
UCLASS()
Class NameModule_API NameClass : (extends OtherClass)
{
  GENERATED_BODY()
};
```

There are three class methods added by default, as shown in the following:

- `ACollectable()`: This is the constructor of the class. Here, the default values of variables are initialized and references are added to other classes or components.

- `BeginPlay()`: This is the initializer. This function is called when the class is called/created during the gameplay. Here, we can set the starting behavior of the class or handle an event in the game.

- `Tick(deltaSeconds)`: This is the `Tick` function, it is a typical function that you can find almost everywhere when talking about game development. It can have different names such as `Update` (like in Unity), `Loop`, `MainLoop`, and so on. Basically, it always follows the same principle—called before every frame update during gameplay.

The `DeltaSeconds` parameter (or DeltaTime) is the time elapsed since the game was last update. This concept was introduced in order to remove the effects of lag on computers that try to handle complex graphics or a lot of code. This is done by adding up the speed of objects so that they will eventually move at the same speed, regardless of the lag.

Collectable

A collectable object is an object that, as the name suggests, can be collected by another object. It is composed of a collision component and a graphic element and it usually performs an event when touched.

Our collectable is the easiest type of collectable. It doesn't spawn, it is simply destroyed when collected and sits where it is positioned, doing nothing, until the player touches it.

Having said this, let's start removing the useless functions from the collectable class that we just created. Delete the `BeginPlay()` and `Tick()` functions from the `.h` and `.cpp` files.

Now, we need to add the two components needed for our collectable, as follows:

- Static Mesh component
- Collision Sphere component

Let's declare them in the header file on top of the `public` keyword:

```
USphereComponent* BaseCollisionComponent;
UstaticMeshComponent* CollectableMesh;
```

We just created two pointers for two components. They still aren't visible in the editor. For them to be visible in the editor, we need to set UPROPERTY before declaring them.

The UProperty variables are declared using the standard C++ syntax with additional descriptors, such as variable specifiers and metadata that is placed above the declaration. The syntax is as follows:

```
UPROPERTY([specifier, specifier, ...], [meta(key=value, key=value,
...)])
Type VariableName;
```

There are different specifiers for many of your requirements. However, in this case, we want the previously mentioned components to be editable from the editor in order to modify them. If needed mesh, size, or any other property can be specified here to be seen and edited within the editor. The final result is as shown in the following code:

```
UPROPERTY(EditDefaultsOnly, Category = Collectable)
USphereComponent* BaseCollisionComponent;

UPROPERTY(EditDefaultsOnly, Category = Collectable)
UStaticMeshComponent* CollectableMesh;
```

Any property can be categorized and, as you see here, we added the `Collectable` category. They are automatically sorted in the editor.

Now, another variable is needed. We know that PAC-MAN can collect two types of pills—the basic yellow ones and a special one that makes the enemies vulnerable for a short period of time. To achieve this behavior, we use a simple Boolean variable. Like the other properties, we want it to be editable in the editor. Add the following lines:

```
UPROPERTY(EditAnywhere, Category = Collectable)
bool bIsSuperCollectable;
```

The final heading looks as follows:

```
#pragma once

#include "GameFramework/Actor.h"
#include "Collectable.generated.h"

UCLASS()
class PACMAN_API ACollectable : public AActor
{
  GENERATED_BODY()

public:
  // initializer of the class.
  // Witout the objectInitializer argument from 4.7
  ACollectable();

  UPROPERTY(EditDefaultsOnly, Category = Collectable)
  USphereComponent* BaseCollisionComponent;

  UPROPERTY(EditDefaultsOnly, Category = Collectable)
  UStaticMeshComponent* CollectableMesh;

  UPROPERTY(EditAnywhere, Category = Collectable)
  bool bIsSuperCollectable;
};
```

Now, let's implement them in the cpp file. Open `Collectable.cpp` and set the tick event frame (`PrimaryActorTick.bCanEveryTick`) to `false`. We don't really need to do this but any performance improvement, even the smallest, is important to any game.

Collisions in the engine are disabled by default. Add this line under the line that we just modified in order to enable the collision to be called by the script:

```
SetActorEnableCollision(true);
```

Now, set the collision component with the following line:

```
BaseCollisionComponent =
  CreateDefaultSubobject<USphereComponent>(TEXT
  ("BaseCollisionComponent"));
```

CreateDefaultSubobject is a method that takes a type class and an input name and adds the type component, if valid, as a component of our class. We will do the same for the Static Mesh and attach it as a child of the collision component:

```
CollectableMesh =
  CreateDefaultSubobject<UStaticMeshComponent>
  (TEXT("CollectableMesh"));
CollectableMesh->AttachTo(BaseCollisionComponent);
```

Now, you can compile the code by clicking on the **Compile** button from the toolbar of the editor and, when finished, you can see this class appearing in **Content Browser** with a little white sphere. This class is now usable as a parent when creating a new Blueprint class, as we saw in the previous chapter. By doing this, you will be able to modify the components that we created in our code and add as many instances as you want in the level.

We can go further. We already know that the mesh will always be a sphere and we can set the collision size directly on the code as it is a static object.

With the help of the code, we can find references to any object on **Content Browser** using the ConstructorHelpers struct. To find a reference of any of our object in **Content Browser**, we can right-click on the object that we want a reference for and click on **Copy Reference**. The code should be as follows:

```
static ConstructorHelpers::FObjectFinder<UStaticMesh>
  Sphere(TEXT("StaticMesh'/Engine/BasicShapes/Sphere.Sphere'"));
```

With this reference, we can simply set the Static Mesh of the component by using the following code:

```
If(Sphere.Succeeded())
  CollectableMesh->SetStaticMesh(Sphere.Object);
```

 Every time you retrieve an object from **Content Browser**, it's good to check whether the object is found by calling the Succeeded() method before assigning it.

We can also set the mesh and collision sizes to fit the game. Remember that with EditDefaultsOnly, we can modify the parameters if required in the editor as well. However, writing them here in the code will save some time in the future:

```
CollectableMesh->SetWorldScale3D(FVector(0.3,0.3,0.3);
BaseCollisionComponent->SetSphereRadius(16);
```

Ok, we are finished with this object for now. It is time to use it in the editor and start populating the level. Just for your reference, the complete code is as follows:

```cpp
#include "PacMan.h"
#include "Collectable.h"

// Sets default values
ACollectable::ACollectable()
{
  // disable the tick call
  PrimaryActorTick.bCanEverTick = false;

  //enable collisions
  SetActorEnableCollision(true);

  //initialize the collision sphere component
  BaseCollisionComponent =
    CreateDefaultSubobject<USphereComponent>
    (TEXT("BaseCollisionComponent"));

  //initialize the mesh for the collectable and attach to the root
  CollectableMesh = CreateDefaultSubobject<UStaticMeshComponent>
    (TEXT("CollectableMesh"));
  CollectableMesh->AttachTo(BaseCollisionComponent);

  // find a reference to the sphere mesh and set it
  static ConstructorHelpers::FObjectFinder<UStaticMesh>
    Sphere(TEXT("StaticMesh'/Engine/BasicShapes/Sphere.Sphere'"));
If (Sphere.Succeeded())
  CollectableMesh->SetStaticMesh(Sphere.Object);

  // set the default parameters of the collectable
  CollectableMesh->SetWorldScale3D(FVector(0.3, 0.3, 0.3));
  BaseCollisionComponent->SetSphereRadius(16);
}
```

Back to the editor, we can see that after compiling under the C++ classes from the content browser, the `Collectable` class has a sphere mesh on it and the size fits the maze spaces perfectly when added on the stage. The only thing that needs to be added in the editor is the material, which can be of two types: the standard ones yellow and the special red ones:

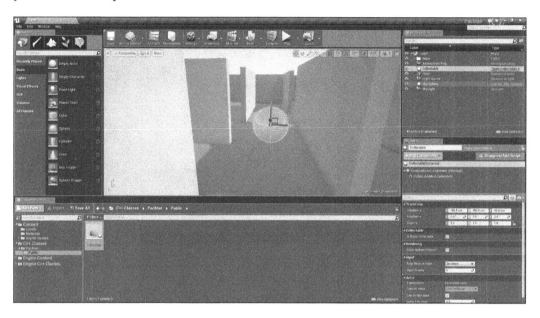

Adding a material to this collectable is the same process used for the symbols in the previous chapter. From the Details panel, just click the **Collectable** mesh component, search for our `M_PacMan_Yellow` material under **Material 0**, and set it to the same. Now, duplicate the whole object in order to have one of them in each cell.

 Use the different viewports to position the collectables correctly and make sure that every position is a multiple of 50 u and exactly in the center of the cell.

You should end with a maze full of collectables everywhere, as shown in the following image:

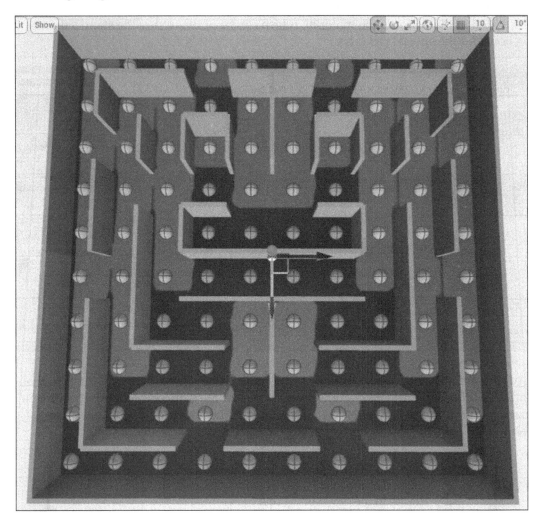

There are obviously some spaces where the collectables shouldn't stay, and we need to convert four of them to special collectables.

First, remove the one at the bottom to the left and the four collectables in the enemy spawn point. These are places where the enemies and player will spawn. We don't want a collectable there!

Second, choose four collectables from anywhere on the map, considering that they should allow, the player to create a strategy while moving through the maze. For these collectables, change the material to a different one (I used M_Enemy_Red; however, you can create another if you desire) and set the **Is Super Collectable** Boolean variable to true by clicking on the instance from the **Details** panel. As you will notice, by setting UPROPERTY to EditAnywhere, we can find it exactly where we want it—under the Collectable category:

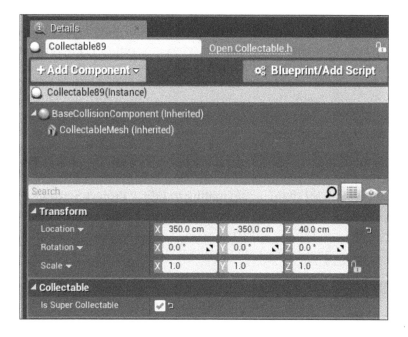

With all the collectables in position, we are now ready to create the hero of our game.

Player character

The character is one of the most important objects needed in a game. The player interacts with the elements of the game through the character, which has a lot of behaviors. In our game, the character needs to be able to move, eat the collectables, die or kill enemies, and be responsible of winning or losing the game.

Let's start by adding a new class from the Wizard, call it `PacManCharacter` and choose `Character` as its parent.

Movements

First, let's implement the movement of the character. In order to achieve this, we override the `SetupPlayerInputComponent` method and through it, we will bind the keys that a player can use.

By binding a key, the code will call a function whenever the player hits the corresponding key. There are two different types of input binding on Unreal: **action** and **axis**. An action rises whenever a bind event occurs (touch the screen, press a key, release a key, and so on), and it can have either one of the two values — `true` or `false`; on the other hand, the axis shows a value range (usually between -1 and 1) besides the `true`/`false` action. For example, this is used to determine the exact value of the throttle on a joystick.

Before binding anything, we need to set the input keys from the editor. The editor allows different kinds of input, right from the simple keyboard button to the Microsoft Kinect Gesture. We can set them by navigating to **Edit | Project Settings | Input**.

For our game, we want to be able to control the movement of our PAC-MAN using the arrows keys and also control the *x* axis and the *y* axis movement. On the **Axis Mappings** section, double-click on the **+** button in order to add an axis control, and rename these two axes as **MoveX** and **MoveY**. For each group that is created, add two key values by clicking on the **+** button. For the *x* axis, search for the keyboard **Left** key | and keyboard **Right** |, setting their values at -1 and 1 respectively. Use the **Up** and **Down** keys for the **MoveY** axis, again with the -1 and 1 values respectively:

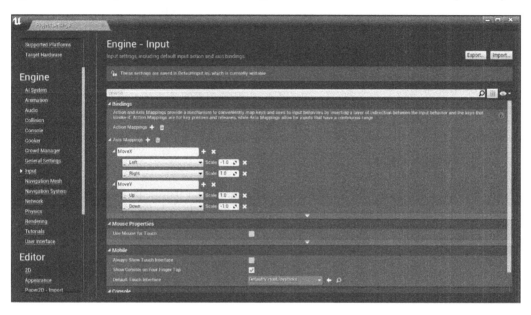

As we are here, we can also add the action value to control the game flow. We want the player to be able to stop, restart, or create a new game.

Add the three **Action Mappings**, call them NewGame, Pause, and Restart respectively, and set three letters key to the mapping: N, P, and R. From the **Action Mappings** section, you can also set the action to only perform if a combination of keys is pressed (for example, *ctrl* + selected key).

With this setup, we are now able to handle the keys actions from the code. On PacManCharacter.cpp, find the SetupPlayerInputComponent function and add the following lines after the super method:

```
// bind the input from the player
InputComponent->BindAxis("MoveX", this,
  &APacManCharacter::MoveXAxis);
InputComponent->BindAxis("MoveY", this,
  &APacManCharacter::MoveYAxis);
```

```
InputComponent->BindAction("NewGame", IE_Pressed, this,
    &APacManCharacter::NewGame);
InputComponent->BindAction("Pause", IE_Pressed,this,
    &APacManCharacter::Pause);
InputComponent->BindAction("Restart", IE_Pressed, this,
    &APacManCharacter::RestartGame);
```

We obviously need to declare these functions on the header in order to use them; therefore, go back to the header, and on the `private` section add them, as follows:

```
private:

// movement handlers
void MoveXAxis(float AxisValue);
void MoveYAxis(float AxisValue);

// key events
void NewGame();
void Pause();
void RestartGame();
```

> Notice how the axis binding functions have a float value parameter. This is the parameter that is returned from the axis input. In this case, it can return only -1 or 1; however, if the input is a joystick, the returned value is between these values and not necessarily exactly these numbers.

We now receive inputs from the keyboard and have a function that handles the key that is pressed. We can now use these functions to set the velocity of the player. In order to do this, we can store the read `AxisValue` read from the Keyboard Inputs in a vector variable. And, thanks to the `AddMovementInput` character method, we can move the player around:

```
FVector CurrentVelocity;// the current velocity of the player
```

We can now implement the axis function, as shown in the following:

```
void APacManCharacter::MoveXAxis(float AxisValue)
{
  CurrentVelocity.X = AxisValue;
  AddMovementInput(CurrentVelocity);

}

void APacManCharacter::MoveYAxis(float AxisValue)
{
  CurrentVelocity.Y = AxisValue;
  AddMovementInput(CurrentVelocity);
}
```

This is the simplest way to add control for our character. There are plenty of methods and functions that are available to manipulate character movements; however, with this simple setup, you will have a simple moving object straightaway. It can also be improved by changing some variables from the editor. We will take a further look at them in the *Chapter 5, Top-Down Shooter*.

Now, let's implement the three game flow keys that we added to our character. In order to use them properly, we need to create a game state enumerator. This will allow us to switch between the different states of a game (playing, in pause, game over, win, and so on) and more importantly, enable us to have a single state for each moment of the gameplay.

Open the `PacManGameState.h` file and just after the `#include` statements at the very beginning, create a new enumerator, as follows:

```
enum class EGameState : short
{
  EMenu,
  EPlaying,
  EPause,
  EWin,
  EGameOver
};
```

Now, this is a little tricky. We want to know the state of the game from the other classes as well; however, we have to make sure that this variable is modified from nowhere except the game state class.

We can modify the state from other places; however, not before checking it with a dedicated function. This is how `getter` and `setter` work.

Add the following lines on the `public` section of the header:

```
public:
// getter of the game state
EGameState GetCurrentState() const;

// setter of the game state that handle further operations
void SetCurrentState(EGameState value);
```

Then, declare the state in the `private` section:

```
private:
EGameState CurrentState;
```

Implement them in the C++ class as shown. As you can see, they simply set or return the value of our currentState private enumerator:

```
void APacManGameMode::SetCurrentState(EGameState value)
{
  currentState = value;
}
EGameState APacManGameMode::GetCurrentState()
{
..return currentState;
}
```

Now that we have the game state code handler, we can go back to the character and complete the game flow functions as we did earlier.

The idea is to simply change the game state of the GameMode class when pressing the binded keys. It is quite simple to achieve this. We need to create a reference to our game mode and call the SetCurrentState() function through the referenced variable.

On the header of the character, under the private declarations, add the following lines:

```
APacManGameMode* GameMode; // pointer to the game mode
```

The game mode heading needs to be included at the very beginning of the file:

```
#include "PacManGameMode.h"
```

We will initialize the GM variable by casting it to our game mode class on the BeginPlay() function, as follows:

```
GameMode =
  Cast<APacManGameMode>(UGameplayStatics::GetGameMode(this));
```

Now, we are ready to change the game state or read its state whenever we want. The three functions for the game flow look similar to the following:

```
void APacManCharacter::NewGame()
{
  if (GameMode ->GetCurrentState() == EGameState::EMenu) {
    GameMode ->SetCurrentState(EGameState::EPlaying);
  }
}

// toggle the pause. action fired only between playing and pause state
void APacManCharacter::Pause()
{
```

```
  if (GameMode ->GetCurrentState() == EGameState::EPlaying) {
    GameMode ->SetCurrentState(EGameState::EPause);
  }
  else if (GameMode ->GetCurrentState() == EGameState::EPause){
    GameMode ->SetCurrentState(EGameState::EPlaying);
  }
}

// restart the game
void APacManCharacter::RestartGame()
{
  GetWorld()->GetFirstPlayerController()->
    ConsoleCommand(TEXT("RestartLevel"));
}
```

As you can see, `NewGame` and `Pause` switch the game state. The only one that doesn't need changes to its state is `RestartGame`. It simply uses a hacked method that forces the whole stage to restart by using `ConsoleCommand`.

Collisions

The player can move as it has a handler for the different states and receives the correct input for a game flow. The next step is to add collision events to it in order to make it receptive of the other objects in the level.

As mentioned, collisions are disabled by default. Therefore, let's set our actor to handle the collisions as we did for the collectable. On the initializer, add the following line:

```
  SetActorEnableCollision(true);
```

Let's analyze what collisions are supposed to do. When colliding with a collectable, the player is supposed to destroy the collectable object, check whether it was the last collectable in order to win the level and whether it was a super collectable in order to debilitate the enemies. When colliding with an enemy, the player is supposed to either die or kill it if the enemy is weakened by then. The most important thing, which is not mentioned in the code, is that with collisions enabled, our PAC-MAN is able to walk around the maze and hit the walls. Without collisions, the player would just pass through the floor and fall.

To achieve the collision, we add a delegate to the `OnComponentBeginOverlap` method and attach it to the collision component of our character. A delegate allows us to call the member functions on other C++ objects in a generic and type-safe way. In this particular case, when the character collides with something, we can raise the collision event in that collided object without being obligated to know exactly which object it is.

The following are the delegated method arguments:

```
Void DelegateFunction(class AActor* otherActor, class UComponent*
    otherComponent, int32 OtherBodyIndex, bool bFromSweep, const
    FHitResult& SweepResult);
```

It looks complex; however, on analyzing it, we know that it just has useful information about the collision detection. The sequence of properties is the follow:

- The actor that it collides with
- The specific component hit
- The index of the body that is hit
- Whether the hit is from a sweep
- The sweep result (useful for calculating bouncing behaviors)

The last two arguments are optional; therefore, our functions look as shown in the following:

```
UFUNCTION()
void OnCollision(class AActor* OtherActor, class
    UPrimitiveComponent* OtherComp, int32 OtherBodyIndex);
```

This should be added on the header in the `private` section.

Now, add the delegate to our collision component. This code is added on the `BeginPlay` method:

```
// set the handler of the collision
GetCapsuleComponent()->OnComponentBeginOverlap.AddDynamic(this,
    &APacManCharacter::OnCollision);
```

Let's implement the `OnCollision` function:

```
void APacManCharacter::OnCollision(class AActor* OtherActor, class
UPrimitiveComponent* OtherComp, int32 OtherBodyIndex, bool bFromSweep,
const FHitResult & SweepResult)
{
    // enter on deeper check only if playing
    if (GameMode->GetCurrentState() == EGameState::EPlaying)
```

```
{
    // check if is a true collectable
    if (OtherActor->IsA(ACollectable::StaticClass()))
    {
        // in any case, destroy that collectable!
        OtherActor->Destroy();
    }
}
}
```

This is a good starting point for our collision method and it is pretty easy to understand. When the player collides with something, firstly, check whether we are in the EPlaying state. If yes, check what is the collider, and if it is a collectable then destroy it.

Winning or losing the game

The win/loss mechanism is very simple. If all the collectables at the scene are eaten/finished, then we win. If PAC-MAN loses all the lives, then we lose.

To handle the winning condition, we do the following: as soon as the game starts, count how many collectables are in the levels and store it in the player controller. Every time the player collects one of them, decrease that variable, and if that value reaches 0, set the game state to win.

Handling the losing condition is very similar: store the number of lives of the player in a variable and decrease that value every time the player is hit by an enemy. If that value reaches 0, set the game state to lose.

Let's start by adding these two variables in the header of PacManCharacter:

```
uint8 CollectablesToEat;  // total collectables in order to win
uint8 Lives;  // player total lives
```

The win handler can be achieved with just a line of code. In the OnCollision function, just after the cast to the collectable object, add the following:

```
if (--collectablesToEat == 0) {
    GameMode->SetCurrentState(EGameState::EWin); }
```

With the double minus math symbol before the name of the variable, we decrease its value by one before evaluating it, and change the game state to Win when that value reaches 0.

In order to count a certain object in a level, we use an iterator. This special function counts all the objects of a certain type in a given world. If used in a loop, it is easy to count them. The function should be added in the BeginPlay() function, and it looks as shown in the following:

```
// find out how many collectables the player need to eat in order to
win
for (TActorIterator<ACollectable> CollectableItr(GetWorld());
  CollectableItr; ++CollectableItr)
{
  collectablesToEat++;
}
```

Dead

The lose condition is not exactly like the win one. There is a middle step called Dead. A player dies when an enemy hits it. Before respawning, we need to decrease the number of lives by one, and if the player has enough lives, he can return to the spawn point and continue the venture.

We need a Kill function and a vector variable to remember where the player starts. Add them to the header:

```
FVector StartPoint;  // the start point of the player
void Kill();
```

Set the start point as the actor location at BeginPlay and implement the Kill function, as shown in the following:

```
// inside the BeginPlay() Function
StartPoint = GetActorLocation();  // simple get the player location
Lives = 3;  // set the full life when start

// kill function
void APacManCharacter::Kill()
{
  if (--lives == 0) {
    GameMode->SetCurrentState(EGameState::EGameOver);
  }
  Else {
    SetActorLocation(StartPoint);
  }
}
```

C++ class to Blueprint class

We are now done with the code for the character. Now, we can complete it by adding a mesh and adjusting this aspect to fit the game.

Go back to the editor and compile the code. Everything should compile without any error. If you receive any error, go back to the previous sections and check the code. If you still don't succeed, remember that you can find all the source code and the games on www.nicolavalcasara.it/packt.

We are going to create a Blueprint class that inherits from the PacManCharacter class that we just created. You can do it by creating a new Blueprint class and searching for our class as parent.

Create a Blueprint folder and name this new Blueprint class BP_PacMan. You should be at a familiar place now. We are going to build PAC-MAN by using a simple sphere as the body and two other little spheres as eyes, just to see where the character is headed towards.

From the **Components** panel, add a new Static Mesh component and set its mesh as the default Shape_Sphere. Move it a little lower in order to be in the middle of the collision capsule and change its material to our M_PacMan_Yellow.

Add two other spheres as children of the the first one, set them to a dark material, and positon and scale them down to be like the eyes of our PAC-MAN.

 Be sure that the eyes are facing the correct direction, which is shown by the big blue arrow.

The whole object needs to be resized to a 0.8 scale and **CapsuleComponent** needs to be resized as well. Set its *half height* property to 60 and its radius to 40 on the **Shape** section of the **Details** panel.

The final result should be as follows:

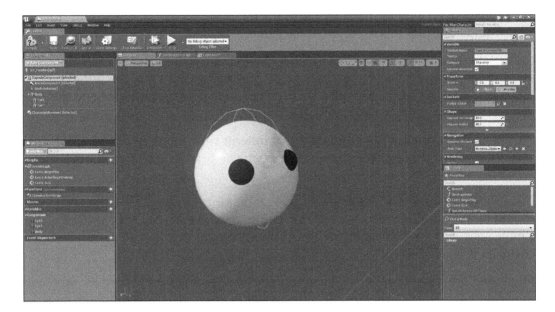

Enemies

After the good guy, there needs to be the bad guy too. We have four of them! The process of making an enemy is similar to the main character: we will create a class extending `ACharacter` and the required functions in it. The only difference is that while we control the PAC-MAN character directly, the enemies need to have their own brains that tell them how to move and what to do.

This is called **artificial intelligence** (**AI**) and there is a dedicated parent that can be used exactly for this called `AIController`.

Create two new C++ classes: the first one called `Enemy` that extends `ACharacter` and the second one called `AIEnemy` that extends `AAIController`. Set them as `public` similar to the other classes.

Enemy Pawn

Let's start with the enemy character class. We will use a simple colored cylinder as mesh. The components that are used are the same as that of the other object: a capsule used for the collision and a Static Mesh used as a graphic element. The idea of this object is that the enemy will continue to walk randomly through the maze and, if the enemy becomes vulnerable, it needs to run quickly to its house in order to recover its life; whereas if it is normal, it will need to kill the player.

We will use two functions to swap between vulnerability and a timer that handles how long the enemy can be killed by the player.

The only variable that we want to be editable in the editor is the Static Mesh. This will allow us to change the color of each individual enemy that is positioned in the map, the other behaviors and variables are all handled in the code. The following is the header of the Enemy class:

```cpp
#pragma once

#include "GameFramework/Character.h"
#include "AIEnemy.h"
#include "PacManCharacter.h"
#include "Enemy.generated.h"

UCLASS()
class PACMAN_API AEnemy : public ACharacter
{
  GENERATED_BODY()

public:
 // Sets default values for this character's properties
  AEnemy();

  // Called when the game starts or when spawned
  virtual void BeginPlay() override;

  // called when colliding with something
  UFUNCTION()
  void OnCollision(class AActor* OtherActor, class
    UPrimitiveComponent* OtherComp, int32 OtherBodyIndex, bool
    bFromSweep, const FHitResult & SweepResult);

  // make it editable in the editor in order to set its starting
    material
  UPROPERTY(EditDefaultsOnly, Category = Body)
```

```
UStaticMeshComponent* EnemyBody;

void SetVulnerable();
void SetInvulnerable();

void SetMove(bool MoveIt);
void Kill();
void Rearm();

bool bIsDead;

private:

bool bIsVulnerable;

FTimerHandle TimerVulnerable;

class UMaterialInterface* DefaultMaterial;
class UMaterialInterface* VulnerableMaterial;

};
```

As you can see, apart from the functions that we have already seen, there is a timer (the FTimerHandle type) and two UMaterialInterface that we use to store the two different materials of the enemy.

Let's implement this in the cpp class.

In the constructor function, we create the enemy object, adding the mesh and setting its size and material. The only new thing that you can notice here is the AIControllerClass call. In that last line, we tell the editor that this character will be controlled by AIController:

```
#include "PacMan.h"
#include "Enemy.h"

AEnemy::AEnemy()
{
  SetActorEnableCollision(true);

  // construct the object with meshes, sizes and everything needed
  GetCapsuleComponent()->SetCapsuleRadius(40.0f);
  GetCapsuleComponent()->SetCapsuleHalfHeight(50.0f);

  // add a cylinder shape to the enemy and set its size
  static ConstructorHelpers::FObjectFinder<UStaticMesh>CylinderObj
    (TEXT("'/Game/StarterContent/Shapes/Shape_Cylinder'"));
```

```
EnemyBody = CreateDefaultSubobject<UStaticMeshComponent>
    (TEXT("Body"));
EnemyBody->StaticMesh = CylinderObj.Object;
EnemyBody->SetRelativeScale3D(FVector(0.7f, 0.7f, 1.0f));
EnemyBody->AttachTo(RootComponent);

// set the vulnerable material, same for all the enemies
static ConstructorHelpers::FObjectFinder<UMaterial>VulnerableMat
    (TEXT("'/Game/Materials/M_Enemy_Vulnerable'"));
VulnerableMaterial = VulnerableMat.Object;

// set our custom AI class as controller
AIControllerClass = AAIEnemy::StaticClass();
}
```

In the initializer, we simply store the actual enemy material and bind the collision event when something overlaps with our collider:

```
void AEnemy::BeginPlay()
{
  Super::BeginPlay();

  // store its material for when he respawn
  DefaultMaterial = EnemyBody->GetMaterial(0);

  // add the collision handler
  GetCapsuleComponent()->OnComponentBeginOverlap.AddDynamic
    (this, &AEnemy::OnCollision);
}
```

The SetMove function will handle the pause/resume state. This is called from the GameMode class. When called, depending on the value of MoveIt, we will stop or restore the movement of the enemy:

```
// called from game mode when paused or restored
void AEnemy::SetMove(bool moveIt)
{
  // need to cast the AI class and call two public functions from
    here
  // if false move to its location in order to stop movements
  AAIEnemy* AI = Cast<AAIEnemy>(AIControllerClass);

  if (bMoveIt) { AI->SearchNewPoint(); }
  else{ AI->StopMove(); }

}
```

Movements and behaviors are handled by the `AI` class.

In this class, we have only movements or object-relative properties to set. In the `Kill` and `Rearm` function, we only want to change its speed and refresh its state:

```cpp
void AEnemy::Kill()
{
  // don't kill twice
  if (bIsDead) return;

  // if is not dead, kill and modify its speed
  // the enemy will go fast at his house in order to respawn
  bIsDead = true;
  GetCharacterMovement()->MaxWalkSpeed = 300.0f;
}

// set invulnerable and restore its original speed
void AEnemy::Rearm()
{
  bIsDead = false;
  GetCharacterMovement()->MaxWalkSpeed = 150.0f;

  if (bIsVulnerable) { SetInvulnerable(); }
}
```

The `SetVulnerable` and `SetInvulnerable` functions are called from the `PacManCharacter` class and they change the material of the enemy and start or clear the vulnerability timer:

```cpp
// when player eat a super collectable, set all the enemies vulnerable
// for a certain period of time
void AEnemy::SetVulnerable()
{
  // set/reset a timer
  GetWorldTimerManager().SetTimer(TimerVulnerable, this,
&AEnemy::SetInvulnerable, 10.0f, false);

  // simple return if is already vulnerable
  if (bIsVulnerable) { return; }

  bIsVulnerable = true;

  // change its material with the transparent one
```

```
  EnemyBody->SetMaterial(0, VulnerableMaterial);

  // make the enemy run slower
  GetCharacterMovement()->MaxWalkSpeed = 50.0f;
}

// when timer ends, clear it and restore the enemy invulnerability
void AEnemy::SetInvulnerable()
{
  // simple clear the timer
  GetWorldTimerManager().ClearTimer(TimerVulnerable);

  bIsVulnerable = false;

  // restore the original material
  EnemyBody->SetMaterial(0, DefaultMaterial);

  // restore the original walk speed
  GetCharacterMovement()->MaxWalkSpeed = 150.0f;
}
```

This is where the collisions are handled. In our case, the enemy simply kills the player or dies, depending on its vulnerability:

```
// when colliding with an enemy
void AEnemy::OnCollision(class AActor* OtherActor, class
  UPrimitiveComponent* OtherComp, int32 OtherBodyIndex, bool
  bFromSweep, const FHitResult & SweepResult)
{
  if (OtherActor->IsA(APacManCharacter::StaticClass()))
  {
    // check whenever the pawn is vulnerable or not
    // simple kill it if is vulnerable
    if (bIsVulnerable) { Kill(); }
    else
    {
      // or kill the player instead if not
      APacManCharacter* PacMan =
        Cast<APacManCharacter>(OtherActor);
      PacMan->Kill();
    }
  }
}
```

Enemy AI

The AIController class is a special class that handles the decisions that a pawn should take in different situations. This is based on state machine mechanics, where every state corresponds to an action, and the end of every state corresponds to a new call, depending on the object that it controls.

The AI of our enemy is really simple. Like zombies, they simply walk around, without thinking about where they are going or where the player is on the map. When they are vulnerable, they simply know that they need to return home and they don't care if they eat a player or not, they just keep walking. The header will be as follows:

```cpp
#pragma once

#include "AIController.h"
#include "Enemy.h"
#include "AIEnemy.generated.h"

/**
 *
 */
UCLASS()
class PACMAN_API AAIEnemy : public AAIController
{
  GENERATED_BODY()

public:

  AAIEnemy();

  void Possess(class APawn* InPawn) override;

  virtual void OnMoveCompleted(FAIRequestID RequestID,
    EPathFollowingResult::Type Result) override;

  void SearchNewPoint();
  void GoHome();
  void Rearm();
  void StopMove();

private:

  class AEnemy* Bot;
  FVector HomeLocation;
  FTimerHandle TimerDead;
};
```

As you can see, the `BeginPlay` or `Tick` functions aren't here. There is only a `Possess` function. This can be considered as the `BeginPlay` function and it is called whenever this AI class controls something. We override the `OnMoveComplete` state of the AI in order to control what to do next when the pawn ends a move, and we use a timer to count how long the pawn needs to stay dead before returning to walk around the map.

Following is the `cpp` class. As it only handles the movement, it is pretty simple to understand. It saves its original location when possessed and starts its behavior. An infinite loop will run; every time the enemy reaches the set point, it needs to find another one and keep walking:

```
#include "AIEnemy.h"

AAIEnemy::AAIEnemy() {}

// when possessed store its location and start to move around
void AAIEnemy::Possess(class APawn* InPawn)
{
  Super::Possess(InPawn);

  Bot = Cast<AEnemy>(InPawn);

  HomeLocation = Bot->GetActorLocation();
  SearchNewPoint();
}

// simple return to the home location and start a timer for the
  deadh
void AAIEnemy::GoHome()
{
  MoveToLocation(HomeLocation);
  GetWorldTimerManager().SetTimer(timer_Dead, this,
    &AAIEnemy::Rearm, 5.0f, false);
}

// call the timer and return to walk
void AAIEnemy::Rearm()
{
  GetWorldTimerManager().ClearTimer(timer_Dead);
  Bot->Rearm();
}

// when the pawn ends a move, return to move if is not dead
```

```
void AAIEnemy::OnMoveCompleted(FAIRequestID RequestID,
  EPathFollowingResult::Type Result)
{
  if (!Bot->bIsDead) { SearchNewPoint(); }
}

// stop the pawn movements
void AAIEnemy::StopMove()
{
  StopMovement();

}
```

The only function that is new here is `SearchNewPoint`. In order to move in Unreal, a pawn uses **Navigation Mesh**. Write it as shown in the following code and take a look in the editor to see what a navigation mesh is:

```
// in order to find a new point we search if there is a navigation
mesh active and
// when found, we simple call the GetRandomPointInRadius function from
the NavMesh
void AAIEnemy::SearchNewPoint()
{
  UNavigationSystem* NavMesh =
    UNavigationSystem::GetCurrent(this);
  if (NavMesh)
  {
    const float SearchRadius = 10000.0f;
    FNavLocation RandomPt;
    const bool bFound = NavMesh->GetRandomPointInRadius
      (Bot->GetActorLocation(), SearchRadius, RandomPt);
    if (bFound)
    {
      MoveToLocation(RandomPt.Location);
    }
  }
}
```

Navigation mesh

The definition of a navigation mesh states: an abstract data structure used in artificial intelligence applications to aid agents in pathfinding through complicated spaces.

At this moment, our enemy is actually blind. It cannot see the environment around itself and obviously it doesn't know where the walls are. One solution for its movement could be to create a loop where the enemy is constantly trying to reach a random point but when it hits a wall, it stops and searches another point to reach. However, there is a smarter way.

Unreal Engine helps us with the **Navigation Mesh Bounds** volume. This mode can be placed in the level like any other volume and when positioned, it automatically traces a walkable map for our pawns. Locate it on the modes panel and drag it in the level.

Position it at the center of the maze, change the size to 1,000 x 1,000, which is the same as the maze, and set the height to just 10 units. Move it in a way that it just covers the floor as shown in the picture. In this way, we don't have to worry about the collectables or other static objects that can disturb the calculation of the mesh:

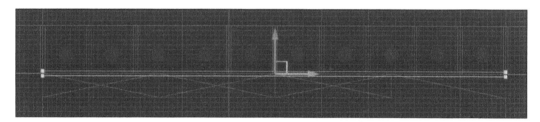

As our cell space is too small, we also need to change the setting on the nav calculation preferences. Navigate to **Edit** | **Project Settings** and click on the **Navigation Mesh** section. Here, you can set all your preferences for the navigation mesh that are generated by the engine. What we need to do is decrease the **Cell Size** to a smaller value; therefore, set it to 5.

Now, you should be able to see the result of the calculation when you toggle its visibility by hitting the *P* key or by navigating to **Show | Navigation** on the viewport window. The highlighted green part is where your pawn will be able to walk:

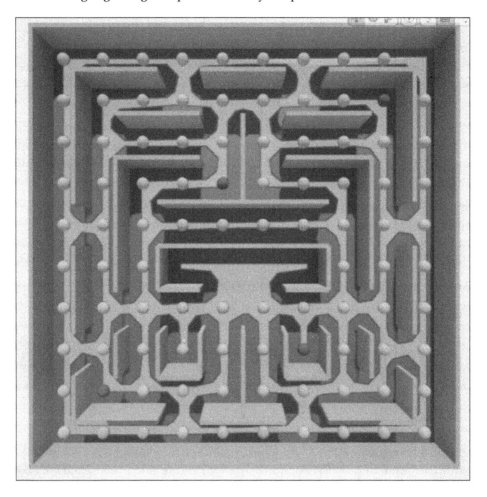

Game mode

We have a character; however, if you start playing right now, you can see that nothing happens. Our PAC-MAN doesn't appear and you can only float around the level in God Mode.

Let's fix the camera first. For the game, we need a single static camera that shows the top view of the maze. From the modes panel, add a camera in the level and position it at the 0,0,1000 coordinates. Rotate by -90 degrees on the x and y axis and, when you select the camera preview, you can see the maze in its entirety.

For this chapter, we want to keep the camera as simple as possible. We will play around with this in *Chapter 5, Top-Down Shooter*. Now, in order to use this camera by default, go to the **Details** panel and set **Player 0** on the **Auto Player Activation** section:

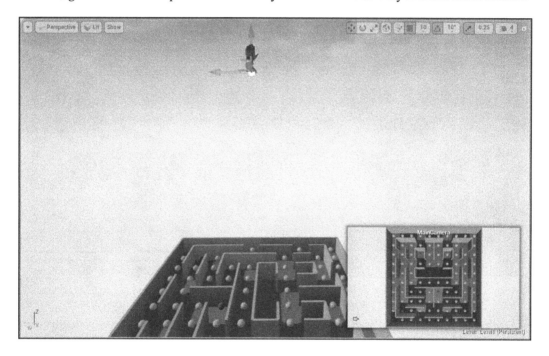

Also, let's add the **player start** object on the lower left-hand side corner of the maze. This key object will be the spawn point for the player. When there's only one **Player Start** object, the player will automatically spawn from there as soon as the game starts:

 When positioning, keep an eye on the sphere collision. It doesn't need to overlap the floor and, in case you position it wrongly, the editor will warn you about it (with a Bad Size label in your object) and the player could be stuck between the floor or could fall forever.

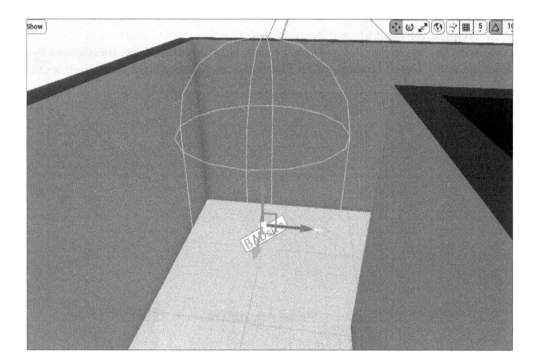

While we are in the editor, we can also add the four enemies. Simply drag the four C++ enemy classes in the level and position them in the middle of the maze. As we did for the collectables, just change their default mesh material. The result will be as follows:

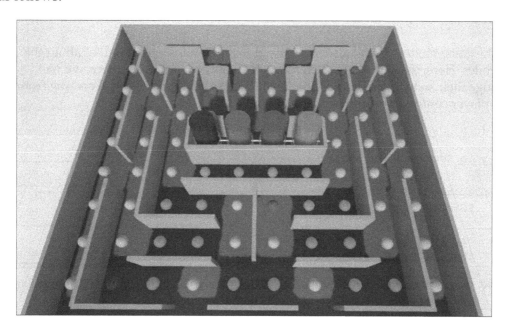

Now, we need to set the default player pawn for the game (our PAC-MAN). When creating the project, UE4 automatically created a customizable **Game Mode** class. It is not set by default; therefore, we need to tell the engine to use it instead of the default empty one. Navigate to **Edit | Project Settings** and on the **Maps & Modes** section, set the default game mode as our **PacManGameMode**.

About the code, the class created by the engine is completely empty. We need to declare the constructor and set the default pawn as our Blueprint class in it using the constructor helper and a reference to it, as follows:

```
// in PacManGameMode.cpp
// there is no initializer by default, we need to add one
APacManGameMode::APacManGameMode()
{
  //search our custom pacman and set as default pawn if founded
  static ConstructorHelpers::FClassFinder<APawn>
PlayerPawnOb(TEXT("Blueprint'/Game/BP_PacMan'"));
  if (PlayerPawnOb.Class != NULL)
  {
    DefaultPawnClass = PlayerPawnOb.Class;
```

```
      }
  }

  // in PacManGameMode.h
  // at very beginning under the public: section
  APacManGameMode();
```

In the game mode, we will also store the global functions and variables about the enemies. Here, we will create a reference to all of them and from there, we will change their state in one single call, depending on whether the call is coming from the player controller or from a change in the game state.

On the header, add these variables and functions, as follows:

```
  void SetEnemyVulnerable();

  private:
    EGameState currentState;

    TArray<class AEnemy*> Enemies;
    Class APlayerController* PlayerController;
```

Now, we use the same function that we did for the collectables in order to populate the enemies array. In this case, an array is useful as, most of the time in our game, the enemies will change their state all together.

Override the BeginPlay() function and add the following lines after the constructor:

```
  void APacManGameMode::BeginPlay()
  {
    Super::BeginPlay();

    // set to be on menu state as soon as the game start
    SetCurrentState(EGameState::EMenu);

    // find the first player controller and set it to our pc
      reference
    PlayerController = GetWorld()->GetFirstPlayerController();

    // find the ghosts in the scene and store them to our array
    for (TActorIterator<AEnemy> enemyIt(GetWorld());enemyIt; ++
      enemyIt)
    {
      AEnemy * enemy = Cast< AEnemy >(* enemyIt);
      if (enemy){ Enemies.Add(enemy); }
    }
  }
```

We find the iterator once again in the `SetEnemyVulnerable` function and while handling the change of state:

```cpp
// iterate all the enemies and make them vulnerable
void APacManGameMode::SetEnemyVulnerable()
{
  for (auto Iter(Enemies.CreateIterator()); Iter; Iter++) {
    (*Iter)->setVulnerable();
  }
}


void APacManGameMode::SetCurrentState(EGameState value)
{
  currentState = value;

  // for each enemy inside the level, use a switch case to handle
    the new state

for (auto Iter(Enemies.CreateIterator()); Iter; Iter++) {
  switch (value)
  {
    case EGameState::EPlaying: // if start playing, initialize the
enemies

      (*Iter)->SetMove(true);

    break;

  case EGameState::EGameOver:
    (*Iter)->Destroy();
    break;

  // same of gameover.
  case EGameState::EWin:
  (*Iter)->Destroy();
    break;


  case EGameState::EPause:

  (*Iter)->SetMove(false);
    break;

    default:
```

```
        // nothing
        break;
    }
}
```

Now, only the UI is missing and soon we will be able to test the game.

User Interface

For this game, we will use a simple text-based user interface, similar to what we did in the previous chapter. We want to only show the basic information on the screen, without any buttons or fancy animations. In order to achieve that, we will create a class that extends the HUD class. This class is responsible for showing the information that is needed on screen.

It has a main function called DrawHUD. This function, like Tick, is called every frame Update. In this function, we will switch the game state and refresh the screen with the player's lives and the game state.

To draw the text, we use the DrawText function. It accepts strings, Unreal font, size, color, and position as arguments of it. It is pretty intuitive to handle a UI this way and it can be useful even for simple debugging purposes.

Create a new class and call it PacManHud. Its header can be left as it is. Now, we just have to add a font property as reference. We use the default engine font called RobotoDistanceField as font; however, you can create your own font in the editor if you prefer:

```
#pragma once

#include "GameFramework/HUD.h"
#include "PacManHUD.generated.h"

/**
 *
 */
UCLASS()
class PACMAN_API APacManHUD : public AHUD
{
    GENERATED_BODY()

    APacManHUD();

    UPROPERTY()
```

```
UFont* HUDFont;

virtual void DrawHUD() override;
};
```

We will now implement the function as shown in the following. First, with the constructor helper, we find the font that we need and set it appropriately:

```
APacManHUD::APacManHUD()
{
  static FObjectFinder<UFont>HUDFontOb
    (TEXT("/Engine/EngineFonts/RobotoDistanceField"));
if (HUDFontOb.Object != NULL) {
  HUDFont = HUDFontOb.Object; }
}
```

In the `DrawHUD` main function, at every call, we check the screen dimension from the canvas, and depending on the game state, we show a different string using the `DrawText` method:

```
void APacManHUD::DrawHUD()
{
  FVector2D ScreenDimension = FVector2D
    (Canvas->SizeX, Canvas->SizeY);

  Super::DrawHUD();

  class APacManGameMode * GameMode =
    Cast<AFooManGameMode>(UGameplayStatics::GetGameMode(this));
  switch (GameMode->GetCurrentState())
  {
    // show a simple menu text
  case EGameState::EMenu:
  {
    DrawText(TEXT("Welcome to Pac Man! \n\n N to start a new game
      \n P to pause the game"), FColor::White, 50, 50, HUDFont);
  }
  break;

    // show the lifes remains
  case EGameState::EPlaying:
  {
    // get the lives and set them
    APacManCharacter* PacMan = Cast<APacManCharacter>
      (UGameplayStatics::GetPlayerPawn(this, 0));
    if (PacMan)
```

```
      {
        FString LivesString = TEXT("Lives: ") +
          FString::FromInt(PacMan->lives);
        DrawText(LivesString, FColor::Black, 50, 50, HUDFont);
      }
    }
    break;

    // show a gameover text
    case EGameState::EGameOver:
    {
      DrawText(TEXT("GAME OVER! \n\n R to restart"),
        FColor::White, 50, 50, HUDFont);
    }
    break;

    //show that the game is in paused
    case EGameState::EPause:
    {
      DrawText(TEXT("pause"), FColor::White, 50, 50, HUDFont);
    }
    break;

    // show a win text
    case EGameState::EWin:
    {
      DrawText(TEXT("YOU WIN! \n\n R for another match ;)"),
        FColor::White, 50, 50, HUDFont);
    }
    break;
    default:
      // nothing
      break;
    }
  }
```

The last thing to do with the code (I promise that after this, we are finally going to test the game) is to add this HUD class to the default HUD in the GameMode class as we did for playerCharacter. Add the following line above the DefaultPawnClass initialization:

```
HUDClass = APacManHUD::StaticClass;
```

Collisions – custom presets and types

Finally, back to the editor, if you compile and run the game right now, you will notice that you can move your PAC-MAN character around. If you have already added the enemies, they will start moving as well; however, both of the player and the enemy are blocked by the collectables, instead of the collectables disappearing.

This is because we haven't set our collisions types yet and the engine, by default, sets the new objects to block everything else.

Every object and most of its components has a collision channel, where it is decided how the object should respond to external stimulations. We are going to modify the object that we created in order to only respond to these stimulations on the capsule collider and ignore everything else.

Navigate to **Edit | Project Settings | Collision**. From there, you can set new channels and create a preset for your object. We want to create three different channels and three different presets referring to them, as follows:

- The **Enemy** (which blocks, by default, and can interact only with the player, completely ignoresing the collectables and itself)
- The **Player** (which blocks, by default, and overlaps with collectables and enemies)
- The **Collectable** (which interacts only with the player)

Create three new channels on the **Object Channels** section by clicking the **New Object Channel** button with the settings that we just discussed, as follows:

Now, extend the **Preset** section by clicking on the little arrow near its name. Here, you can see and edit all the different presets and also, of course, add new presets. Click on **New** and create three new elements, as follows:

Save and build. If you have done everything correctly, you will be able to play a fully enjoyable PAC-MAN clone game.

Summary

I hope you enjoyed this chapter; however, I can understand if some of you found it a bit tedious and difficult to handle. I wanted to focus on the code part of Unreal Engine, but don't worry, the next chapters will be easier and more enjoyable.

Like the other chapters, after my guidance, I will give you some tasks that you should try to implement on your own to improve the final product, as follows:

- Add a door to the enemy spawn point that only allows the enemies to pass through. Use BSP volumes, transparent material, and play with collision preset.

- Create a Level 2. Hint: we didn't see the level transitions so far; therefore, just create another maze near the first one and teleport the player there when he finishes the first one.

- Make the enemies smarter. Play with the **MoveToLocation** button and the player position.

- Improve the HUD. Try to also show how many collectables need to be founded or the countdown till the enemies respawn.

- Add a score, use your imagination. A score could depend on the enemy hit, the collectables taken, or even new types of collectables that can have timers or can move around.

In the next chapter, we will go back to Blueprint, discovering the way to create wonderful user interfaces thanks to Blueprint widgets, and also creating our first particle system.

4
UFO Run - Play with the Environment Effects

I hope you survived through the last chapter, maybe it was too complicating and confusing for some of you. As I promised, in this and the future chapters, we will not use any code, just the engine and its tools.

The aim of this chapter is to learn about the fundamental tools of the engine and the common elements that are used in video games and, following the style of the book, create an entire game using the tools that you just learned about. In this chapter, we will focus on the following important parts of a game:

- Particle system and particle effects
- Unreal Motion Graphic UI Designer (UMG)
- UI Blueprint wizard
- HUD

Before creating the game, let's introduce the two new main concepts of the game; the particle system and the UMG tools.

Particle system

A particle system, for those of you that don't know, is a technique in computer graphics that uses a large number of very small graphic objects to simulate a certain kind of fuzzy phenomena, which is otherwise very hard to reproduce with conventional rendering techniques. Examples of particles could be fire, explosion, smoke, waterfall, spark and so on.

Having said that, you can imagine how essential it is to know how to create and manipulate particle systems (pfx from now) in your projects. A few well-made pfx around the level can drastically change a scene from static and boring to dynamic and enjoyable.

UE4 has a robust and extremely powerful particle system creation tool called **Cascade.**

Cascade

Cascade is a fully integrated and modular particle effects editor. It offers real-time feedback and modular effects editing, allowing fast and easy creation of even the most complex effects.

Particle systems are also very closely related to the various materials and textures that are applied to each particle. The primary job of the particle system itself is to control the behavior of the particles, while the specific look and feel of the particle system as a whole is often controlled by the materials.

Cascade offers a modularly designed particle system to the users. That means that when you create a new particle in the editor, only a few bones property and default behavior modules are created.

It is your choice to decide which module to use and in what order, this is to avoid the calculation of unnecessary properties. Each module is relative in itself and can be easily added, removed, and copied, making intricate setup very easy to achieve:

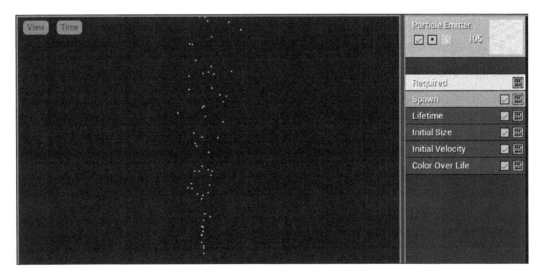

Modules

When you create a particle system, a few modules are added by default, as shown in the following:

- **Required**: This module and the next one are the only permanent modules that cannot be removed. This contains the minimum required properties that are necessary for a particle system in order to work.

- **Spawn**: This module contains information about how a particle will spawn if in burst or linearly.

- **Lifetime**: This module controls how long a single particle lasts, it can live forever, at a constant time, or simple random.

- **Initial Size**: This module controls the scale of a particle at the moment of its spawning.

- **Initial Velocity**: This module is of the same size, it controls the velocity.

- **Color Over Life**: This module contains the properties to change/control the color/alpha of the single particle during its lifetime.

However, there are hundreds of modules that you can use in your particle emitter.

Emitters

A particle system is formed by a collection of particle emitters. Each emitter works as an individual element with its own modules and behavior and can be activated or deactivate singularly at any time.

A particle emitter, regardless of the type, is a sprite emitter at the start. You can change the type by adding type data modules to it and choosing between one of them:

- **Sprite emitter**: This is the default and most used type. Particles are emitted as polygonal sprites that always face the camera.

- **AnimTrail Data**: This is used to create trails.

- **Beam Data**: This is used to create lasers, lightning, and similar effects. They have a start and end point that can be set by Blueprint or script dynamically.

- **GPU Sprites**: These are a special type of particle. The runtime calculation is handled by the GPU, allowing the number of possible particles to be several hundred thousand.

- **Mesh Data**: This emitter will emit polygonal meshes instead of emitting sprites.

- **Ribbon Data**: This emitter produces a string of particles that are attached end to end from a ribbon that trails behind a moving emitter.

Level of detail

As you can image, a particle system can easily become very expensive to calculate and it is important to consider the value of calculating the particles from which the player is too far away or adequately appreciate.

The UE4 uses an easy setup for this, the LOD system. This system allows you to set up the custom distance ranges at which your particle system will automatically simplify. For each range, you can set a custom property for any module or emitter such as lower values, enable/disable certain modules, and so on. There is no limit to the level of detail that you can have, usually two or three levels are more than enough.

 You will soon see how important it is to set your LODs. Maybe for small projects you will not notice the difference; however, for medium or big games, it can lead to a difference from an enjoyable to a horrible and laggish game.

The Cascade interface

Now that you know the basic concept of particle system, let's take a look at the Cascade tool and its interface. When you open any particle system in the editor, the engine automatically opens Cascade as it opens the Blueprint class interface for any Blueprint file, as shown in the following screenshot:

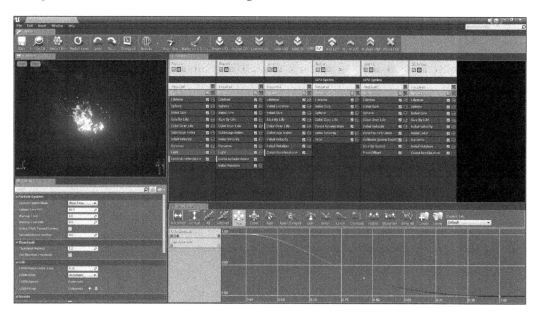

Let's take a look at the different sections of the Cascade Interface:

- **Menu bar**: On the very top, you have the familiar menu bar, where you can load, save, find any asset that you need, and personalize your window view.

- **Toolbar**: The Toolbar, like Blueprint, has the most used functions that you could use when creating your particle system. It contains a large part that is dedicated to the LODs, some useful functions such as save, undo and redo, restart the particle effect preview, show the bounds, change the background color, and create the thumbnail of the particle preview based on what is shown from the preview camera.

- **Viewport panel**: It is on the left-hand top corner, just above the toolbar. It shows the current particle system (including all emitters that are active at that moment).

- **Emitters panel**: This is where you can add, select, and work with the various particle modules and emitters that control particle system's look and behavior. Each column represents a single particle emitter, its top contains the emitter name, type, and buttons that control the whole emitter behaviour. Right-click on this panel to open a context-sensitive menu.

- **Details panel**: Like the **Details** panel of Blueprint, this panel contains the detailed property of the selected module or emitter.

- **Curve Editor**: Here, you can adjust any value that needs to change during the life of a particle or across the life of an emitter.

UMG

As mentioned in the previous chapters, UE4 has a very powerful tool that helps the users to create and handle all the UI elements of a game: Unreal Motion Graphic (UMG).

At the core of UMG are Widgets, which are a series of premade functions that can be used to construct your interface (buttons, checkboxes, sliders, progress bar, and so on). They can be edited in a specialized Widget Blueprint, which is divided into two tabs for construction: a **Designer** tab for the visual layout of the interface and a **Graph** tab that provides the functionality behind the Widget.

Widget Blueprint

The main tool when talking about UMG is the Widget Blueprint. Let's take a deeper look at it:

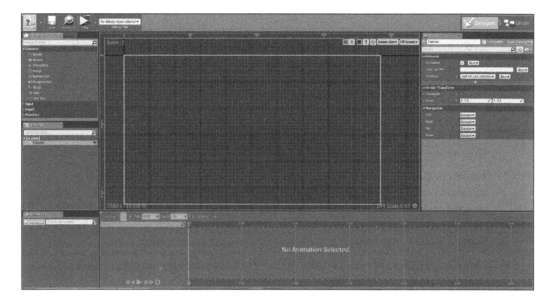

- **Menu bar**: On top of it we find our familiar menu bar. It is the same menu bar that we can find in any Blueprint class.

- **Tool bar**: This is a simplified version of the Blueprint class toolbar from where you can save, compile, and play your game.

- **Editor Mode**: This is on the right-hand side of the toolbar and it switches the Widget Blueprint editor between designer and graph modes.

- **Palette**: This panel contains a list of Widget that can be dragged in the visual designer. They are divided into categories and they inherit the content from UWidget.

- **Hierarchy**: This is similar to the **Content** panel of a Blueprint class, it contains the parenting structure of the user Widget.

- **Visual Designer**: This is the main panel where a visual representation of the layout is shown. Here, you can set up the UI by adding or moving around the Widgets.

- **Details panel**: As usual, this displays the details and properties of the selected item.

- **Animations**: Here, you can add animations to your UI by creating the keyframe states of any Widgets.

HUD class

The **Heads-up display** (**HUD**) class is a Blueprint class that handles all the user interfaces in your game. While a Widget Blueprint contains a single graphic layout, the HUD is responsible to handle the different Widgets that you can have for your game, such as Main Menu, In-game UI, Leaderboards, and so on.

It is not necessary to use the Widget Blueprint as you saw in the previous chapter that an UI can only be handled by the HUD class. However, it becomes really useful, if not essential, to set it when talking about bigger projects.

 An HUD class is a part of the essential items that are needed to run your game. Just to remind you that they are The Game Mode (GM), the Default Pawn, the PlayerController (PC), the Game State and the HUD class.

You can create the HUD class by extending it like any other Blueprint class and you can set your custom HUD by navigating to **Edit** | **Project Settings** | **Maps & Modes**, as follows:

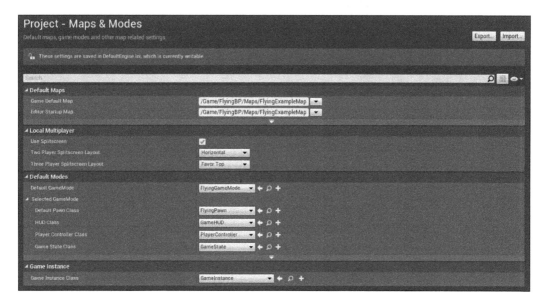

I know that only talking about the theory does not make it easy to understand; however, don't worry, we are now going to create our game, looking in detail at these two tools.

The game

For this chapter, we are going to extend the flying template of UE4. The final result will be a beat-the-time game where the player will fly around the level, trying to collect as many collectables as possible before the time ends. There will be a menu with buttons, particle system for the player and collectables, and a user interface that shows the score. We will also implement a power bar that increases when a collectable is collected and decreases when the player uses its boost.

Without further ado, let's open the launcher and create a new project, starting from the flying Blueprint template. Call it UFO_Run and, as usual, leave the other settings as the default:

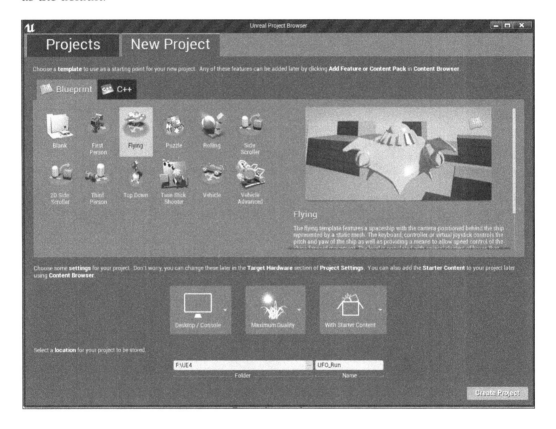

What you will see once it opens is a stylized city, a nice sky and a pawn character that is ready to be used. The gameplay of the template allows you to fly around with your ship, move using the arrow keys, and accelerate/decelerate using spacebar or other keys (you can check the key binding of the level by navigating to **Edit | Project Settings | Input**).

The movement and the input keys are perfect for our purpose, the map as well is big enough and, even if not graphically pleasing, it fits our needs well:

Blocking volumes

The first thing that we notice while playing is that the player can easily leave the playing area and float in the empty space around the map. We will want to limit the movement of our player in order to be inside certain bounds. Usually, this purpose is achieved on adding physical elements around the map; however, it was not rare to find these bounds being represented by invisible walls, especially in old games.

Under the **Volumes** section of the **Modes** panel, we can find exactly what we need; **Blocking Volume**. A Blocking Volume serves as a collision shape through which the objects are not intended to pass. You can choose which type of objects will be allowed to pass using the collision properties (this is similar to how we set the PAC-MAN collisions) and can be positioned, scaled, and moved around the map as we did for the BSP volumes:

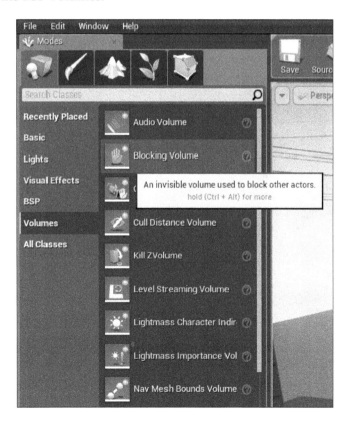

We want to create a perimeter around the entire level, including a roof above the city. When creating a blocking volume, you can choose among some brushes in order to create a shape that fits your needs better. For our purpose, we can see the entire map as a giant box; we could create four box volumes as walls on its perimeter and a fifth box volume for the roof.

It will certainly work; however, it is not a smart solution. A nice and clear solution is to create a single box volume with a hole in it and position the entire map in the hole.

Drag and drop **Blocking Volume** in your map and search for the **Hollow** property, under the **Brush Settings** from the **Details** panel. If you set it, you will notice that the editor immediately creates a smaller second box volume in the first one to represent the hollow space. With just a couple of clicks, we created our giant cage for the entire map. Now, you only need to change its size in order to fit the map and we can go ahead with the game.

 Sometimes it could happen, especially with high speed objects, that the blocking volume doesn't work properly. In this case, most of the time, it is enough to change the **Wall Thickness** property to a higher value in order to fix the problem.

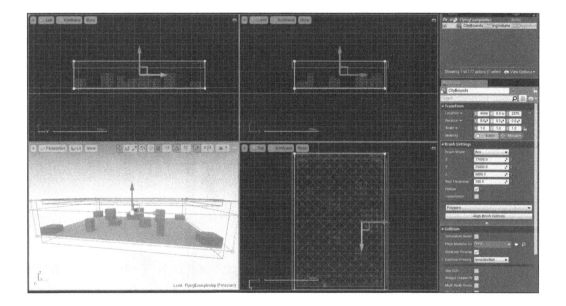

The menu camera

A menu is typically composed of buttons, text information about what is in the screen, and a static background image. Lately, thanks to the new technology and resources, the menu and the UI elements have started to be more dynamic, adding animations and 3D elements to it.

As background for our menu, we are going to show the top view of the whole city using a second camera actor, instead of a static image. Position a new camera actor anywhere in your level and rename it **menuCamera**.

Now we need to move it in a suitable position. There are two ways to smartly move a camera around; the first one is to manually pilot the camera in the desired position and the second one is to move around in the viewport and, when you find a good spot, snap the camera actor to that point.

They are both good alternatives and both of them are easy to use. To pilot a camera, right-click on the object and select **Pilot 'CameraActor'** (or *Ctrl + Shift + P*). Move with the arrows and mouse, and then, click on the eject button on the left-hand top corner of the viewport:

The second method is even simpler. Just right-click on the camera object from your point in the viewport (if you cannot reach the camera, remember that you can always find all the objects in the scene from the **World Outliner** panel) and select **Snap Object to View**.

 These two methods work for any other object in your level; however, they surely give their best when talking about cameras.

The following image shows exactly that second method:

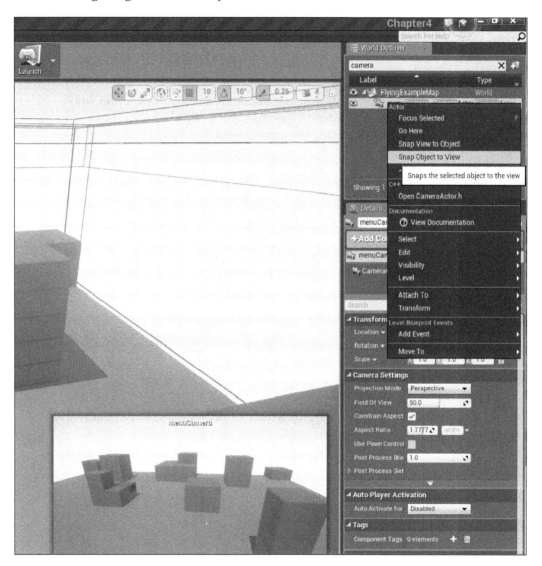

Wizard Blueprint

Let's finally create the UI. In the Blueprint folder of the project, right-click and navigate to **User Interface | Widget Blueprint**. Call it **UI_Menu** and open it.

What you see here is a two-dimensional canvas for your UI. The underlined rectangle in the scene represents the resolution that you are actually using in the project and what is actually seen by the user. You can easily switch to different resolutions using the **Screen Size** button and you can even set up a custom **Dots per inch** (**DPI**) scale curve if required:

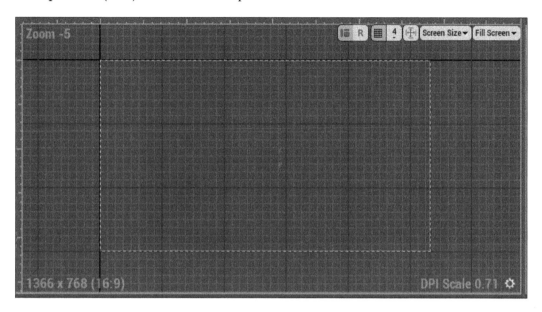

The greatest feature of this tool is that you don't need to worry about how your UI is seen in different resolutions (one of the common problems when developing a game) as the engine will automatically fit itself according to your setup.

Let's start by adding a text to the canvas. From **Palette**, drag a **Text** Widget (from the **Common** category) to the canvas. This will be the title of our game, therefore, under the **Details** panel, change its **Text** property from the **content** section to **Ufo Run!**.

The **Slot** section controls the position and size of any Widget in the canvas. The first field is **Anchors**. This is an important property and it is the point in the canvas that the object refers to for the resolution-position calculation. In this case, we want to set the anchor as a center point at the top. By clicking on it, you will see all the different anchors that are possible for the canvas.

When using anchors, you can even offset it by dragging the anchor symbol directly in the canvas.

In order to always be centered on the screen, the easiest way is to set the position of the Widget (with a centered anchor) to be at half the size of its axis. With this setting, you can test it by changing the screen size and notice how the title is always perfectly in the middle of the screen:

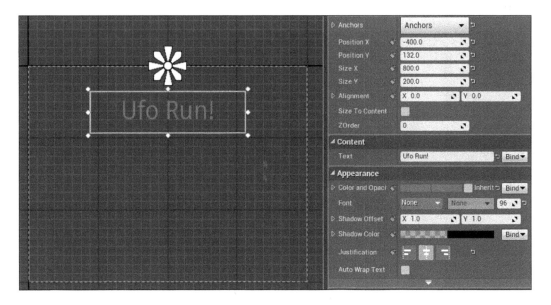

Import a custom font

The default Arial could be boring and you would soon want to use your fonts in the UI. The editor doesn't allow the direct usage of traditional font files such as **TrueType Format** (**TFF**) or **OpenType Format** (**OTF**) but its own font asset file. There is a handy font editor tool in the engine, where you can import your font and create family and subfamily for your font (for example, the same font can have a family for its bold, italic, light, and dark style as its subfamily).

To create a font asset, we first need to have its text file. You can use one of your default system, create one on your own using an external tool, or download one from the Internet community. I found www.dafont.com really useful and full of freeware content.

 If you like to use the same asset that I'm using here, remember that you can find this and all the other files of any project that we are developing at www.nicolavalcasara.it/packt.

Once you have the font, return to **Content Browser** and add a new font from **User Interface | Font**. Call it **GameFont** and open it.

Pretty intuitive. There are only two panels here; a **Composite Font** panel, where you can import and set the different families and the familiar **Details** panel.

Import your custom font to **Default Font Family** by clicking on the three dots, leave everything else as it is and you have created your first basic custom font! Now, you can go back to the UI and use it straightaway in the title of the game:

Buttons

It is time to add some control here. The main menu will have two buttons: a **START** game and an **EXIT** game button. Drag the two button Widget to the UI menu use a center-center anchor and position/resize them to fit the screen and position one above and one under the anchor.

You will immediately notice that there isn't a **Text** field in the properties. This is because, by definition, a button is just a button—a clickable/touchable item that answers to an input. To add text on them, simply drag a text Widget in the button itself. The engine will automatically set the text as a child and fit it in the centre of the button.

Add the **Start** and **Exit** text to them and the following image should be the final result:

Click events

From the button Widget, you can add events in order to handle when a button is clicked, pressed, or released. They work like any other Blueprint event and simply click the **+** button on the **Details** panel of the button of the event that you want to handle to add them.

Implement the **OnClicked** event for both the buttons and let's implement the **Exit** button for now. For the exit, we only need a single node: an **Execute Console Command** node with, as **Command Exit**. This node allows you to send console command to the game.

The console is made available by pressing the ` key in any of your running projects.

There is quite a long list of commands that can be sent to the engine and this node allows a direct communication between Blueprint and the engine:

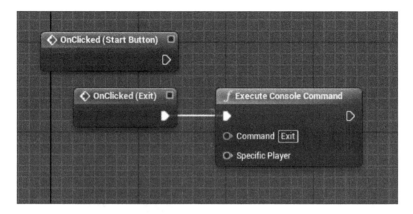

Set the default camera

If you run the project right now, you can see that nothing changes. The UI doesn't show up and the game looks exactly the same as it did in the beginning. This is because we didn't initialize the Widget, we didn't set which camera is to be used, and, most importantly, there is a pawn in the scene that is being possessed by the player controller as soon as the game starts.

First, remove **Flying Pawn** from the scene. We want that our player is initialized only after clicking the start button.

After doing that, we want to use the camera that we previously added as the default one. We can set it using the Level Blueprint class and a node called **Set View Target With Blend**.

This node is used to change the view target between two target actors. As a parameter, it accepts a blend time and type and the node automatically blends the transition between the two cameras, nice and smooth. For the node, we will use the **Player controller** as **Target** and the camera Actor that we previously placed as the new target.

To have a direct reference to any of the actors in a scene, you can simply select the desired object, go to the Level Blueprint, and on right-clicking, you can see the **Create a reference to...** option:

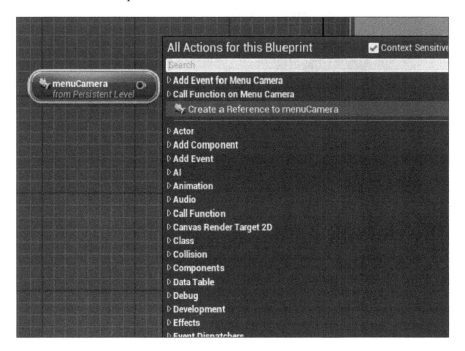

Now, search for the **Set View Target with Blend** node (if you don't see it, you can remove the **Contex Sensitive** option on the right-hand top of the menu) and connect it to **Event BeginPlay**. Set the **Blend Time** to **0** and that's it. We don't want a smooth transition from an empty camera to ours, we simply want an immediate jump to our camera.

To get a reference to the player controller, search for the **Get Player Controller** node and set the index to **0** (there is only one player in this game, therefore, the **0** index will always be our PC):

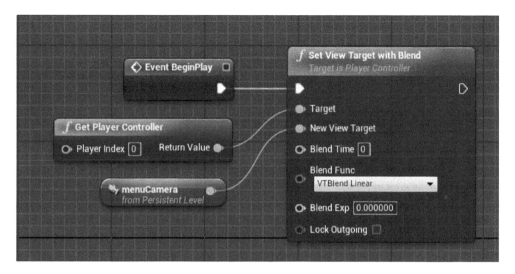

Now, if you run the game, you can see that the camera is correct; however, it is still missing the UI. We can fix it in a second.

HUD class

As said in the beginning, we need two different UI Widget Blueprint classes and to handle the transition between them, we need to set an HUD class. In this game, this class will simply switch between the UI Widget according to the state of the game.

From **Content Browser**, add a new Blueprint class and choose HUD as parent. Call it GameHUD and open it.

From the **Event BeginPlay** node, search for Create Widget and connect it. This node will take a Widget class and create an instance of it that is ready to be placed in the viewport. We can immediately set the return value to viewport; however, as we need it in the future, we can promote the output pin to a variable. Right-click on **Return Value** and select **promote to variable**. Then, connect the final output to an **Add to Viewport** node:

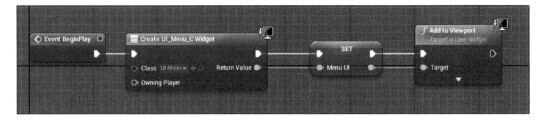

Yet nothing happens when you try to play. This is because this HUD is not set on our **Game Mode** class. Search for the **FlyingGameMode** class in **Content Browser**. Open it and search for the **Classes** section in the **Details** panel. Set the **HUD** class to be our **GameHUD** and **Default Pawn** to **None** (as discussed, we don't want a pawn to immediately spawn when click **Play**). Now, once we click **PLAY**, we finally see our UI and if you try to click **EXIT**, you will be able to close the game as expected.

Player controller class

We need to create a player controller class that will handle various things in our game, such as the score and the energy of our Ufo. A PC class is also useful when we need to store references to the persistent objects in the scene. Level Blueprint is the only place where you can have references to any object in the scene; however, you are not allowed to directly reference the Level Blueprint from a class Blueprint. This would prevent you from using it in different maps. This is where a PC is helpful.

When a player clicks start the dynamic of the action that we want is the following: remove the UI menu, gently slide the camera to the player spawn point, switch the camera to our pawn camera, and start the game.

To do this, we first need a physical spawn point target for the **view blend** node and we need to be able to access it anywhere in our Blueprint scripts.

On the **Modes** panel, search for a **Target Point** Actor and place it where the player pawn was:

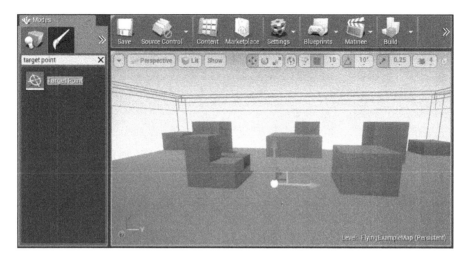

Now, create a new Blueprint class and select Player Controller as parent. Call it PC (PlayerController)and open it. For now, we simply need to add a new variable of the **target point** type and call it **TargetStart**. Change it to **Editable** and add **Tooltip** to it (similar to what we did in the tic-tac-toe game):

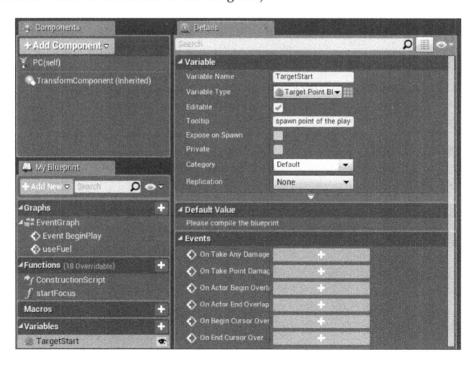

Now, go back to the Level Blueprint class and we are now able to initialize this variable by casting the Player Controller to the PC class.

After the **view target blend** node, search for the **Cast to PC** node, connect the **Get Player Controller** node to the **Object** input pin and simply set the **Target Start** variable in the **As PC** output to be our reference for the target point:

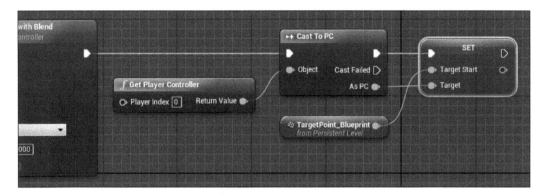

As a last thing, remember to set this **Player Controller** class in the classes section of the **Game Mode**. Now, you can access this Actor from anywhere in your Blueprint classes and we can go ahead to add the behavior of the start button.

Start button

Back to the **UI_Menu** wizard, we now have all the elements required to complete the start event. First, you need to remove the Widget from the scene. You can use the **Remove from Parent** node with the **self** variable as **Target**. We do this to the first node as we don't want anything on the screen during a camera transition.

Now, search for the **Set View Target With Blend** node and connect **Player Controller** as **Target** and the **Target Start** Actor from the PC class that we created as new target. This is pretty simple. Just add **Cast To PC** before connecting the target and use a get node for the referenced object:

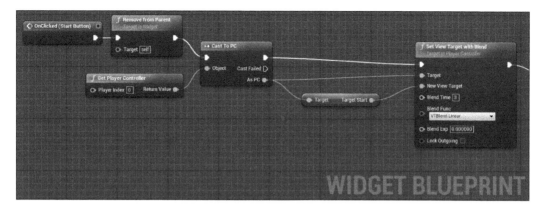

Add a **Blend Time** of three seconds and leave a linear blend function. If you play now and try to click start, you can immediately see a smooth movement of the camera from the starting point to the point where the pawn should appear.

We can now spawn our player using a **SpawnActor** class node. Add this node after the blend one, search for the **Flying Pawn** Blueprint class, use **GetActorLocation** as **Spawn Transform** on the **Target Start** and convert the vector result into a transform variable.

Doing this, a pawn will spawn; however, not as expected. This is because the graph flow doesn't wait till the end of the blend transition and executes all the nodes as soon as it can.

To avoid this problem, just add a **Delay** node of the same amount of time as the blend time between the blend and spawn and you can finally see the transition and the spawning working perfectly when played:

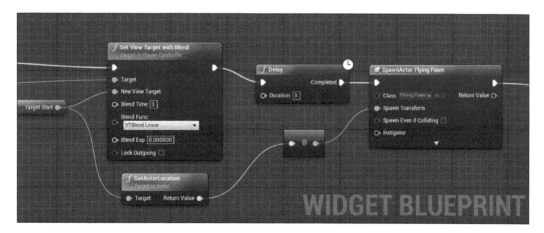

You have a main menu that handles the game start and a player that can fly around at the right time in order to search for collectables. It is time to add the second UI Widget for the In-Game state and our gameplay elements.

In-game screen

Create a second Widget Blueprint and call it **UI_InGame**. This interface will show two progress bars for **TIME** and **ENERGY** and a text that updates the number of collectables that are collected during the game.

Let's start by adding these wizard position two **Progress Bar** wizard and three **Text** wizard using the correct anchor for each element according to what you learned, as shown in the following:

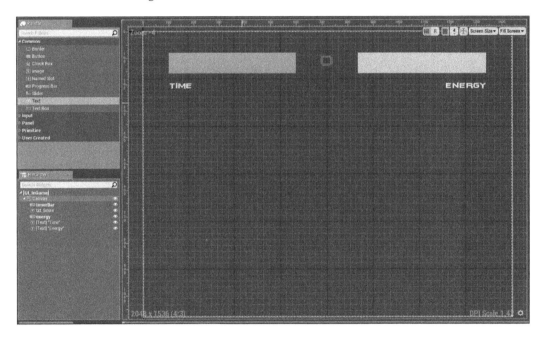

The **Progress Bar** accepts a percent value from 0 to 1 and allows different color or image for both the fill or the empty state. I set a background color with 0 value in its alpha channel in order to just have a single bar showing on the screen without any background.

Property binding

One of the most useful aspects of UMG is the ability to bind properties of your Widgets to Functions or Properties in the Blueprint. By binding a property to a function or a property variable in your Blueprint, it will reflect in the Widget anytime this function is called or a property is updated.

Let's create the properties that will bind on the Widget in the Player controller. We need three float public variables, called energy, time, and score.

Before binding, it is also better to store a PC reference directly in the UI wizard. For this, we use **Event Construct** of the Wizard Blueprint. This event is similar to the **Event BeginPlay** and it is called when the UI is initialized at the scene.

To get a reference of the PC, do what we did in the Level Blueprint; get the player controller, cast to our PC, and promote the **As PC** output pin to variable:

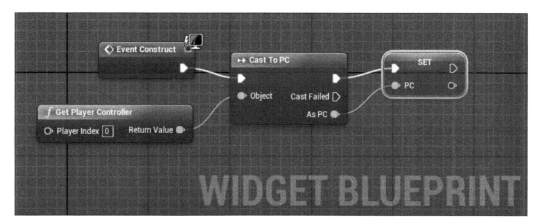

Now, with the reference that is just created, return to the designer window and click the **Score** text. In the **Details** panel, under the content **Text** place, navigate to **Bind | Create Binding**. A new function will be added and bound to this variable, all you need to do is get the score variable from the **PC** reference, convert it to text, and set it in the input node of the output function that was just created:

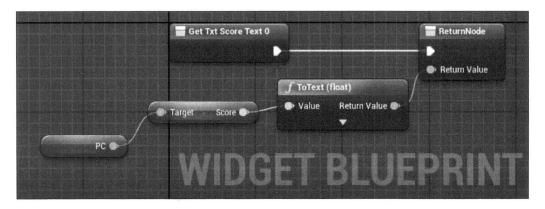

For the **Time** and the **Energy** bar is even simpler. We don't need to implement any function, we need to simply bind the corresponding variable of our **PC**:

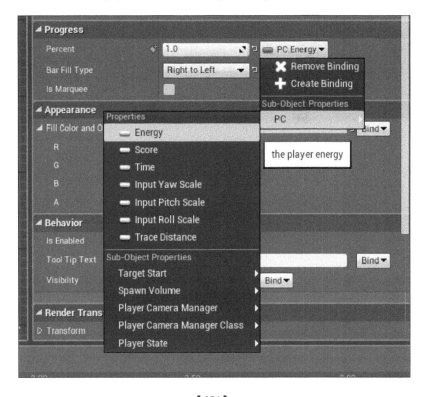

Switch user interface

It is now time to show this interface in the game. From the **HUD** class, create a custom event called **BeginLevel** and copy what we did earlier for the menu. The only difference is that target is the **UI_InGame** class instead of **UI_Menu**:

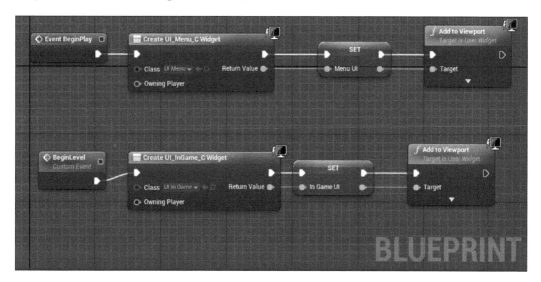

Now, we can call fire this event exactly when the pawn is spawned in the level. We can use the **onClick** event and add the call just after the **SpawnActor** node.

To have a reference to HUD, we need to get the player controller, from it **Get HUD**, cast to our **GameHUD**, and finally call the **BeginLevel** event:

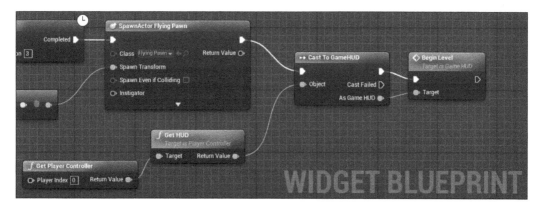

The game will show the new Widget correctly. It is the time to create the collectable and finally work with particles.

Collectables

Create a new Blueprint class and call it **BP_Collectable**. We will use a sphere static mesh as a collectable in this game, we will add an aura around it for it to be easily localized by the player and add some fancy particles that go up in the aura.

First, simply add a Static Mesh in the components, set it to be a Sphere Mesh and replace it with the default root component. This will be the item that receives collisions by the player, therefore, set the collision of the mesh as OverlapAll. All the further components need to be set as NoCollision.

Add another Static Mesh to the root one, set it as **Cylinder** mesh and change its z scale to a higher number. This will be the aura of the object, therefore, it should surround the sphere, starting just under it and going up as much as it can.

Materials

We now create two materials for the sphere and the cylinder. The cylinder will be a simple translucent material, you can use the one that we used for the ghost or recreate another on your own.

For the collectable itself, we don't want a boring static color, we want something attractive. Therefore, let's do some math to see if we can create a fancy sphere that shines intermittently.

The idea is to use the time that is passed as input for a **Sine** node that gives us a changing value between -1 and 1. Use this result in **ConstantBiasScale** that converts -1/1 in a more useful value that scaled according to our setting, **Multiply** it with a color and apply it to **Base Color** and **Emissive Color** of our material node:

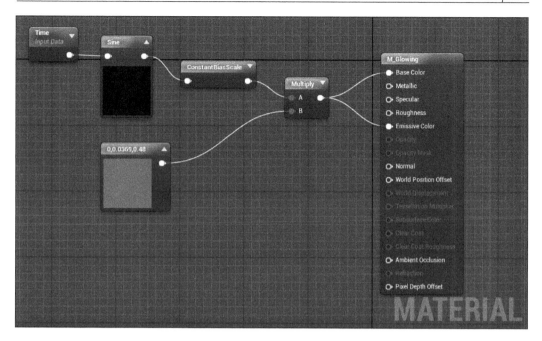

Set the nodes as shown in the preceding image. The **Sine** period is 1, the **BiasScale** node uses this formula to create the output: *(input+bias)*scale*. Set the bias to be 2 (so that the final emissive value will not be less than 0) and a scale of 5 (in order to give enough shine for it to be seen in the material). The end result will be a wonderful shiny material.

Go back to the Blueprint class and apply these materials to the two meshes.

Particle system

Before creating a particle system, we need a material as the required field of the particle emitter needs a material to show. A material for the particle is usually a translucent blend type with the **Unlit** shading model. For our object, we want to use a colored texture that goes up following the translucent cylinder.

Search for a star image on the Internet or import the Star.png file from the asset folder that you will find at www.nicolavalcasara.it/packt to **Content Browser** by dragging and dropping or by navigating to **File | Import**.

Now, create a new material and call it **M_Collectable_PFX**. First of all, in the **Material** section of the material node, change **Blend Mode** to **Additive** (in order to completely dissolve the background color of the texture) and **Shading Model** as **Unlit** (in order to have the material completely not responding to external light sources).

Search for the **Texture Sample** node and add it to the graph and set the texture to the image that we just imported. You could now just connect the RGB pin in the **Emissive Color** and the Alpha pin in the **Opacity** and the material is ready to be used by a particle system; however, as we want to change its color, we need another node. Search for the **Particle Color** node, multiply its nodes with the texture as this image and we have the material ready:

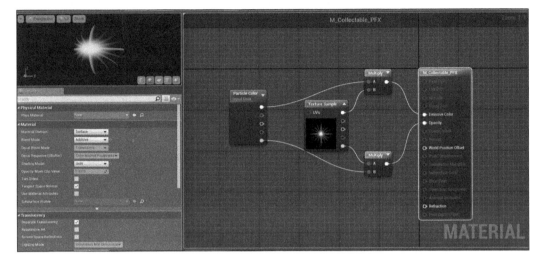

You can finally go to **Content Browser** and add a new particle system. Call it **M_Collectable_PFX** and open it. We use a single emitter for this particle. The modules used are shown in order as follows:

Required

Here, we set **Material** as the **M_Collectable_PFX** material that we just created. Nothing else changes in the required setting.

Spawn

We want a higher rate of spawn, therefore, change the rate constant distribution value to a value around 100. We don't want to use higher numbers because of the CPU-expensive calculations. If you desire to use a higher number, you should also add the **TypeData** module called **GPUSprite** to use the GPU directly for the calculations. Leave the other settings as they are, we don't need a **Burst** spawn and the **Rate Scale** needs to stay at 1.

LifeTime

We need our particles to reach at least half of the cylinder before disappearing. Change the constant lifetime field to three seconds.

Initial size

Initial size depends on the texture that you used; change this value when we are finished with the other modules and you have a better preview of the whole system. If you use the same image as I did, you can set it to have a constant size of five for each axis.

Initial velocity

Remove this module, we don't use an initial velocity.

Color Over Life

In the **Color Over Life** module, we can set how the particle changes its color during its lifetime. In the constant curve of the **Distribution** field, you can see two points. Each point has an in value (the time in a single particle life where the color will change), an out value (the effective color), and a few other setting for smooth transition.

We want to have a shiny blue color at the beginning, which fades to a bright white before disappearing. At point 0, set an in value of 0.1 and out value as **R**: 2, **G**: 2, **B**: 15. You will see something strange now. Usually an RGB color single value is between 0 and 1 for traditional plain color. If any of these values are higher than 0, the color immediately becomes a combination of white and the desired color, which is adjustable thanks to the saturation field:

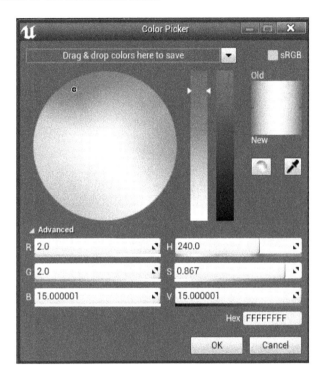

The other point is easier: in value set as 3 (the arrival point of the particle) and out value as plain white (**R**:1, **G**:1, **B**:1).

Size over life

It has the same principle as the **Color Over Life** module. It has two points by default and the properties are very similar. Just set the point 0 to a scale of 1 when spawning, which grows till it is five times its original size at the end of the particle life.

Cylinder

This module can be found in the **location** section. It sets the starting location of the particle to be on a cylinder surface. You can leave everything as default. If you see that the particles are too close, you can change the start radius field.

Acceleration

Acceleration is used instead of the initial velocity module. This module allows a more dynamic movement, where we can set a minimum and maximum range for the random acceleration. Just set the **Z** field to a positive number between 100 and 500, as follows:

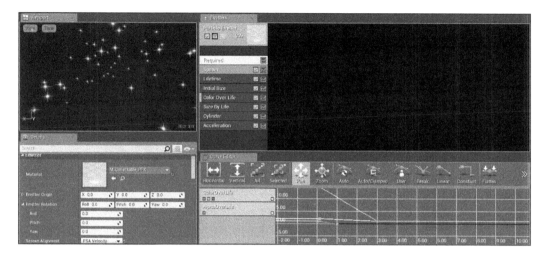

Save it and you can now add this particle in the Blueprint class of the collectable. Position it under the sphere, scale it to fit the object correctly, and admire your beautiful final result.

Blueprint script

The script needed for this object is not much. We need to destroy when hit by the player and fire an event that is stored in the player controller.

Open the Blueprint file **BP_collectable**, search for the **ActorBeginOverlap** event and add it to its the event graph.

This node has an output pin containing the information of the actor that hit it. We can use this to cast to our **Flying Pawn** and, if successful, simply destroy itself.

Now, in the **Player Controller** class, add a custom event called **Collect Item** (as a placeholder, we will implement it the second time) and, back to the **Collectable** class, call it by casting our PC class as we did multiple other times:

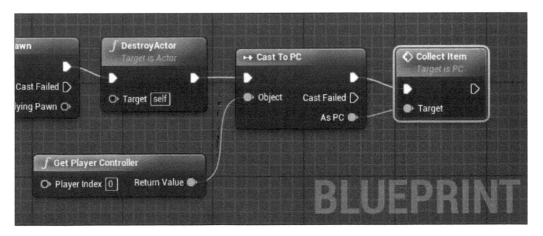

Now, you can manually insert as many instances of this class as you want. You can even start to fly around and collect them; however, placing the collectable manually is tedious and not fun. We want the collectable to spawn randomly around the map, being delayed randomly during the time and not altogether. To achieve this, we need to create a custom volume that will handle the random spawn.

Spawn volume

A random spawn can sound easy to handle; however, you will soon see how hard it can be to achieve a not-so-random result. We have a huge map with static objects and a three-dimensional environment. We want to find a random point at a fixed distance from the object above it in the whole game map that is not in a mesh, or in the middle of the floor, or high in the sky.

Components

Let's proceed step by step. First, create a new Blueprint class by extending an Actor class. Change the default root component to a **Box Collision** component. This will be the bounds volume that is used to calculate the random point.

No other components are needed for this class. The representation, when placed in the level, is like any other volume; a fully transparent box that can be adjusted to fit any dimension / position / rotation.

When having more than one volume around the level, the line color around the box is sometimes not enough. There is a component called **Billboard** that can help you to easily find your volumes. It shows a two-dimensional image in the center of the volume, which is completely invisible to the player; however, useful for the developer.

Random point function

Getting a random number is achieved using the get **Random Point in Bounding Box** node. On giving it an **Origin** point and a box extension, this node will return a random vector point in the range of the box.

Knowing this, we can use getter of the **Box** component to get the Actor location (as origin) and, thanks to the **Get Scaled Box Extent** node, we can get the three dimensions of the box (scaled) to use as **Box Extent** and calculate our random vector:

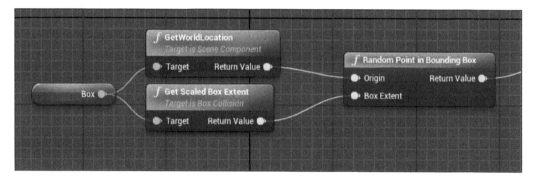

The next problem to be solved is that if we apply this volume to cover the whole map, how can we be sure that the random is not in a building? To solve this, we use **Raycasts**. This method simply traces a ray from a desired point to a desired location and, if the ray hits something (and it is something that can be hit) it returns with the information of the object that is hit by the ray.

In this way, we can place the volume to cover the whole ceiling of the map and, from the random location, use a Raycast from it and down on the *z* axis as direction and, from the hit result, use hit location to spawn anything that we want.

A Raycast can be achieved using the **LineTraceByChannel** node. This will be the execution node of our function. We set the random point as **Start** and the random point subtracted by 10000 (it should give us enough units to pass through the whole world) as **End** on the *z* axis:

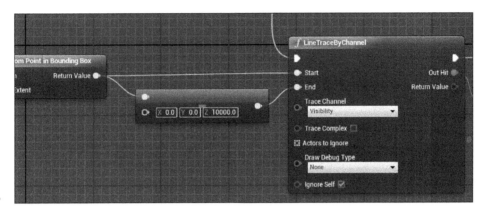

Finally, break the *Out Hit* node in order to find the impact point and offset it to find our *not-so-random* point that is ready to accept our collectable.

The whole script will go to a function in the **SpawnVolume** class. To add a new function, just press the **+** button from the function section of the **My Blueprint** panel. This works similarly to the macros that we saw in *Chapter 2, Tic-Tac-Toe*. It has an enter and exit node, both with the possibility to add input and output pins as required. For this function, we don't need any input pin, only an output pin on the exit node that returns the **Transform** variable of the **Random Location**:

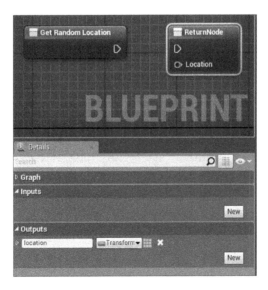

Now, simply connect them with the correct nodes we just did as shown in the
following image and the script is completed. You can now add the volume to the
scene. The volume needs to cover the whole sky on the top of the map. The **Z** scale
doesn't matter as long as it doesn't touch any building roofs:

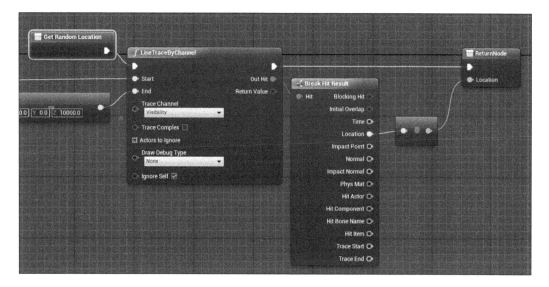

Actor reference

The player controller will handle the spawning system of the collectables, therefore,
it is essential to have a reference to it. From the Level Blueprint, use the same node
that we used to set the **Target Point**, get a local reference to the volume in the scene,
and simply set it on our PC (of course, you need to create the object variable in the
PC first):

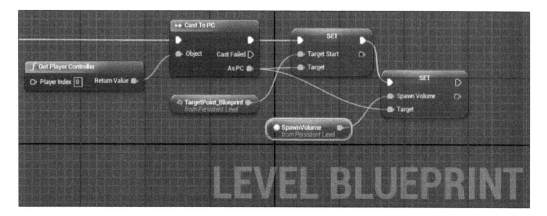

Gameplay

It is time to complete this project, merging together what we did so far and adding the gameplay scripts.

The game mechanic of the game expected:

- A timer that goes down each second
- An energy that is used by the player when accelerating the ship and a ship that can accelerate only if it has enough energy
- A score that increases each time an item is collected
- A game over that is shown when the player ends its time
- The possibility to restart the game as many times as the player desires
- Collectables that spawn periodically

For **GameOver**, we can create a third UI window that shows the score and the button of the main menu; however, let's keep it simple. We can connect a second event called **GameOver** on an **HUD** class **BeginPlay** event. This will be called by the PC when the game is over and it simply shows the menu together with the ingame UI. Not so pretty but fast and useful:

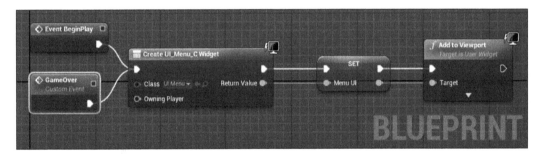

Prepare the needed references

In order to communicate between the player pawn and player controller, the easiest way is to set a reference variable on both classes. The logical place where these references should be set is on the **BeginPlay** event of **Flying Pawn**.

To understand it better: the **player controller** class is unique each time the game start. The **Flying Pawn** is an Actor that can be destroyed and replaced by other instances of it during the game's life. Setting both **PC** and Pawn references at this point in that class allows you to always have the correct reference, as follows:

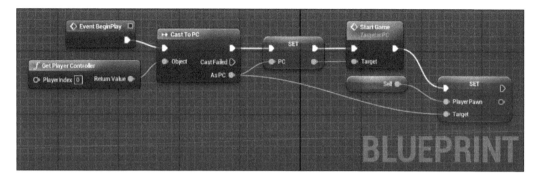

The player controller class

This is where all the magic happens. Here, we already have the two required variables: the target start reference and the spawn volume reference. We need to add a **PlayerPawn** variable (of the **Flying Pawn** type, for the reference that we just discussed) and two other float variables: **TimeScale** and **GameLength**. Most of them are public and to make sure, just double check whether you have them, as shown in the following image:

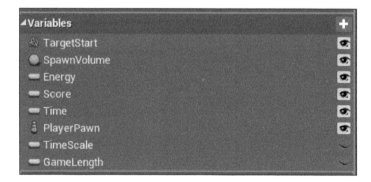

Now, let's create the required events.

StartGame

The **StartGame** event is fired from **Flying Pawn** at its spawn in the game. Here, we reset the UI variables (**Energy**, **Time**, and **Score**) and create the two main timers of the game.

A timer node is, as the name suggests, a timer that will call an event (or a function) at the end of its life. It can remotely call functions, can be looped, and you can set as many timers as you want. Just keep it in mind that everything consumes resources, therefore, when you set a timer, remember to have a place where the timer can be removed.

The first timer handles the end of the game and calls its function just once. A second timer is looped each second and calls the main **update** function of the game each second a new collectable is spawn and the time left is refreshed.

We use the following three variables for the time management for this reason:

- **GameLength**: This value shows the time (in seconds) for which the game lasts. It is a constant variable and is used to adjust the game length easily without any calculations.

- **Time**: This is the value bound to the progress bar. It will contain a value between 0 and 1.

- **TimeScale**: This is the result of 1/**GameLenght** and it is the amount that will decrease in the Time variable:

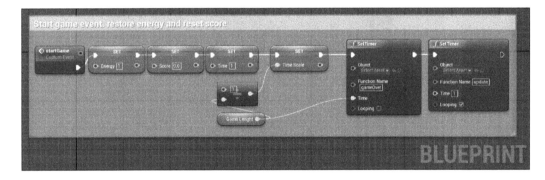

The useFuel event

This method simply decreases by a fixed variable of the **Energy** value. It will be called for each frame that the player is accelerating:

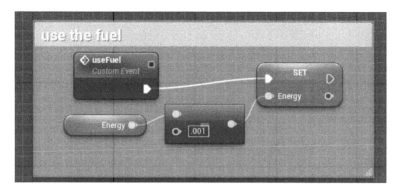

Spawn Collectable function

I chose to add a function that handles the spawning of a collectable as this function will be called from two different events: when the game updates and when a player collects an item.

Thanks to the **Get Random Location** function of **Spawn Volume**, this function is really easy to implement. Just spawn an object at the random location:

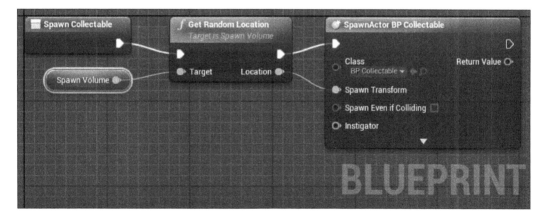

Update

This event, thanks to the functions that are created, is short and easy. Simply call the spawn function, decrease the time by the timescale, and that's it:

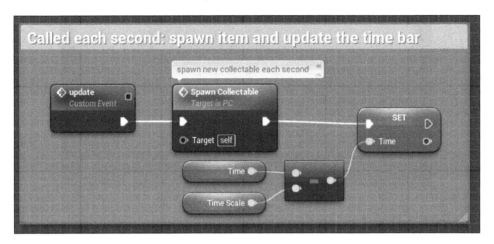

Collect Item

This event is called by the **BP_Collectable** class. Each time it is called, the score is increased and also a little bit amount of energy is added to the ship. We want to add the energy only if necessary and not overcharge the progress bar with useless values:

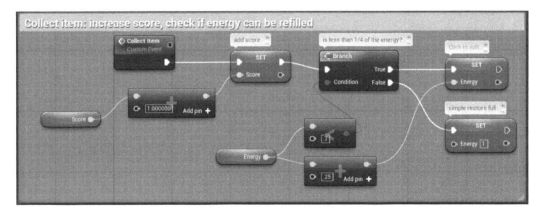

The gameOver event

For **gameOver**, we want the following in order:

- Clear the update timer. It is not needed anymore.

- Destroy the pawn. As this is not needed, it ends its playing time.

- Destroy all the collectables left at the scene: This is achieved with the help of the **Get All Actors of Class** node. This node returns an array of all the objects of the specified class found in a level. With this array, we loop all the items and can destroy them.

- Call the **gameOver** event of the HUD class, as follows:

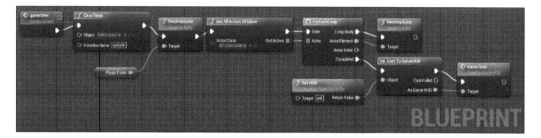

That's it! Compile the whole project, save, and play it. Everything should work as described and, when the time is over, the ship should disappear, showing you only the main menu with the score. Also, thanks to the behavior of the start point target, you can notice how the camera smoothly moves in the correct position independently on where you end the previous run.

Summary

It is hard to explain all these concepts and at the same time, create a whole game without using lot of words and pages. I wish I had more space to show you more about particle systems and UI; however, at the same time, I hope you correctly understood all the steps of this chapter and are now able to create your own particle system, choosing between different modules and achieving the result that you have in your mind.

As usual, here is some homework for you:

- **Spot the missing behavior**: You should notice that there is something missing when you play the game. We created the fuel variable and the code that handles it; however, we never actually implemented its usage in the game. The fix is pretty easy; check **Flying Pawn**, the nodes needed are an AND boolean and a branch.

- **More time**: Instead of increasing the energy, try to change the behavior of the collectable item to add a little bit of time (or both energy and time) when one of them is collected.

- **A game over UI**: Try to create a new UI that handles the **gameOver** screen; keep using the menu UI as we did for our game over and just switch the **inScreen** with a new screen Widget that shows only the score and a text.

- **Create an exhaust particle for the ship**: A texture is not needed. When creating, don't think about the movement of the particle. Remember that each single particle has its own life with duration, size and so on. If the particle system doesn't move in the preview, it doesn't necessarily mean that when its attached to a moving object, its aspect will change.

In the next chapter, you will learn how to create a shooter game. We will manipulate a mannequin by creating our own animations and see how a pawn can be controlled by artificial intelligence.

5
Top-Down Shooter

In this chapter we are going to create one of the most interesting and popular types of video game, especially on the mobile market: a top-down shooter. This kind of game is characterized by a fixed view from above the player, which shows the action around it from a top-down perspective.

This technique, also called bird's eye view or helicopter view, has being used in a lot of types of games such as **role-playing game** (**RPG**) (*Final Fantasy* series), action **Grand Theft Auto** (**GTA**), and **Adventures** (the *Legend of Zelda*), and lately it is being adopted in mobile games thanks to the possibility of creating a really interesting environment even with the typical limitations of the portable devices.

A top-down shooter gameplay is usually a frenetic action game, where the player needs to survive as long as they can as the continuous waves of enemies attack. The top-down perspective is perfect for those games. A player can see far around them, giving a perfect immersion into the problem of being surrounded and constantly in danger.

In this chapter, you will learn:

- Animation Blueprint
- Aim offset and blending animation
- State machines

Animations

It is assumed that you already have knowledge about basic 3D animation concepts such as Skeletal Meshes, Bones, Frames, Rigs, and so on. We aren't going to create new animations from a mesh, but we will work with them so, if you don't know anything about them, I suggest you to take a break from this guide to find out more about those concepts using Google or Wikipedia.

The animation system of UE4 can be divided into three main tools: **Persona**, **Skeleton**, and **Animation Sequences**. These tools, combined together, give you the ability to manipulate and control your Skeletal Meshes. You can play and blend animations within an Animation Sequence, create customized moves using **AnimMontages**, create complex facial expression with **MorphTarget**, and do much more.

Skeleton

Skeleton is a hierarchy of bone locations and rotations used to deform a Skeletal Mesh. The difference between a traditional 3D environment is that Skeleton in UE4 are abstracted from Skeletal Meshes in their own assets, and this means that animations are applied to the Skeleton rather than the Skeletal Mesh. In this way, multiple Skeletal Meshes can share the same animations:

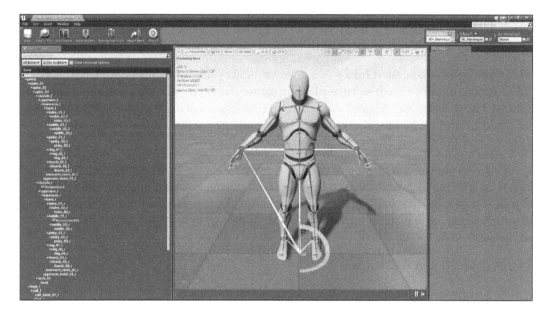

In the preceding screenshot, you can see the **Skeleton Tree** on the left and the familiar **Details** panel on the right. Here, you have full control of your Skeleton. You can modify the root position of any single bone and check your modifications from the preview viewport panel. The preview panel has the same tools of any other preview window of the engine, with functions to toggle visibility of different aspects of the Skeleton or the preview zone itself.

Persona

Persona is the main toolset for animation editing of the Engine. From there, you will be able to edit Skeletons, Skeletal Meshes, AnimationSequences, and so on. Although a deeper manipulation is available inside the other tools, here you can preview your Animation Sequences, set **BlendSpaces** and **Montages**, control sockets, and do much more:

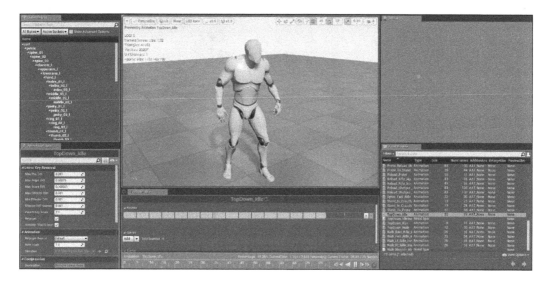

As you can see from the preceding image, this window is similar to the Skeleton window but there are three additional panels. On the right-hand side, you have an **Asset** panel, which shows you all the Animation Sequences, BlendSpaces, and AimOffset files relative to that skeleton. From that panel, you can simply double-click on one of the files to see its preview and manipulate it in the other two panels.

Just above the preview, you can see the Anim Sequence Editor. This panel provides functionality for previewing and editing the selected Animation Sequence. From here, you can add animation notification events (or **Notifies**). They allow camera effects, particle effects, sounds, or custom events to be triggered on a specified frame.

From here, you can also add **Curves**, which is useful when you want to change, for example, a variable value dynamically during the animation.

At the bottom, you can see the frames of the animations, loop the entire animation, or stop it on an exact frame:

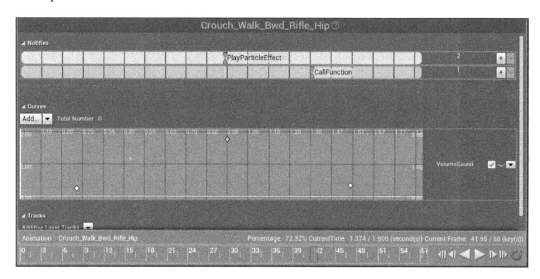

In the bottom-left corner, there is the **Anim Asset Details** panel. This is a context-sensitive property editor (exactly like the **Details** panel) that allows you to change setting on various animation assets, such as Anim Sequences, Blend Spaces, AnimMontage, and so on:

Animation Sequence

An Animation Sequence is a single animation asset that can be played on a Skeletal Mesh. It contains keyframes that specify the position, rotation, and scale of a bone at a specific point in time. The animation is generated by playing in sequence all the keyframes, blending between them to make the animation smoother.

When opening an Animation Sequence, the Persona window will be opened and any modification in a single animation sequence will be made there.

When talking about Animation Sequences, there are three different ways to use them.

Additive animations

An animation can be used as absolute or additive at any time. The system performs the appropriate calculations to convert the data to offset when necessary. This makes the system much more flexible than that of previous versions of the engine, since you don't have to specify beforehand that an animation is to be considered additive.

An additive animation can be used when you have two specific animations and you want to merge them smoothly. For example, when you have a walking loop animation and you want to modify the walking loop with the hands of your character opened. With Unreal, the only thing you need to do is to create the hand open pose and use that pose as additive animation at the walking loop.

Blending animation

Blending animation is the most used type of animation you will see. Animations can be blended together to create more complex final poses through the use of **Blend Nodes** and **Blend Spaces**. This type of animation allows you to populate your animation asset by reusing the single sequences instead of having a dedicated sequence for each situation. For example, you can blend between run and shoot to be able to aim and shoot at a target while running, walking, or crouching.

Animation poses

An Animation pose is essentially a snapshot of the Skeleton, including the position and rotation of all of its bones. Think of a pose as what you see if you pause the playback of an animation. Poses are useful to create addictive animations or aim offset.

Animation Blueprints

An Animation Blueprint is a special Blueprint class that, like any other Blueprint class, uses graphs to control the animation of a Skeletal Mesh. It can perform blending of animations, directly control the bones of the Skeleton, and output a final pose for a Skeletal Mesh in each frame.

Each Skeletal Mesh, in order to be animated, must have an instance of an Animation Blueprint associated to it. The Animation Blueprint, through its graph, can access to the properties of the owner (that can be a pawn or any other Actor) of the Skeletal Mesh and uses those values to deliver the correct final pose of the skeleton:

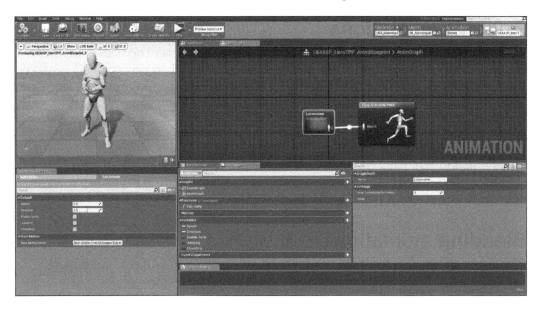

There are two main components in an Animation Blueprint that work in conjunction to create the final animation for each frame: the **Event Graph** and the **Anim Graph**.

The **Event Graph** is a standard graph like any other Blueprint class. It uses a collection of special animation-related events to initiate sequences of nodes. The typical usage of the Event Graph is to check the values of the controlled pawn and update the corresponding values of Blend Spaces or other blend nodes to drive animation within the Anim Graph.

The **Anim Graph** is used to evaluate a final pose for the Skeletal Mesh for the current frame. By default, each Animation Blueprint has a single AnimGraph, which can have animation nodes placed within it to sample AnimationSequences, perform animation blend, or control bone transforms using skeletalControl.

The game

As usual, after a brief theoretical introduction, let's use what I explained and create a game. For this project we use the **TopDown** Blueprint template, but we also need some external assets.

UE4 recognises a vast amount of files extensions, from `.fbx` for a 3D object (almost any 3D software can create an FBX asset file either from an internal exporter or external plugin) to the `.wav` audio file, from the `.bmp` texture to the `.wmv` video file created by an online tool.

For this game, we need a bunch of animations contained in the **Unreal Animation Starter Pack** and a couple of weapon 3D models. If you are an artist you can use your own models, but my advice is to use the files suggested here for 100 percent compatibility with what I'm going to teach you.

The **Animation Starter Pack** is a free package released by the Epic team and it can be found directly from the **MARKETPLACE** section of the launcher at `https://www.unrealengine.com/marketplace`:

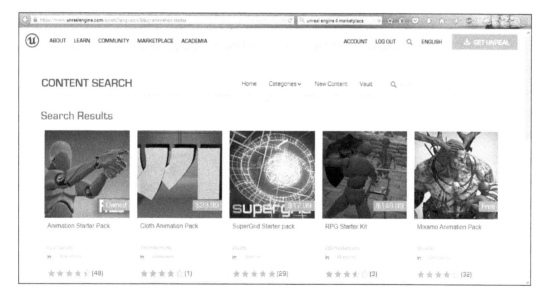

This package is compatible with the mannequin used on the template and contains a vast amount of useful animations for a shooter-type game, such as aim, reload, die, crouch, and so on.

When you buy a package from the marketplace, as soon as it is downloaded, you can find it in the **Vault** section of your **Library** and it can be added at any of your projects by clicking on **Add To Project** button. A popup window appears and shows you all the projects compatible with the package. When you select them, even if your project is open, you immediately have that package available in your **Content Browser**.

The external files are slightly different to import but the process is very simple and intuitive.

We are going to import a weapon model for our main character. It can be found, like always, at www.nicolavalcasara.it/packt. As soon as you download it, you can import it into the editor by dragging and dropping that file into the **Content Browser** (wait a couple of seconds before releasing the mouse, it takes a little bit of time for the editor to process the file and recognize it). You can also right-click and select **import to...**:

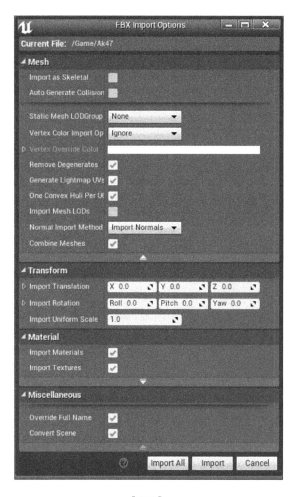

A context-sensitive popup appear showing the different settings that can be applied to the imported file. In our case, we are importing an FBX file. Because an FBX is a complex file that contains usually animations and materials instead of only a simple mesh here we can choose what to import, and how.

The steps to prepare our project are as follows:

- Create a new project from the TopDown Blueprint template, call it `TD_Game`, leave the other settings as default, and launch it.
- Download the Animation Starter Pack from the unreal marketplace and add it to your project.
- Import the `ak47.fbx` file into your project. Leave the FBX settings as defaults and create the corresponding folders for the imported files (meshes and materials). You will notice that the mesh just imported is shown to you as a white plain mesh, even if the materials are correctly linked. Don't worry, we will soon fix this problem.

Cleaning the unnecessary files

A clean and tidy project can be developed faster and is surely more enjoyable than a messy project, so let's do some cleaning on this project.

About the map, the default one is fine for our project; just remove the top-down template text from the floor.

On the template, you can find some Blueprint script in the controller. Since we will hardly modify the code, simply create a new Blueprint class extending from `PlayerController` and remove the existing `TopDownController`. When you remove this file, the editor gives you the possibility to choose to replace the file that references it (in this case, the `TopDownGameMode` file). If you don't succeed in retargeting the file, delete and manually set the controller of the Game Mode to our new controller.

Let's now go inside the Animation extension package and remove all the animations that we don't need. The player will be able to walk, run, aim, shoot, and reload.

Before deleting take a look at those files. You can easily identify the different kinds of animation thanks to the colored underlines:

- Green: Animation Sequence
- Light Orange: BlendSpace
- Dark Orange: Animation Blueprint
- Blue: Blueprint class

Let's delete every animation sequence for crouch, prone, jump, jog, and hit. Remove the Blend Spaces relative to those animations too. The showcase map is useless, so is the Blueprint class for this mannequin and its Animation Blueprint. We don't need this mannequin as well, as we will soon discuss how to redirect animation. For the moment, your folder should look like this:

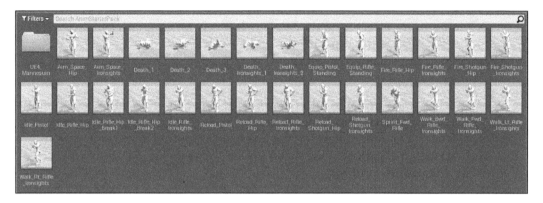

You should have only Animation Sequences in this folder. You can now move all of them inside the animation folder of your project. From that folder, remove the TopDown_Anim_Blueprint file; we will create a new one when the time comes.

Adjust the imported files

When you import a file into the editor, especially complex ones such as .fbx files, it is often necessary to adjust them to be correctly used in your game. As you already noticed, the weapon imported lack of texture. This is a common issue and easy to fix.

Open one of its materials (wood or metal). There is only a none node connected to the base color. We simply need to change the none node to a **Texture Sample** one and that's it. Search for this node and search for the **T_AK47** material in the **Texture** field from the **Details** panel. Apply to the base color and do the same to the other material. The mesh is already waiting for this material, so you should immediately notice the correct texture applied to it as soon as you save:

From this starting point, you can play with **Metallic**, **Roughness**, or the other pins as we did in the previous chapters to give your weapon a more realistic view. The mesh UV mapping will apply the correct piece to your object.

Skeletal Mesh retarget

You might want to use the same animation you created with a Skeletal Mesh of another model or, like in our case, you want to unify all the animation to the same target.

At the moment, we have two copies of the same mannequin (one from the template and the other from the animation package), and that will be a problem when we want to create the Animation Blueprint. An Animation Blueprint can work only on a single Skeletal Mesh. Because we need to blend, for example, the walk without weapon and walk with weapon animation, we need to have the same reference mesh.

When you retarget an animation, you are saying: use this skeleton inside the other model. The engine will create a copy of the same animation based on the new model, but as you can imagine, the models can be slightly different (even if they're usually humanoids). A goblin, for example, is different from an elf. When changing model after retarget, you can adjust the bones position using the **Retarget Manager**, a tool available from the skeleton window that allows you to fit the skeleton to the new model:

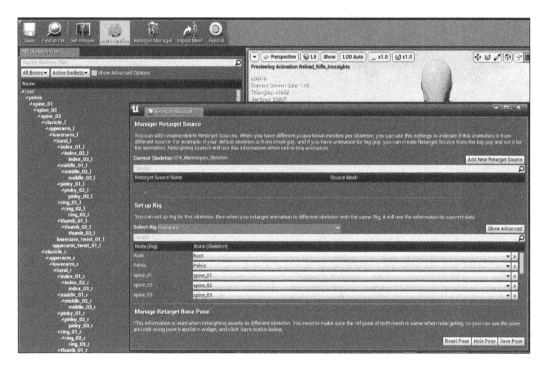

In our case, we have the same model. So, we have to simply switch between them. Go to your `animation` folder and select all the TopDown animations files (four files), right-click, select `Retarget Anim Asset`, and go to `Duplicate Anim Assets and retarget`.

In this window, you can see a preview of the actual model and the final target. Just select the correct `UE4_Mannequin_Skeleton` file and click on **Select**. If you don't see the Skeletal Mesh, just uncheck the **Show Only Compatible Skeletons** option:

Now, you are free to delete the original four animations you just retargeted and replace the existing files under the `Mesh` folder with `UE4_Mannequin` one. Remove the (now useless) `AnimStarterPack` folder and prepare to animate it.

Animations

It's time to plan our game to see what is needed in terms of animations. The gameplay consists of a typical shoot 'em all: the player needs to shoot as much as they can at the infinite waves of enemies. The enemies can be killed with the weapon but the player must move around constantly because the enemies never end and never stop chasing the player.

The environment is a flat plane, with some random tall obstacles useful to avoid the attack. It doesn't contain slopes, doors, or jumpable obstacles.

Considering this and seeing what animations sequences we have available, we can implement the following:

- **Aim offset**: An animation offset that allows the animation to aim the correct point to use as addictive animation at the final pose

- **BlendSpace idle-walk while aiming**: We already have an idle-walk-run Blend Space without aiming, but the player surely will need to shoot while moving

- **Animation Blueprint**: The animGraph of our player can use a single State Machine that goes through idle-move-shoot-reload steps according to the player controller

Aim Offset

When talking about AimOffset and BlendSpaces, the engine allows you to choose between one or two-dimensional sequences depending on how you want to interact with it. A two-dimensional Blend Space, for example, can take the direction and the speed of the character in order to create a correct moving result. A single dimension, for example, can take only the speed of a falling object to modify its shapes.

A typical two-dimensional AimOffset for our character take the pitch and the yaw degrees to calculate a final pose, but it is not what we need. Because we are watching it from the top-down perspective, we can use a single dimensional offset and take only the yaw of the player, irrespective of whether they are looking down or up. The following screenshot explains the concept:

From the preceding screenshot, you can see that **0** is the point where the player is aiming in the pose shown. By creating the offset, we will rotate only the upper part of the body by calculating the angle between the **0** point and the aiming cursor (in our case, the mouse position). This screenshot also shows how a pitch calculation is hard to find and useless.

To create an aim offset, we need to create three additive poses for our character. If you search in the available sequences, you will notice that we have an `Aim_Space_Ironsight` sequence. On opening it, you will see that it loops between all the possible aiming positions. It's a good starting point to extrude the poses that we need.

Create a new folder and call it `AIM_Offset`. Copy the `Aim_Space_Ironsight` sequence inside that folder, duplicate it two times (by using *Ctrl + w*, or by using right-click and selecting **duplicate**), and rename those three sequences: `Aim_Center`, `Aim_Right`, `Aim_Left`.

Now, open `Aim_Center` in Persona and stop the preview from the Animation Notification panel:

From any of your sequences, you can extrude a pose. Here, we want to find the frame where the model is aiming at its center and generate an additive pose for the aim offset. The center point is easy, drag the red rectangle from the frame bar to the Frame 0. Notice how the preview is updated instantly while dragging.

Now that we found our frame, we can delete all the others frames by right-clicking on the red rectangle and selecting remove from frame 1 to frame 87:

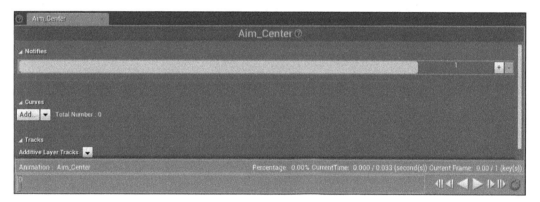

You should get an empty frame bar with a single key on it. If you play, you can see how (logically) the mannequin doesn't move at all.

Now, we need to set this pose to be additive. From the **Anim Asset Details** panel, find the **Additive Settings** section and choose **Mesh Space** as **Additive Anim Type**, choose **Selected Animation by Frame** as **Base Pose Type**, and search for **Idle_Rifle_Ironsights** as **Base pose Animation**. We are basically telling the system that whenever this pose is used, it has to calculate the addition based on the bone transformation of the first frame of the idle with weapon animation:

Repeat the same process with `Aim_Right` (frame 35) and `Aim_Left` (frame 62). When cleaning frames from a middle point, there is a second step but the process is the same: first remove frames *0* to frame *x* and then remove from frame *0* to end of clip.

With these three poses, from the **Content Browser**, right-click and go to **Animations | Aim Offset 1D**.

The window that appears is different only in the Animation Notification panel. This new panel has a **Parameters** section where you can set your dimension values (axis name, starting point, and ending point of the dimension) and a single line graph where you can drag poses or sequences that you want to be executed according to the value of the dimension parameter.

Set the parameter name to `Angle` and **Range** to be `-90` to `90`. **Apply Parameter Changes** and notice how the graph changes:

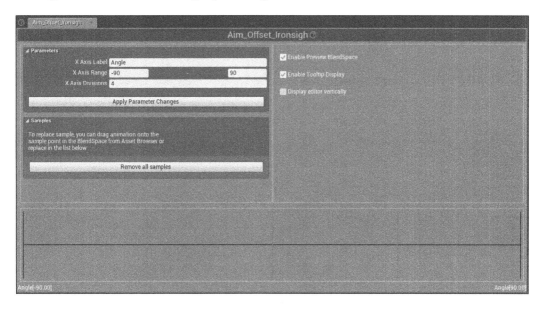

You will soon see the meaning of all this. From the **Asset** browser on your right, drag the `Aim_Center` pose and drop it on the center of the graph line. Do the same for `Aim_Right` and `Aim_Left`, positioning them on the end points of the line. Now, you can move your mouse around the line to check the result of the blended offset.

The mannequin moves its torso to the left and the right, but it is not embracing a gun! This is because we didn't set the preview base animation of AimOffset. Fix this by going to the **Details** panel and setting the `Idle_Rifle_Ironsigh` sequence in the **Additive Settings** section. The AimOffset is done and ready to be implemented in our future Blueprint:

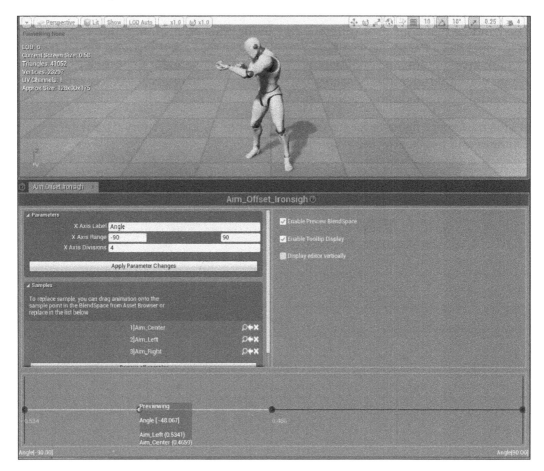

Blend Space

We now need to create a Blend Space to handle the animation between an idle aim and a walking aim. A two-dimensional BlendSpace is what we need. The x dimension will be the 360 direction of the character and the y dimension will be its speed.

Right-click on the Content Browser and go to **Animations | Blend Space**. Set our mannequin, name it `Idle_Walk_IronSight`, and set the **Preview Base Pose** to be `Idle_rifle_ironsights`.

About the parameter, name the x axis `Direction` and give it a range from `-180` to `180`. The y axis will have the name `Speed` and a range from `0` to `200`. Click on **Apply Parameter Changes** and notice how the graph is a 4 x 4 grid.

When the speed is 0, it means that the player is not moving but aiming at something. You can drag the `Idle_rifle_Ironsigh` sequence to all the five intersection bottom points of the graph. We need to do it for all the intersections because we want to be sure that the animation is not moving at all at 0 speed, irrespective of the direction.

To figure out the correct sequences, try to think about the image we saw for the aim offset angles. If the direction is 0, it means the player is moving forward and if the direction is nearby 180 or -180, the player is walking backward. Similarly, for the 90 and -90 degrees, the player is moving to their left or their right.

Drag the **Walk_Bwd_Rifle_Ironsights** sequence to the top corners of the graph, the **Walk_Forward_Rifle_ironsights** sequence to the top-center, and **Walk_Rt_Rifle_Ironsights** and **Walk_Lt_Rifle_Ironsight** to the 90 degrees intersections:

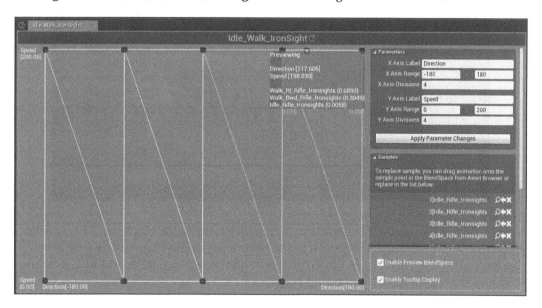

Animation Blueprint – AnimGraph

It's time to create the `Blueprint` file that will handle the animation. In the Blueprint folder, right-click and go to **animation | Animation Blueprint**. From that popup window, you can select a parent class for your animation. Like a normal Blueprint class, you can have a main Animation Blueprint that handle the basic movement of a character and create extension of that class that will handle only the different animations for different characters.

Select **AnimInstance** (the basic class) and our mannequin, and name it `AnimBP`.

Opening the file will immediately show you the AnimGraph, with the final Animation Pose node waiting for the result input pin to be connected with a State Machine.

A State Machine is a special node and provides a graphical way to break the animation of your Skeletal Mesh into a series of states. These states are then governed by **Transition Rules** that control how to blend from one state to another. This tool simplifies the design process for animations. You can create a graph that easily controls how your character can flow between the types of animations without having to create a complex Blueprint network.

Thanks to a State Machine, it is really easy to create and handle an animation flow. To create a new State Machine, right-click anywhere in **AnimGraph** and search for **Add New State Machine...**. Call it `Locomotion` and connect to the **Final Animation Pose** node:

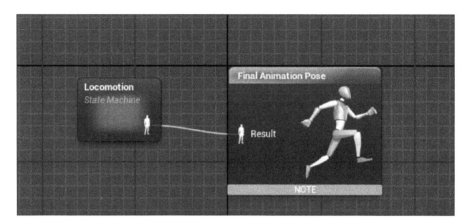

Now, double-click on the Locomotion node to open the **State Machine**. This special graph is made by the logic block, each one contains a single sequence or a blended sequence. What we need is an idle/move state that can move from and to a shooting state and that can handle a reloading state.

Before creating our states, let's add the variables that will be used by them. From **My Blueprint** panel, add these variables:

- `Speed`: Float
- `Direction`: Float
- `Angle`: Float
- `isReloading`: Boolean
- `isShooting`: Boolean

To add a new state, drag the new arrow from the `Locomotion` State Machine, click on **Add state**, and name it `Idle/Run`:

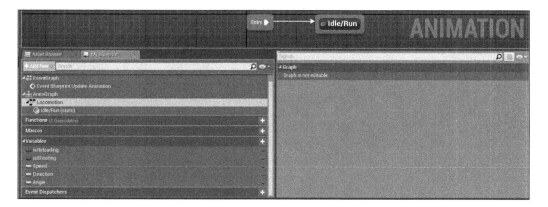

The **Idle/Run** state will be the entry point of the State Machine. The animation will use this node without a Transition Rule by default as soon as the model spawns on the level.

Open the state you created. Notice how every state node you create has a final animation pose. You can connect a single animation sequence to this node or connect a complex result from a Blend Space and other animations. This **Final Animation Pose** is basically the same node of the AnimGraph and any animation connected here directly affects that final result of the root. For example, you connect the Idle sequence on the Idle state. If the actual state is Idle, the Final pose of the animGraph will be the Idle loop animation.

For our state, we want to use `TopDown_IdleRun_2D`, a default BlendSpace that takes as a parameter a speed value and blends the animation according to it.

When inside animGraph, you can simply search for the exact name of a sequence/ BlendSpace and add it as a graph node. Search for it and add to **Final Animation Pose**. Now, simply get the **Speed** variable we created and connect it to the animation **BlendSpace**:

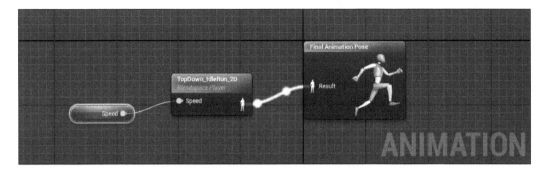

If you compile, you can see that the preview now is changed and the mannequin is now in idle animation. From the default value inside the AnimPreview editor, you can change the speed to check if the state you created works as expected.

We can go ahead and connect a new state to the idle one. To do this, simply click on the **Idle/Run** node, drag out a new state, call it Shooting, and notice the type of graph the editor created. The wire is not, like Blueprint, a straight line that connects two nodes. It's a unidirectional arrow, with a symbol on top of it. This is a transition wire and it is a special arrow that handles how two states are connected. Here, you can set the rules to handle when and how a state will change:

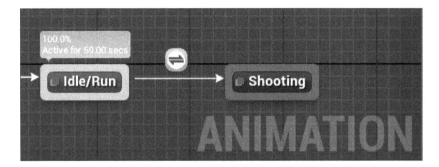

Double-click on the symbol at the top of the arrow to set the Transition Rule. In our case, we want that the state should change from idle to shooting and vice versa based on the isShooting variable.

From **Idle** to **Shooting**, simply get the `isShooting` value; from **Shooting** to **Idle**, use a **NOT** node to find when the player is not shooting:

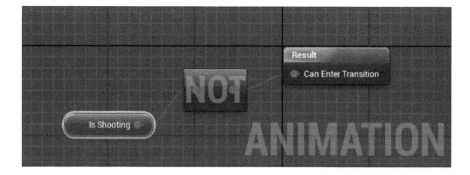

You can create as many Transition Rules you want by dragging and connecting the two states node borders.

About the **Shooting** state, it is time to use the two animations we created before. Take **Idle_Walk_IronSight**, connect the result to **Aim_Offset_Ironsight**, add the corresponding variables, and connect the end to the **Final Animation Pose**:

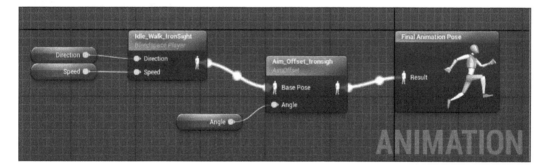

Compile and enjoy the result. Everything works smoothly and according to the input values.

There is a known incongruence between the template mannequin and the Animation package root bone that makes a blend between those two unpleasant. To hotfix this problem, under the blend settings of the transition rule from idle to shooting, change the duration field from 0.2 to 0 seconds.

As last, handle the **Reloading** state. Create the same transition we did before, use **isReloading** instead of **Shooting** and connect it from entry to the shooting state:

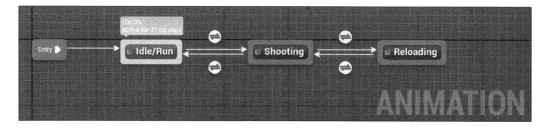

Inside the reloading state, we simply want to **Play Reload_Rifle_Ironsights** sequence and blend it with the direction the player was aiming on the **Aim_Offset_Ironsigh**:

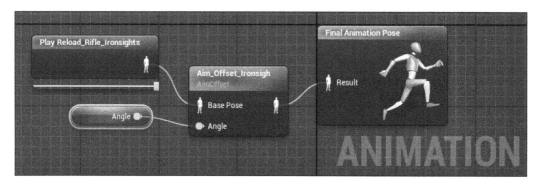

Animation Notifies

All those variables are updated each frame from the evenGraph and their values are handled by the player controller. There is a variable that can't be handled by the controller: **IsReloading**. How will a player know when an animation ends playing? (In this case, when it ends to reload the weapon?). It's here that an animation notify can help. From Persona, we can set a notify to be fired on an exact frame that says to any listener (in this case, the animation Blueprint) that an animation ends.

Open **Reload_Rifle_Ironsights**, right-click on frame 62 in the **Notifies** panel, and go to add **Notify | New Notify...**. Name it `Reloaded`. It should appear correctly on the time frame like this:

With this setup, we can go back to our Animation Blueprint. Within EventGraph, we can simply search for the Reload event and use it like any other nodes within Blueprint:

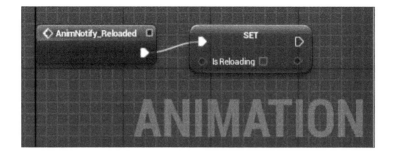

Compile and check if it works correctly. On selecting `isShooting` and `isReloading` as true, the animation should automatically return to the shooting state as soon as the reloading animation ends.

Inputs

For our game, we need to change the default input values. The player will move the character using the WASD or the arrow keys, aim and shoot with the mouse, and they have the option to equip/unequip and choose between two weapons by using the 1 or 2 keys. Go to **Edit | Project Settings** and create the following actions and axis:

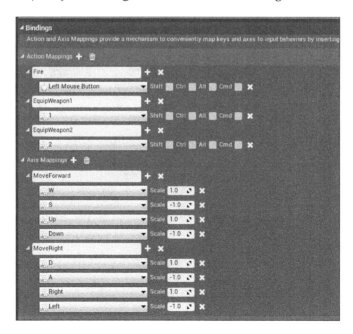

Player movements

It's time to implement some logic in our project. We can start by handling the movement of the character. Like most of the logic of a player, this will be handled by the player controller.

 It's good practice to use the player character (or pawn) to store and handle only the pawn-related information such as health, equipped weapon, speed, and so on, and handle all the logic of it with a player controller class. This leads to a better reusability of the code and a cleaned and ordered workflow.

Open the `TD_Controller` Blueprint class and enable the cursor and the mouse events from the mouse interface section. Then, open the full Blueprint editor and insert the movement event nodes: **InputAxis MoveForward** and **InputAxis MoveRight**.

We saw a similar event in the previous chapters: those events are fired in each frame the event occurs (in this case, one of the move key is pressed and held). When a key is pressed, we want to add a movement input (remember to uncheck the contex-sensitive option if you don't find the node) with the player pawn as target and a direction vector up (1,0,0) or right vector (0,1,0) as direction, correctly scaled by the axis value. With these nodes, we have a walking character that faces the direction it's pointing and moves correctly in the four directions:

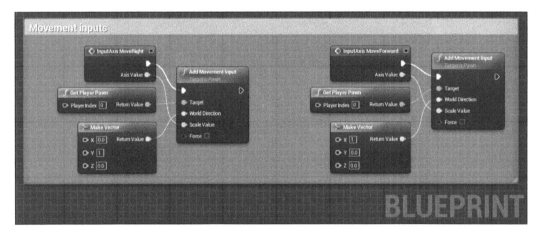

This setup doesn't allow acceleration or a clear passage between walk and run because the value is always 0 or 1. You can make the transition smoother by multiplying the created vector by a custom float value and play with the character movement properties.

Aim logic

At the moment, the pawn is rotating automatically by facing the direction of the movement (still without animation but we will fix that soon). This behavior - check and apply throughout is fine if the player is not shooting. As soon as a player embraces a weapon, we want to be able to aim at the mouse position and to keep aiming the mouse while moving.

To achieve this result, we will create two functions. The first one physically rotates the character to the cursor position and stores a reference to its rotation. The second one updates on every tick an angle value based on the cursor position and the rotation of the player.

Rotate To Aim

Inside the player controller class, create a new function and call it `RotateToAim`. This function simply rotates the character to face the cursor. To find the cursor location, we use **Get Hit Result Under Cursor by Channel**:

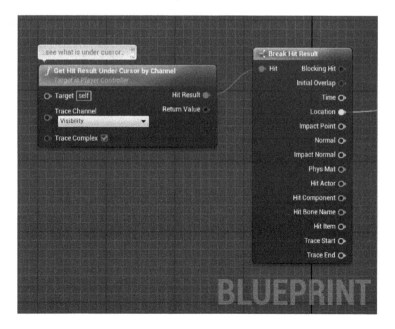

This node checks whether the player hit a traced object and returns a hit result; it is similar to the raycast node we saw in other chapters. Thanks to this node, we can get the exact position of the cursor and we can use the **Find Look At Rotation** node to get the exact rotation to apply to our character to face the cursor:

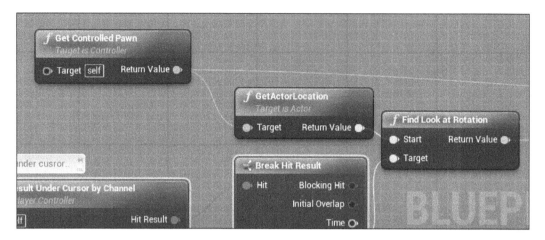

Before changing the rotation, break the rotation and nullify pitch and roll. We only want to rotate the player by its yaw:

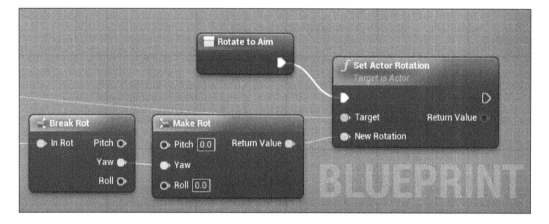

Set Aim angle

The set Aim angle function is similar to the preceding one, the only difference is that it doesn't rotate the Actor but it refreshes a stored variable that will be used in the animation Blueprint. We use **Get Hit Result Under Cursor**, we find the rotation toward the cursor and we subtract the actual actor rotation to find by how many degrees we need to rotate our AimOffset.

Create a new float variable and call it `LookAngle`, create a new function, call it `SetLookAngle`, and copy the same nodes we used before, applying the modifications we just discussed. The final result should be something like this:

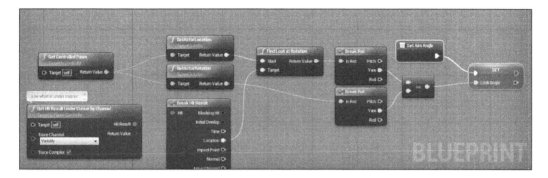

Gate

We now need the ability to control whenever a player is firing or is simply moving. To do this, we use a Gate node.

A **Gate** node is used as a way to open and close a stream of execution. The **Enter** input takes in execution pulses and the current state of the gate (open or close) determines whether those pulses pass out of the **Exit** output or not.

In our case, we use the player controller tick as the **Enter** input, the **Pressed Fire** button as **Enter**, and the **Released Fire** button as **Exit**. As soon as the player hits Fire, the `RotateToAim` function is called. Until the player stops firing, the execution node is called and the `lookAngle` is updated with the `SetAimAngle` function:

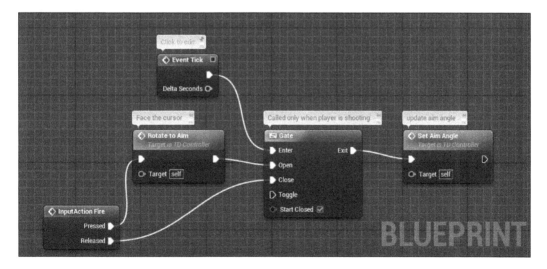

Start and stop shooting events

This gate is a good starting point but there is still some work to do. First, as you notice, as soon as you move after clicking fire, the player returns to face the direction where it is moving and there isn't a place where to communicate to the animation what we are doing.

Create two custom events, call them `StartFire` and `StopFire`, and connect them to **InputAction Fire**. Fire just before the **Gate**:

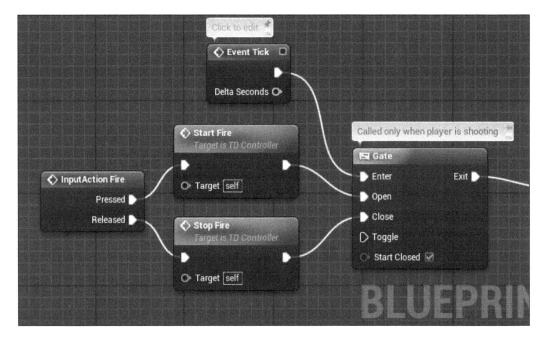

It is much cleaner than before and it gives you the possibility to implement nodes a second time without needing to move around everything.

On the start and stop fire, first we want to toggle the autorotation. This is achievable thanks to the set orientation to movement node of the character movement component of the player pawn.

To get a component of another Blueprint class, we can cast to the correct class our pawn or (and it's preferable this way if you need to cast multiple times components in your Blueprint) create a casted reference of that class on the **BeginPlay** event:

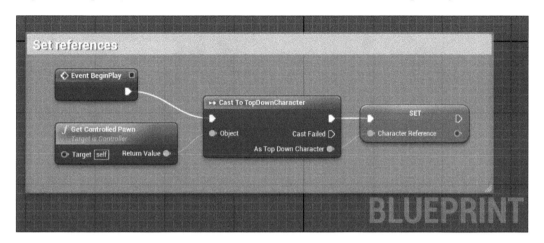

Character Reference is of the type **TopDownCharacter** Blueprint class. With this way, we don't need to cast anymore during the gameplay and we are now able to get any component of the topdown character pawn.

Get the Character movement component, search for **Orient Rotation to Movement** node, and apply it to the stop and start fire like this:

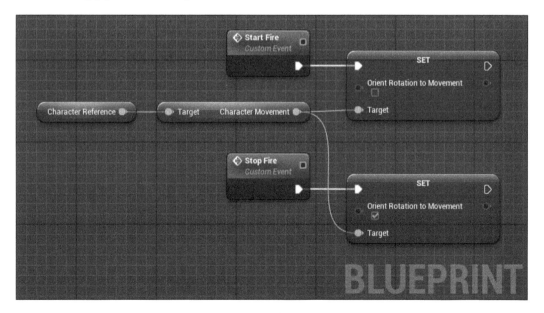

About the animation, we need to set a Boolean value here that will be used by the animation. Just create it, call `isShooting`, and set true or false on the according event. Lastly, remember to reconnect the **Rotate To Aim** node at the end of the **Start Fire** event:

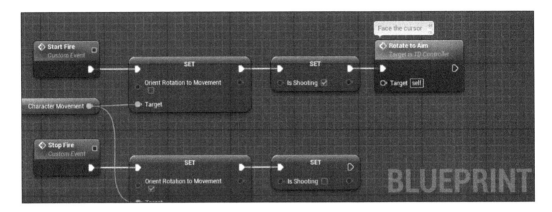

Flip the player

If you return to when we created the AimOffset, you will notice that is handled only from -90 to 90 degrees from the point 0. This is because, as a humanoid player, it cannot rotate its torso all the way around to cover 360 degrees all around it. This means that when we start to fire, we are able to cover only half of the space available.

This is a common problem in this kind of game and usually the solution is a compromise between realism and practice. Most of these games simply don't care and rotate the whole mesh constantly to face the cursor. The ideal solution is to blend an animation between the left and right aim pose, but, because the action is so frenetic that this kind of animation will barely notice, a rotation of 180 degrees when the angle exceeds a certain value is more than enough.

First, create a function called `FlipPlayer` and set its rotation after adding 180 degrees to its yaw. It's an easy function and the final result should look like this:

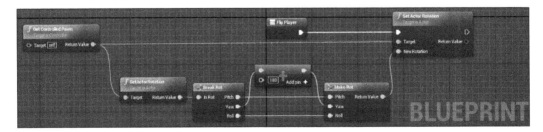

Secondly, implement this function just after setting **Look Angle**. If the angle calculated is more than 90 degrees, then flip the player:

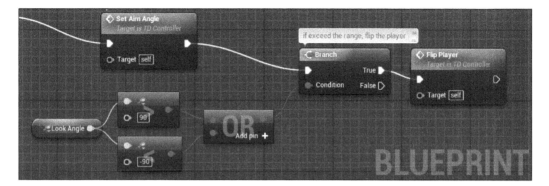

Weapon

The weapon in our game is an Actor object that can be collected and dropped, can be attached to our pawn thanks to a Socket, and can handle the spawn of bullet objects. We will create a super class weapon that can be used as a parent to create different types of weapons for your games.

Socket

First, let's talk about socket. A socket is a special object that can be placed as child of any bone of a Skeletal Mesh. It has its own translation properties (location, rotation, and scale), it is totally invisible to the player, and it can be used to attach a mesh to another object. Because the socket is attached within a bone, it will follow the animations automatically without needing to use additional calculations.

For our game, we need two sockets: one in the hand of the player when it is aiming, and one on the shoulders when the weapon is in the inventory. To create the first socket, open **UE4_Mannequin** skeleton and locate the Hand_R bone from the **Skeleton Tree**.

Right-click and select **Add Socket**. Call it `ArmedSocket` and that's it; you have a socket ready to accept a mesh. You can add a preview mesh to the socket you created by right-clicking on it and selecting **Add Preview Asset**. This is really useful when you want to adjust the socket properties to fit the mesh you know will be added there. Search for the AK47 mesh and adjust the values of the socket to something like this:

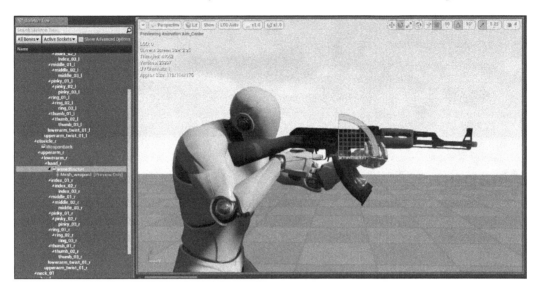

Repeat the process for the secondary weapon by adding a new socket at the **Clavicle_R** bone, call it `WeaponBack`, and adjust its values to something like this:

The weapon meshes here are only available inside the preview. If you run the project, you will not see them until we will attach them by code.

Weapon Blueprint class

Create a new Blueprint class extending Actor and call it `Weapon`. A weapon can be collected from the floor and needs to have a reference point for the bullets. On **Viewport**, add a **Sphere** collider component, a **Skeletal Mesh** component, and an **Arrow** component. Make the **Sphere** collider as root, change the collision type to generate overlap events, and set collision preset as overlap all.

The Skeletal Mesh as you can image is our AK-47. Position it inside the **Sphere** collider and disable its collision. The arrow needs to be moved on the fire point of the mesh, with the big red arrow pointing forward from the weapon. The result is something like this:

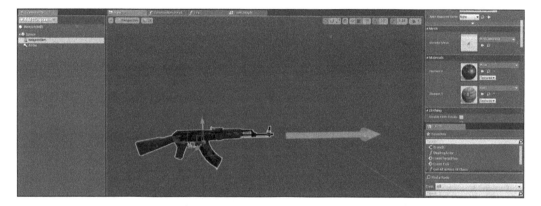

We need the following variables:

- `MaxAmmo`: Float and public; the maximum amount of ammo available for this weapon

- `Loader`: Float and Public; the actual number of bullets available. This and the previous variable are public to be used within the HUD

- `FireRate`: Float; the fire rate (in seconds) of the weapon

- `IsReloading`: Boolean; used to stop fire while the weapon is reloading

The fire will be handled by two custom events and a **Fire** Function. The events will be called by the player controller and they simply start and stop an infinite timer based to the **Fire Rate**:

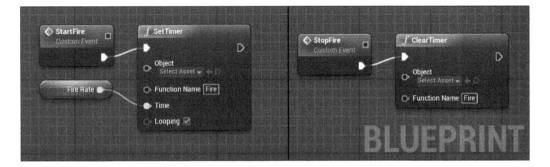

When called by the timer, the **Fire** function uses the **SpawnActor** node from the `Arrow` location:

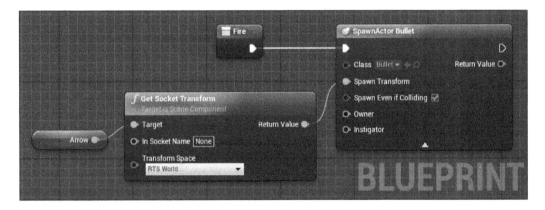

On this function, before firing the bullet, we need to check if there are bullets available in the loader and if not, we set the Fire to unavailable until the player has reloaded it.

Because the player could want to keep the button **Fire** pushed even when reloading, we add an **AND** condition to the check this value together with the weapon loader to prevent an accidental and unwanted bullet spawned until the weapon is ready to shoot again:

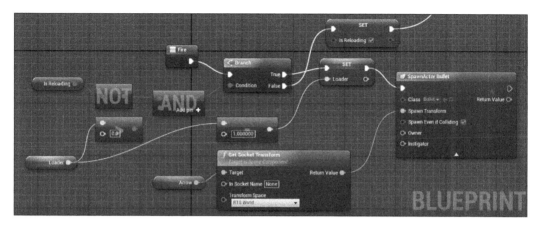

Animation reloading

Remember that we need to update the variables used by the animation as well. So add two new custom events, **OutOfAmmo** and **Reloaded**, inside the player controller. These two events toggle the player input movements (to prevent it from moving while the reloading animation is playing) and update the **Is Reloading** controller variable:

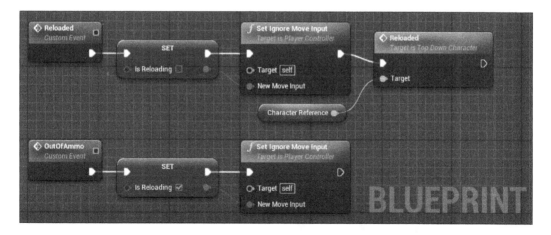

In the preceding screenshot, you can see a **Reloaded** event called to the **Character Reference**. This event is needed to tell the character that the animation has ended and its weapon can be topped up. This chain of events is called a bubble chain and is often used when a single event needs to be fired inside different classes, each one with its own variables to update and actions to call.

In this case, the weapon used by the player stops to fire and communicates to the controller to end the ammo, the controller tells the animation Blueprint that it needs to start the reloading animation. As soon as the sequence ends, the controller can re-enable the input movements and communicate to the character that it can start to fire, and the character closes the loop by communicating to its weapon to topup its loader and fire again.

This is the event called inside our player character:

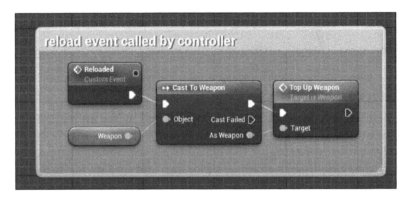

The **Weapon** variable is a **Weapon** class variable; it is used to store the actual equipped weapon. We will implement it soon.

This is the last part of the chain, the **top-up event** inside the weapon class. It simply restores the maximum ammo available for the selected weapon and resets the **Is Reloading** variable:

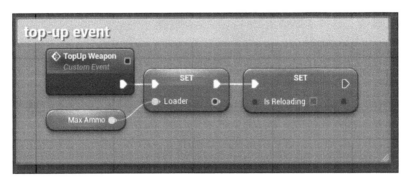

Bullet

As bullet, we use a sphere Static Mesh with a glowing material. The code for our bullet is really easy: just a single node `DestroyActor`. When it hits something, we will handle the damage taken directly within the enemy classes.

Create a new Blueprint class extending from an Actor and call it bullet. On the viewport, add a Sphere collision (`OverlapAll`) and a Static Mesh component (`SimpleSphere`). Then, create a new material for it with a plain color for the base color and a multiplied version of the same color for the emissive field. This is similar to what we did for the collectables in the previous chapters.

For the bullet physics behaviour, Unreal offers a dedicated component: **Projectile Movement**. This component will add realistic bullet behaviour to your Actor, such as acceleration, gravity, direction, and so on.

Add this component and change its **Speed** to **1500**, gravity to 0, and check if the direction is a forward vector (1,0,0). This should be the final result:

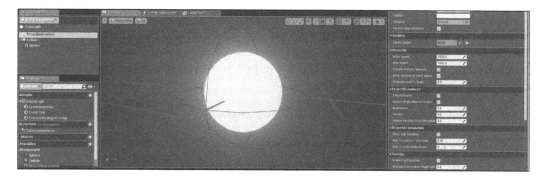

On the event graph, just add this node and that's it for the bullet. As soon as this Actor is spawned into the scene, the **ProjectileMovement** component will take care of its movements:

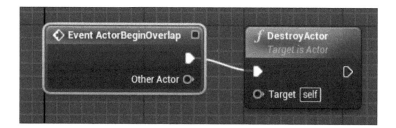

Save and set this class to the **SpawnActor** node of the weapon class. The last thing to do is to communicate to the player controller that the weapon is out of ammo. Add these nodes inside the fire weapon function, just after the `isReloading` variable is set:

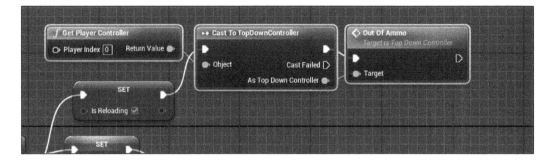

Player character weapon slots

We want to be able to collect the weapons we find around the level; we should be able to carry two of them and switch between them with the input keys we set earlier.

This behaviour is handled inside the player character (it's the character pawn that carries the weapons, not the controller). From this class, we will control whether there is space for a new weapon, when a weapon is equipped or dropped, and the code to equip them by the player inputs.

Go to the player character class and add these variables:

- **WeaponSlot1**: This is a weapon class and the first slot of the inventory
- **WeaponSlot2**: This is a weapon class and the second slot of the inventory
- **WeaponEquipped**: This is a weapon class and the actual equipped weapon
- **IsCollected**: This is Boolean and used with the collect function when a new weapon is found

First, when a player presses the equip key, we want to check if the corresponding slot has a weapon. If yes, switch the weapon in the slot with the equipped one and attach the weapon mesh to the socket we created earlier.

To do this, we use the **AttachActorToComponent** node. This node accept as input a **Target** actor (the weapon, a parent actor (our character mesh component), and a socket name for where to place the new actor (in this case, the **armedSocket** socket):

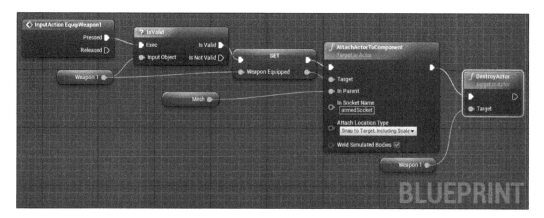

This event is for key 1, and key 2 is exactly the same. Simply use the **WeaponSlot2** variable. The **IsValid** node will check if the input object is a valid object; in this way, we can easily know if there is a weapon in this slot.

The second function we need here is to handle whenever a collected weapon can be stored into a slot or not. Create a new function and call it `Collect`.

Set an input weapon class variable (the collected weapon that needs to be stored) and an output Boolean result that will say to the caller if the weapon is collected. Thanks to a couple of **IsValid** nodes casted to the slots, populate the output variable and the corresponding slot. Remember that if you create an output value on a function, you always need to cover all the possible cases of the nodes inside this function:

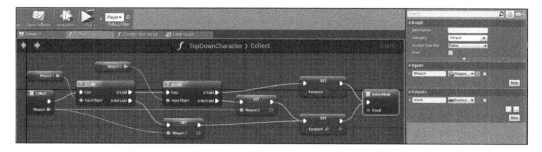

Explaining this graph: check if in the slot one there is actually a weapon (using an **IsValid** node), if yes, go ahead and check the second one. If both exist, simply return false. If there is a free slot, set the collected weapon on the slot and return true.

Weapon collectables

Now that we have implemented a little inventory, we can create the events that handle whenever a player collects a new object. Go back to the weapon class and extend the **ActorBeginOverlap** method. From there, we can call the character `Collect` function. If it returns true, move the weapon Actor to the back socket of the mesh using the **AttachActorToComponent** method we used earlier and specify the socket as **WeaponBack**:

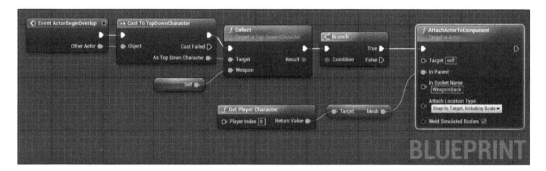

Mono-use weapon

When creating different types of weapon, you might want to make them with only a fixed amount of ammo and without the possibility to top them up. Implementing this behaviour is easy. Within the weapon class, add a new variable and call it `SelfDestory`. This variable, if set to **True**, as soon as the player ends its ammo on the fire function. It will destroy the Actor and call the stop shooting event without the possibility to recover it.

On the fire function, add a new branch node immediately after ending the ammo like this:

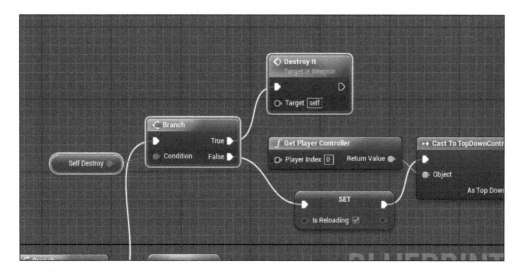

The **Destroy It** function simply destroys the Actor and calls the stop shooting event:

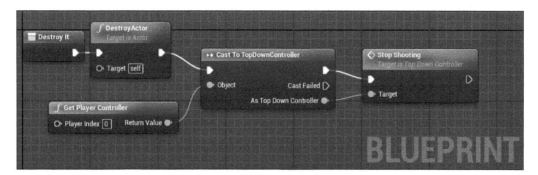

Spawner

The spawner is usually a place where a random collectable object is spawned in the level. It's an essential object for a shooter because it is the only place where a player usually can top up their weapons or heal themselves.

We are going to create a generic spawner, which is placeable anywhere in the level that can accept an array of objects and that can be reusable or customizable for your needs.

Create a new Blueprint class, extending Actor and call it `Spawner`.

Only a **Cylinder** mesh is used as platform visible for the player and an arrow component that will store the location where the object will be spawned.

The variables needed are two: an array of classes called `Spawnable` objects and a Boolean variable called `ObjectExist` used to know whenever an object can be spawned or not:

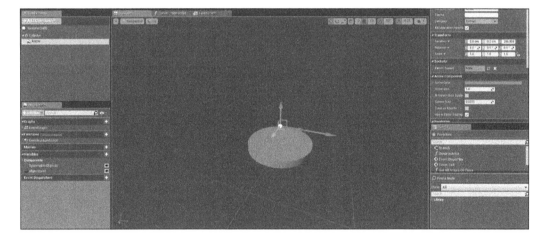

We don't care about collisions; they are handled by the spawned object itself and the only logic to be implemented is to start a looped timer as soon as the spawned object is activated. At its loop call, it takes a random object from the array and spawns it in the correct position (if it can).

So, set a timer with a delay of 30 seconds on **Event BeginPlay** and toggle the **Looping** variable:

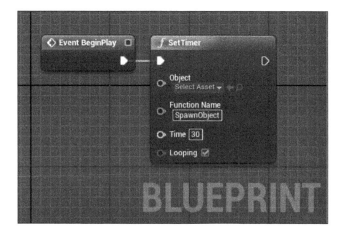

To get a random item from an array, use a get node with as index a random integer number between 0 and the length of the array like this:

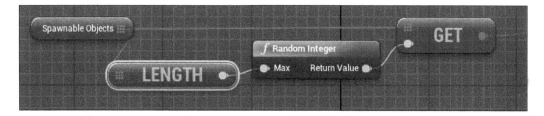

Connect the result to a **SpawnActor** node only if an object don't exist:

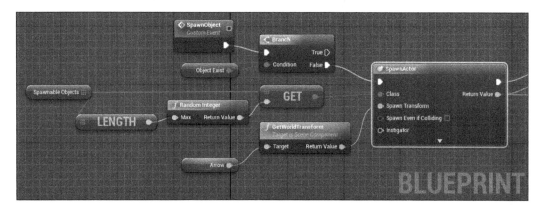

We can now add a little bit of dynamism and add a **RotatingMovement** component to the spawned Actor. A rotating movement component is a special component that rotates the Actor and it is attached to each frame by the rotation rate set on its details. This makes the spawned object easier to notice by the player.

Custom component

The `ObjectExist` variable raises a question: how can we change this variable when the player collects the spawned object? We could add a reference for each spawner on the level to the character, and loop all of them to find the owner. But it is a very expensive way and not good practice.

An easier solution is to create a custom component to attach to the spawned object that will simply contain a reference to the owner.

In this way, when a player collects something, it simply checks if the object collected has this component and changes the `objectExist` variable.

Create a new Blueprint class, extend **ActorComponent**, and call it `SpawnerComponent`. This object has an **Owner** Variable of type Spawner class and two functions: `SetOwner` (called from the spawner whenever this component is attached and a `ResetSpawner` (called from the player whenever it collects an object that has this component attached):

With this component, you can go back to the spawner object and add this node just after the spawn node:

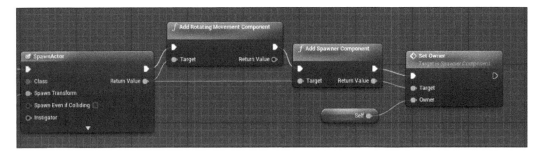

With this setup, for any object that you want to be spawned into the spawner, you can use **Get Component by Class**. If this component is found, call the corresponding function.

In our case, because we only have the weapon object that will be spawned, we want to destroy **Rotating Movement Component** and reset the spawner of **SpawnerComponent**:

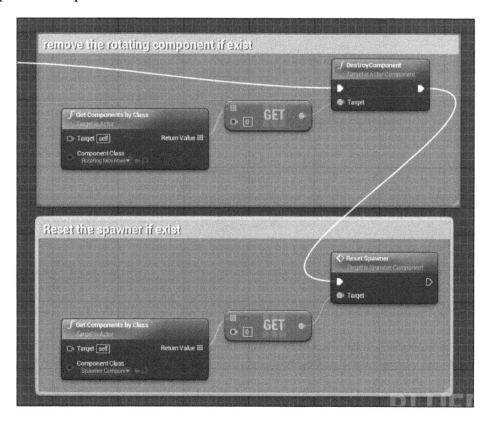

Animation Blueprint – EventGraph

At this point of the project, it is time to finally see the animation in action by completing eventGraph of the Animation Blueprint with some communication nodes.

We have all the elements needed inside the player controller, ready to be collected by the Animation Blueprint. First, create a handy function inside the player controller called **Get Parameters**. It simply returns the value of aiming, look angle, and reloads whenever it is called. It looks like this:

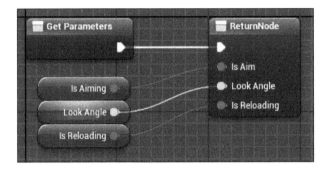

Now, open the Animation Blueprint and go to its eventGraph. First, create a setter for those three values we just made the getter for:

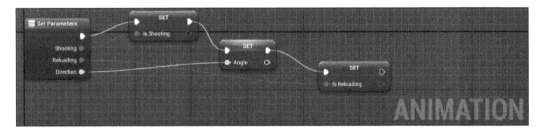

On the main graph, we use the **Event Blueprint Update Animation** event to get those references and update them, along with the direction and the speed of the player.

To calculate the movement speed, we simply take the vector instant velocity length:

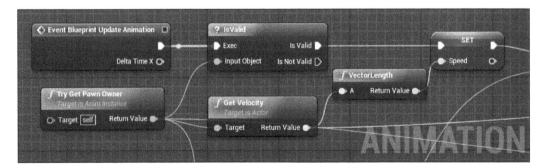

After calculating the speed (we will see soon why we calculate it first instead of calculating it together with the other values), we can cast the pawn owner to our controller and get/set the parameters. Lastly, we calculate the direction of the player by using the **Calculate Direction** node, with **Base Rotation** and **Velocity** of the pawn as input:

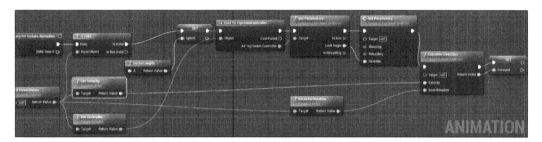

Everything needed for the animation is in place. Compile it and test it. You can finally see your player animating nicely when moving around and if you hit fire, you should see the animation changing and the player aiming correctly (yes, without a weapon at the moment but will it be fixed soon) at the mouse position, rotating the torso as the AimOffset wants and flipping its direction when exceeding a certain angle.

About the aiming without weapon issue, add another check at the **InputAction Fire** event of the player controller. Enable the fire only if a weapon is actually equipped:

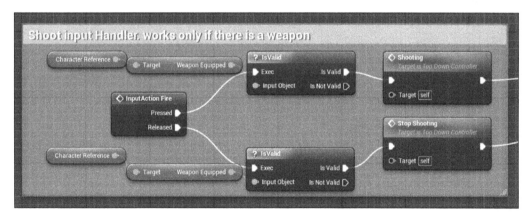

Now, place a spawner object anywhere within the level and try to collect a spawned weapon (remember to add the weapon class to the spawner array), equip it by the equip key, and shoot around. Now, we only need an enemy to shoot at!

Enemies

Because we are still learning and we did a lot so far in this chapter, the enemies for this project will have a zombie-style brain, without a weapon to shoot through the player. They will slowly chase the player forever and when near enough, they explode -- hurting the player.

The Skeletal Meshes used will be the same mannequin used by the player, and the animation blueprint can be reused by the enemy.

When developing enemies, you can see them like player characters but instead of being controlled by a player controller (that is controlled by the inputs of the player) they are controlled by an AI controller (that is controlled by a logic sequences of actions).

Pawn

So, let's start to create a new Blueprint class by extending Character Actor and calling it Enemy. Set SK_Mannequin as **Skeletal Mesh**, with our Animation Blueprint as **Animation Blueprint Generated Class** and, to make it slightly different from the player itself, apply on **Element 0** of **Materials**, a modified copy of the original one with the **BodyColor** changed to another color:

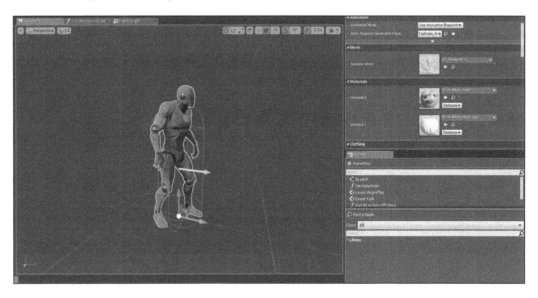

For our enemy, we need to handle two different collision events: the first one, within the capsule, is used when the enemy is hit by a bullet. The second one, used by a bigger sphere collider (the red sphere in the previous image), will handle the impact with the player and is the responsible for the damage sent to the player.

We only need two variables for the enemy: a float **Health** and a float **Strength**. The first one is how much **Health** the enemy has, and it will be decreased by a fixed amount when hit by a bullet. The second one is how much damage this pawn will inflict to the player.

On **Event ActorBeginOverlap** add those nodes:

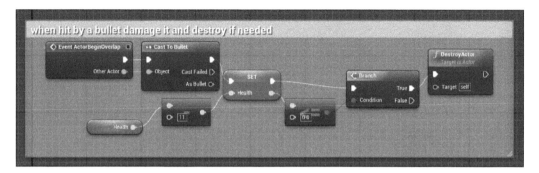

When the root component is being overlapped, check if the collider is a bullet, decrease the health, and destroy if there is no health remaining.

Now, add a sphere collider component to the Actor, chance its collision type to overlap only the player and add these nodes to the **OnComponentBeginOverlap** event:

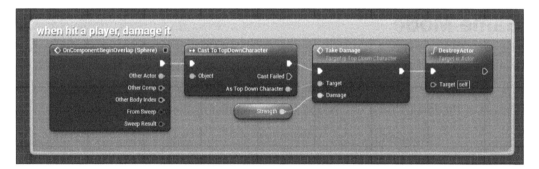

AI

The AI for this enemy is composed by a single main node: as soon as the pawn spawns into the level and is updated on each tick, call the `SimpleMoveToLocation` function.

This node will move the pawn to the goal location (in our case, the player pawn location) using the **NavMesh** to find the shortest route and automatically avoiding obstacles.

We don't need to create a NavMesh like we did in the previous chapter, because the template already has it but if you accidentally delete it, it shouldn't be a problem for you to recreate one.

Create a new Blueprint class extending **AIController** and call it **AI_Enemy_ Controller**. The only code that needs to be added to the EventGraph is the following:

Lastly, return to the EnemyPawn class and on the **Pawn** section from the **Details** panel, set on Auto Possess AI: placed in world or spawned and set the AI you just created as AI Controller Class.

Game Mode

The game mode will be a wave-based one. Every 60 seconds, a new, increased number of enemies will spawn into the level, making the life of the player each minute harder.

First, place four Target points (you can find them in the **Modes** panel) in the four corners of the level. Those will be the spawn points for our enemies.

Now, open the **GameMode** class of the level. We want to get a reference for all the target points inside the level and store them into an array as soon as the game starts. After doing that, call a custom event that takes care to create a new wave of enemies, and lastly we want to set an infinite timer that will call a new wave every 60 seconds:

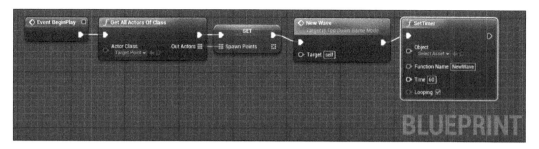

The new wave event will multiply the wave variable by five and use this value in a **ForLoop** node to spawn, with a delay of 1 second, the number of enemies calculated from a random point of the **Target** points array:

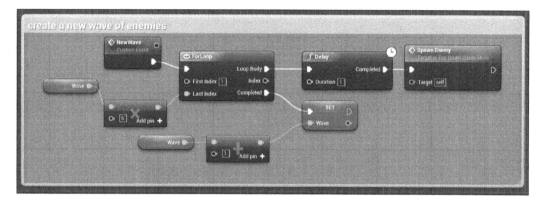

The **SpawnEnemy** event will find a random point (with the same method we used earlier for the Spawner class) and spawn an enemy:

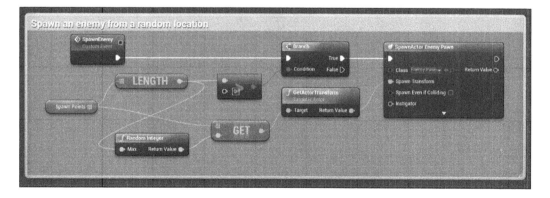

Launching now, the game should show you an almost complete game. You can run around, collect weapons, and hit the enemies that spawn around you and that chases you forever. We only need a HUD that shows us some information of what we are doing.

User interface

The information that we want to show is as follows: the player life, the ammo of the weapon we are using, and the wave we reached.

Remembering what we did in the previous chapter, create a new Blueprint Widget and call it UI_Game. Add four text widgets and a progress bar Widget to create a result like this:

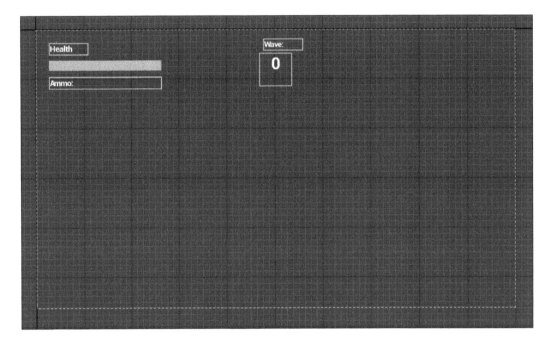

Health and **Wave** are two static texts. The other three Widgets will be updated when needed.

About the health bar, bind the percent value of its progress section with a function that checks the player character's health and divides its value by 100. (It is supposed to have a maximum health value of 100. Change the percentage scale with the maximum amount of health if you change the player life.):

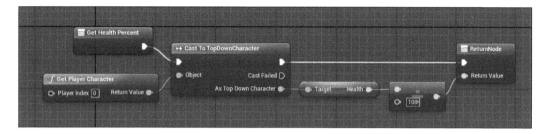

The ammo text bind will check if the player has a weapon equipped and if yes, it uses the **Format Text** node to create the string: Ammo: actual ammo remains/max ammo:

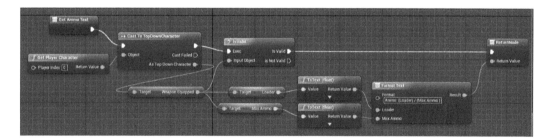

The Wave bind is the easiest one. It simply reads the wave variable of the game mode class and converts it into a text value:

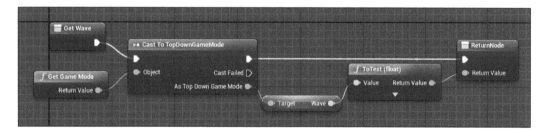

As practice, here are some suggestions to improve this project.

Summary

As usual, here are some suggestions to improve this game:

- GameOver? Yes, like the other chapter, it is missing a piece here also. This time it is the GameOver state of the player. Implement it by checking when a player reaches a value less than 0 on their health and managing this state with a Widget or simply restarting the game.

- Buttons? Try to create a menu similar to the one in the previous chapter that handles the start/pause events.

- New Weapons! Even if simple, the weapon class we created is really powerful; by using this class as parent, you can create dozens of new weapons without being worried to recreate the logic of fire/equip.

- Different walking speed while shooting! Play with the **CharacterMovement** component and the start shoot event of the controller.

If you follow everything correctly, you can now play and enjoy a typical top-down shooter. In this chapter, I gave you all the basic aspects of this kind of game. By tweaking the variables and changing the mesh with better ones, you could have amazing results with relatively less work.

In the next chapter, we will focus on the environment. In this chapter, we focused on player animations and behaviors. In the next one, we will see how to create dynamic objects such as doors, traps, and other items useful for a platform-type game.

6
A Platform Maze

In this chapter, we are going to see some new aspects of a game development. We will create a maze with plenty of traps, where the player needs to use his skills to reach the final destination.

You will learn about modular and reusable elements to create, like in a puzzle, any kind of game level you want by simply positioning them:

- Matinee and cinematics
- Ragdoll
- Destructible elements
- Trigger volumes
- Blueprint Function Library
- Timelines

This game uses the third-person Blueprint template and some of the assets of the starter content. This chapter doesn't have a strict guideline but is divided into sections, each one of them covers a different specific tool or technique. So, without further ado, let's start.

Ragdoll physics

In computer physics engines, ragdoll physics is a type of procedural animation that is often used as a replacement for traditional static death animations. A ragdoll is a collection of multiple rigid bodies (each of which is ordinarily tied to a bone in our Skeletal Mesh) tied together by joints that restrict their movement. When the player dies, each rigid body collapses to the ground and thanks to its constraints the death looks realistic.

This is the ragdoll of our familiar mannequin, and it actually looks quite dead.

This technique is improving year by year thanks to the new technologies, and there are games that use it in a non-traditional way, such as the *FlatOut* series, where you can control the dead mannequin while flying, or *Rag Doll Kung Fu*, where you control one part of the body and the rest follows along.

In Unreal Engine, achieving ragdoll physics is really simple. Any object can be set to answer at the physic stimulations, as long as that object has **Physics Asset**.

For our mannequin, we need to set the physics asset because the default skeleton mesh doesn't have one. Open Persona and set the **Physics Asset** under the **Physics** section of **Mesh Details**:

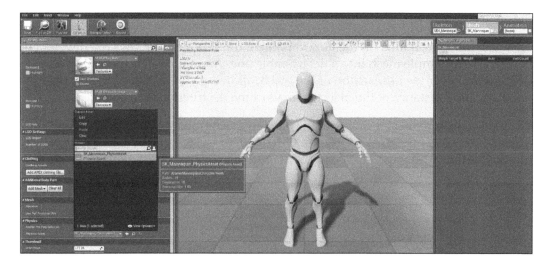

Now, any time we want to convert the player into a ragdoll, we simple have to call the **Set Simulate Physics** node on the correspondent Blueprint event like this:

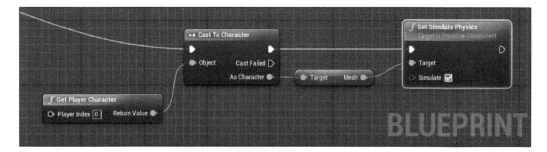

Destructible meshes

A destructible mesh, as the name suggests and different from a simple destroy object node, is a mesh that can be divided into smaller pieces and each piece is treated by the engine on its own.

This new function, added on the new version of unreal engine, allows the developers to convert any simple mesh into a destructible one. An intuitive editor gives you a deep control over the destruction of the mesh, allowing you to choose the number of fractures, the resistance of the object, spread of the destruction, and so on.

To create a destructible mesh, select the desired mesh from the content browser (if you don't have one, create it using a BSP brush or choose one by navigating to **StarterContent | Shapes**), right-click on it, and select **Create Destructible Mesh**:

A new file is created in the same folder with the name NameMesh_DM. Double-click on that file to open the destructible mesh editor:

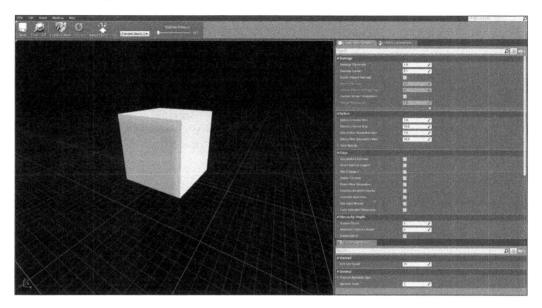

The editor is divided into the following sections:

- **Menu bar**: This is the familiar menu bar, where you can customize the aspect of the tool, navigate to and from the content browser to change mesh, and save/load other assets.

- **ToolBar**: This is another familiar element. From here, you can fracture the mesh according to your settings, import an external file for the chunks, and (thanks to the Explode Amount slider) watch a preview of it.

- **Destructible Settings panel**: This is the main setting panel. From here, you can set damage and debris parameters, set the material of the chunks, add flags conditions, and so on.

- **Chunk parameters panel**: This panel is available when you select a single chunk. It allows deeper settings for the individual piece.

- **Fracture Settings**: This decides how the mesh will be fractured by the tool.

Let's now investigate the main properties of this tool:

- **Damage Threshold**: This is the amount of damage needed at a single chunk to be fractured.

- **Damage Spread**: This specifies how the damage is propagated to the destructible Actor.

- **Enable Impact Damage**: If enabled, the destructible mesh takes damage on colliding.

- **Debris lifetime**: This is time (in seconds) that a chunk will be destroyed after being separated from the other chunks. Ensure that you enable the flag Debris Timeout and set the correct debris Depth.

- **Damage Cap**: Set a limit of damage that can be applied to a chunk. This is useful for preventing the entire destructible from getting pulverized by a very large application of damage.

- **Accumulate damage**: If set, chunks will remember damage applied to them (by default, only a single damage must exceed the threshold to break the mesh).

- **Particle System**: This will set a particle system to spawn when a chunk breaks.

- **Sound**: Same of the Particle System property: set a sound to play when a chunk breaks.

- **Material**: This will set the material per level of detail.

- **Cell Site Count**: This is the number of chunks that will be generated during the fracture process.

A destructible mesh usually doesn't need to be controlled by a Blueprint class; its customizations make this a wonderful component to be placed as is in your scene.

If you need to control that mesh destruction, for example, by a trigger, you may need to create a Blueprint class dedicated to it. Let's create a Blueprint with the destructible mesh we just created. Create a new Blueprint class and choose Actor as parent.

Add a component and search for destructible. Make it the root component and under the **Destructible** component from the **Details** panel, search for **Shape_Cube_DM**:

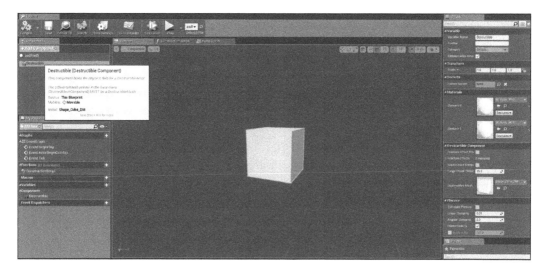

We are now able to control this component like any other component on the Event Graph. We can use the **Apply Damage** node, launched by **Custom_Event** and with as **Target Destructible Component**. In this example, when the event is called, **Damage Amount** (bigger than the threshold of the destructible mesh) is applied to our component. We use the center of the component as **Hit Location**, we choose the direction where the chunks will move as impulse, and **Impulse Strength** will control the strength of the explosion:

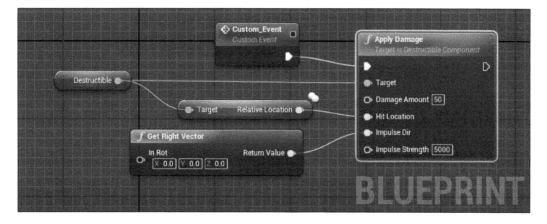

You can test this by using the event begin play. The following images show the result of the previous nodes on three different phases of the break:

Physics constraint

A physics constraint is a joint that allows you to connect two Actors or component together and also apply limits or forces on them.

UE4 has a very flexible and data-driven constraint system that allows you to make many different types of joints simply by changing some options. With these components, you are able to create many different objects such as swinging balls, wheels, and gears mechanisms, or simply keep a physics body in a general area.

You can create a Physics Constraint within the scene using Physics Constraint Actor from the **Modes** panel, or using Physics Constraint Component within a Blueprint class. They are basically the same object with the same properties. The Actor has three prefab settings (ball and socket, hinge, prismatic), but they are only a preset of common usage of the constraint—nothing that can't be reproduced in the Blueprint class:

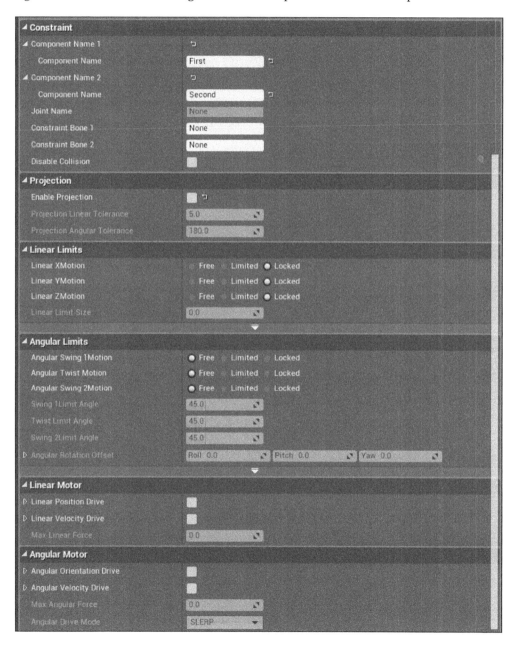

Let's take a look at the properties of this component:

- **Component Name 1** and **Component Name 2**: These are the two Actor/Components where the constraints will be applied. If placed inside the level, a list of usable Actors will be provided. If used within a Blueprint class, you need to set the exact same name of the component manually.

- **Constrain Bone**: If the object/component is a skeletal mesh, you can set a specific bone to apply the constraint.

- **Projection**: Enable this setting to prevent your two objects from looking detached when moving too fast. This will project all bodies so they still appear attached to each other.

- **Linear Limits** and **Angular Limits**: This will set movement limits on the three axes.

- **Linear Motor** and **Angular Motor**: Enable these parameters to add a constant motor to the constraint. A linear motor try to move the constraint to the set vector, the angular motor try to spin the constraint by the given rotation. Both can be driven by velocity or position.

There are plenty of objects that can be made using constraint. Let's now create a wrecking ball to test it with a destructible mesh.

Create a new Blueprint class using Actor as parent and call it `WreckingBall`.

Use a billboard as root of this class. This is a simple 2D image that is visible only on the editor and useful to keep track of the objects inside your levels. The secondary function of this billboard is to be the primary component of our constraint.

Add **Sphere** and enable **Simulate Physics** (when using constraint, one of the components must be physic in order to work). Search for a **PhysicConstraint** component and position it just above the billboard. Set the first component as the billboard and second component as our **Sphere**. In **Viewport**, you can see a red and a blue rectangle showing the constrained components:

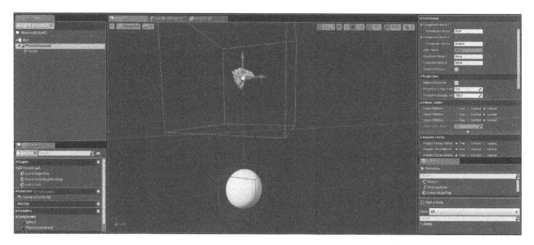

That's it. To test it, you can add it to your scene just near the player and when hit by the player, the ball should start swinging.

At the moment, it is just a floating ball, surely not so realistic without a chain attached to it. The ideal solution is to create a Skeletal Mesh with an external editor and attach two components at the first and the last bone of it, but we can achieve something acceptable even only within Unreal.

A chain is a series of metal rings connected together. We can replicate this object by using a series of cylinders connected together with physic constraint. Four joints are enough to give at our wrecking ball a slightly more realistic behavior.

Add four cylinders and four physic constraint. Connect them in order (constraint-cylinder-constraint-…-sphere), being careful to add at least 2 cm of space between the cylinders. If you attach them too close, they will not move. Be careful to check that all the components simulate physic and have a block collision set:

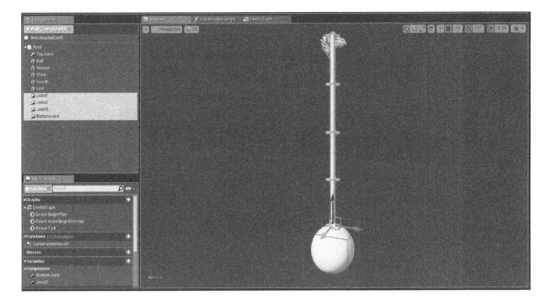

Test again and notice how the joints work in a slightly better, realistic way. As said before, a rope/chain made with a skeleton by an external program is surely better but, without it this solution is more than acceptable.

Matinee

The ability to create cinematic sequences or even dynamic elements within the engine is covered by the Matinee animation tool. This system allows you to manipulate the properties of an object over time and its framework is based on keyframes (like any animation or video editing software such as Flash, Maya, and so on) where each key positioned within its timeline represent a value of an Actor in the level:

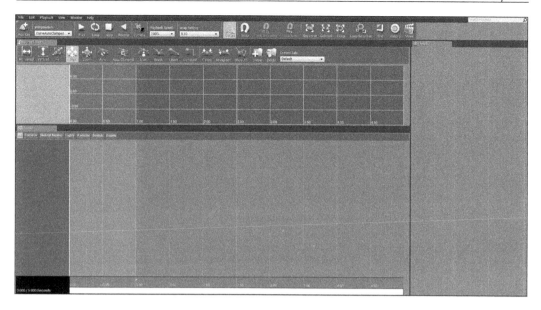

Let's take a look at the interface:

- **Menu bar**: At the very top, we find the menu bar. From here, you can import/export the Matinee or part of it, manipulate keys and sections, toggle and customize the viewport.

- **Toolbar**: From this toolbar, you can find buttons to preview the Matinee (such as play, loop, reverse, or playback speed) and buttons to navigate through the sequence.

- **Curve Editor**: This editor allows you to graphically visualize and edit the animations curves used by the tracks in the sequencer. Tracks that have animation curves that can be edited in the Curve Editor in Matinee have a toggle button on the right side. Clicking on this button will send that track's curve information to this panel, where the curve will become visible and editable.

- **Track View**: The track view contains a list of all the folders, groups, and tracks contained within the Matinee sequence and shows their keyframe information on a timeline where they can be edited.

It is worth explaining the curve editor and the track view.

Curve Editor

Curve Editor is composed of a toolbar, a track list, and a graph editor:

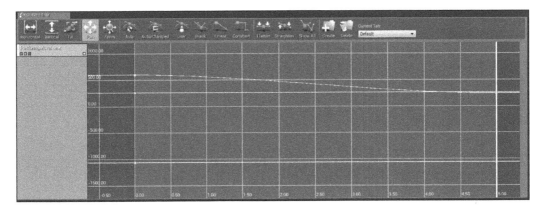

The toolbar is divided into three sections: the first one allows you to **Fit, Pan**, and **Zoom** the graph curves as per your needs. The second one has buttons that allow you to manipulate the interpolation mode of the curves. The last section is used to create and manipulate tabs group for your curves.

The track list displays all the curve tracks currently loaded into the current tab:

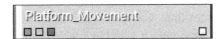

A track contains the name of the property associated with it and a series of buttons that can be used to toggle the visibility of each single value within the graph.

In this example, the track is controlling the movement of a platform and the colors are corresponding to the vector X (red), Y (green), and Z (blue).

The graph editor is a graphical representation of the curve with the time along the horizontal axis and the property value along the vertical axis. Keys along the curve are displayed as points that can be selected and manipulated to visually edit the curve:

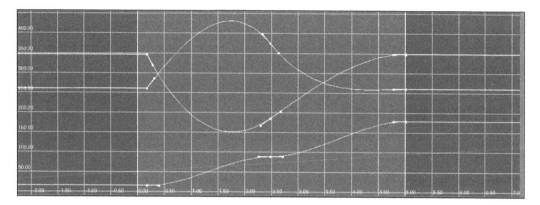

This image shows the movement of the platform during a 5-second period. It has three keyframes that control how the values will change on all the three axis.

Track View

Track view is divided into: group tabs, groups, track list, and a timeline.

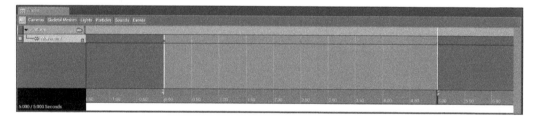

The group tab, found at very top of the panel, shows all the group that exist in the current Matinee sequence. Group tabs are handy way of organizing groups and tracks based on their functions. This is useful in complex sequences, like those used to create in-game cinematics, you will do best to make use of these tabs as the number of groups and tracks in the sequence can quickly add up and become unwieldy to navigate. You can create your own custom tabs in addition to those provided by default to further organize your groups and tracks based on any criteria you choose.

The group and track list, situated on the top-left corner of the panel, shows all the groups and tracks in the currently selected group tab. In this case, there is a group called **Platform** that contains a **Movement** track.

The black rectangle on the bottom left is a timeline info panel that displays information about the timeline, including the current location of the time cursor and the total length of the scene.

The timeline goes together with the graph editor of the curve panel; it contains all the keyframes of all the tracks in the sequence. From there, you control the loop section (available only in the preview of the Matinee and represented by the green triangles) and the actual sequence length (represent by the red triangle).

Create a Matinee

Let's create our first Matinee, a moving object. Add a cube anywhere in the scene and open the Matinee editor.

To create a Matinee sequence, you can use the Matinee button in the toolbar or drag the Matinee Actor inside the scene from the **Modes** panel.

In order to create a new track, we first need to create a group. To add a group, right-click from the **Tracks** panel and select **Add New Empty Group**:

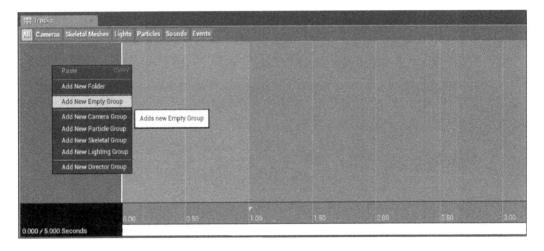

Call it Cube and hit enter. If you right-click on the newly created group, you can see all the possible tracks you can create inside it:

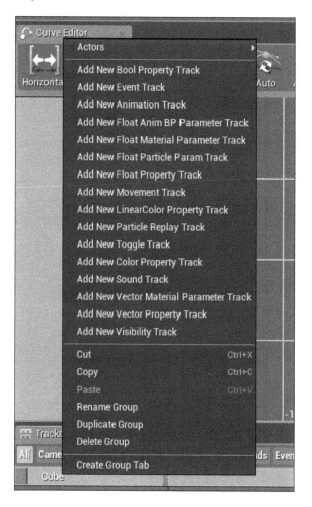

We now need to assign which Actor will be affected by the Matinee. If you have an Actor selected while creating a new group, that Actor is automatically assigned to it but if we didn't select the cube actor, we can add it a second time.

Select the **Cube** from your level, right-click on the **Cube** group, select **Actors**, and select **Add Selected Actors**:

Now, you can add new movement track on its group tab and start to play with its movements.

To add a new keyframe, move the selection inside the timeline and position it at the desired second. When ready, hit enter and you should see the keyframe added thanks to the red triangle and the time (in seconds) written above it:

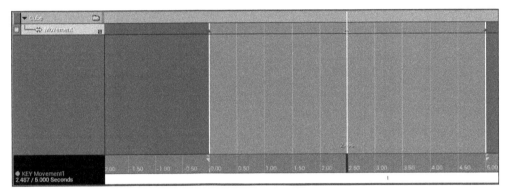

In the timeline details, you can see a red dot with written the name of the key. Similarly, in the level viewport, a red advice script is saying that now you can adjust the key movement you just created. Move around the cube and notice how automatically a yellow line shows the path that your Actor will follow:

You can add as many keyframes as you want, and you can freely modify rotation and location of your object. To modify the single value curve, you must enable the curve editor by clicking on the little gray button at the right-hand side of the track.

By default, only the location curves are shown on the graph. If you want to individually modify rotation and location, you must split your track by right clicking on the **Movement** track and selecting **Split Rotation and Location**:

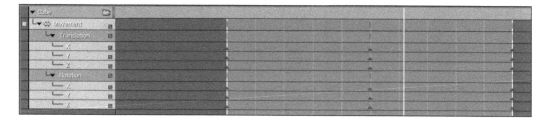

Fake platform corridor

Let's create a corridor using some destructible mesh we discussed before. The idea is to create a long corridor composed of a lot of tiles where some of them are fake and will break as soon as the player steps on them.

The easiest way is to create a simple tile mesh, create a destructible one from it, and position the single tiles one by one inside the level. We want to be smarter than this and use Blueprint to our advantage.

We will create a Blueprint class that contains a single row of static tiles and as soon as the game starts, swap a random tile with destructible ones.

Using BSP brushes, create a tile frame of 200 x 200 x 20 with a hole of 180 x 180 and a plain tile of 180 x 180 x 20 like this (I used the material `M_Plains_Floor_Block`):

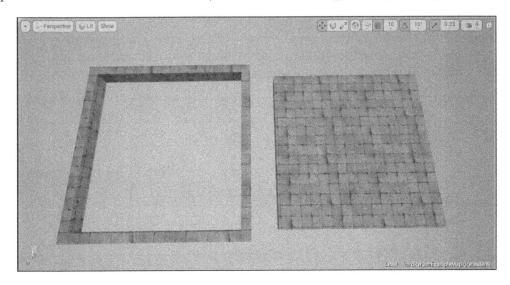

We create the tile in this way for a practical reason. When a destructible mesh is destroyed, it sends a force signal around its corner, and without a border, this signal inevitably touch the other destructible meshes, starting an endless chain until all the other meshes along the corridor will be destroyed.

Now, we must add a collision box around the big tile. When you create a mesh using a BSP brush, there aren't collision bounds on it. You can create a custom collision using the editor from the mesh window. Open the tile you just created and from the menu bar, go to **Collision | Add Box Simplified Collision**:

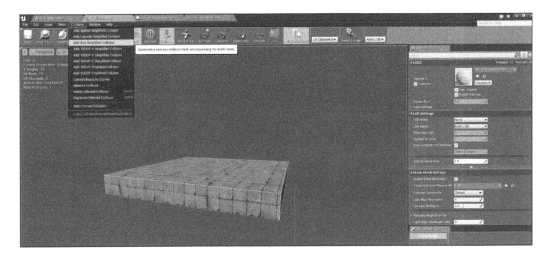

This will create a collision box (it is highlighted in green in the preceding screenshot) around the mesh. You can move and scale this box by clicking on his border.

Create a destructible mesh from this tile. We want to enable the impact damage and have a damage threshold of a very low value. Leave all the other properties as default ones. In this way, the meshes will break completely as soon as the player touches them.

Create a new Blueprint class starting from Actor and use a billboard as root component. Position the meshes we created in a row of three elements like this:

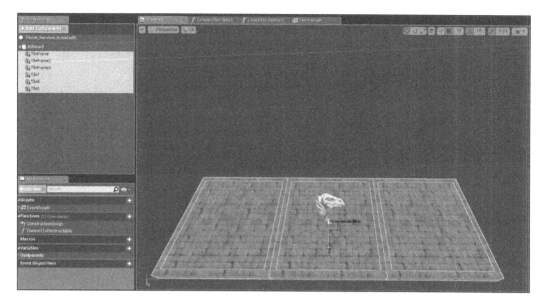

At the moment, all the meshes are static ones—a perfectly stable row of tiles. We now need to set on the graph editor the code to swap one of those platforms with a destructible one.

On the Graph Editor, add a new function and call it ConvertToDestrucible. Add an input pin of type Static Mesh. This input node will be the mesh to swap, with this value we can find the location where the destructible component will be. As soon as the component is placed, we can destroy the original one.

To add a component by Blueprint, you can use the **Add Destructible Component** node and set the right mesh from the **Details** panel. This node needs a **Target** reference and **Relative Transform**. By default, the component is attached as a child of the root component but you can attach manually by toggling the **Manual Attachment** option.

Be sure to get **Relative Transform** and not the world transform. A relative one is referenced to the root component transform, a world one is relative to the whole world. In this case, by simplifying the values, the relative location of the first tile on the left is (-1,0,0) but a world location could be anything. A wrong choice of this getter could result in disappearing meshes without apparent reasons.

The code will look like this:

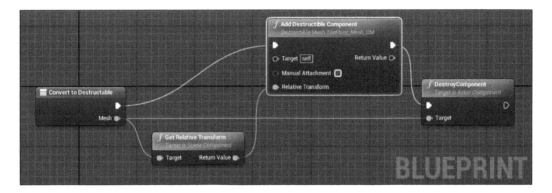

To choose randomly which tile to swap, we use a Switch node. This flow node has an input value and depending on this value, we will launch the corresponding execution node. This is a very useful node when you have multiple choices but need only one to be executed.

Attach a **Switch on Int** node to the **BeginPlay** event, add three output pins by clicking on **Add pin**, and connect the input to a **Random Integer in Range** node:

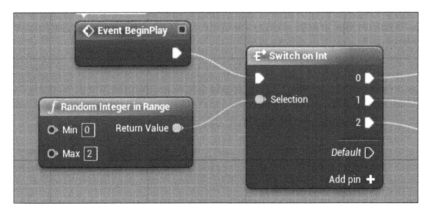

It's usually a good practice to connect the default output pin as well. This output is executed if none of the conditions of the selection pin are confirmed but in this case, we are sure that a number between 0 and 2 will arrive so we don't need to connect it.

In the output, we can now call the `ConvertToDestructible` function, using the tiles as input:

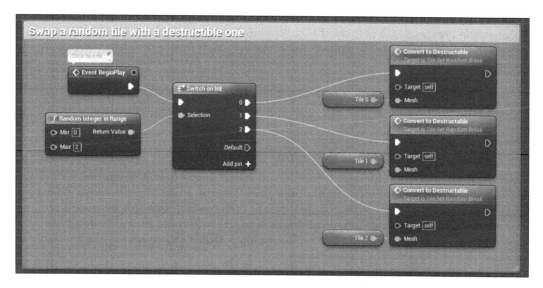

Blueprint Function Library

Because there are plenty of objects on this game that can damage the player, it's useful to create a universal component that can be set into any of your objects in a few steps and that contains any kind of common function you need.

A Blueprint Function Library is exactly what we can use for this purpose: it's a collection of static functions that provide utility functionality not tied to a particular gameplay object. These libraries can be grouped into logical function sets.

We could put the function to kill the player into a library, and access this function on any object that has to kill the player when a particular condition rises. A ball, a spear, or a projectile are all different elements but all have one big purpose: kill the player.

Actually, there's already an element that can be used (but not for our purpose): the **Kill Z volume**. This volume essentially destroys any Actor that enters (including the player) and is usually positioned at the very bottom of an open space or anywhere you want to destroy the elements that fall down into it.

Let's first create the kill and respawn events on our Blueprint player and when ready, create a common callable function.

Kill and respawn a player ragdoll

The killing process on our game must be different from a simple destroy Actor. Because the player could die lots of times before reaching the end of the maze and because the typical death is caused by being hit by something, we would like to use a ragdoll that shows a player falling dead and respawn it on the starting point after a short period of time.

To achieve this, we can simulate the physic of the mesh on death and on respawn, we can remove the simulation and reset the Actor to the original location.

The default player pawn is composed by a collision capsule with a skeletal mesh as child and a camera that follows the capsule movements. When playing with ragdolls, there are some consequences that must be considered and solved. First, because we modify the physic only on the mesh and not the parent, those two elements will become separated and must be attached when respawning. Second, because the camera is following the capsule (and that is correct), when the player is dead the ragdoll could move around far from the capsule collider. We need to find a way to refresh correctly the focus of the camera.

Let's open the **ThirdPersonCharacter** class and on the Event Graph, create two custom events, Kill and Respawn, and three new variables, SpawnLocation (of type vector), SpawnTransform (of type Transform), and IsDead (of type Boolean).

On the Event **BeginPlay**, store the actual **Relative Transform** of the mesh and the location of the Actor:

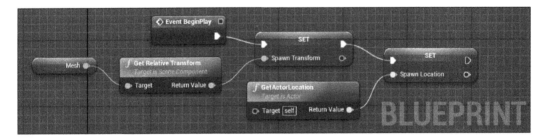

We can store only the original vector location of the whole Actor, but we must have the whole relative (of the capsule) transform of the mesh in order to reset it.

Now, in order to partially solve the natural detachment of the mesh from the capsule, instead of simulating the whole mesh, we could use **Set All Bodies Below Simulate Physics**. This node simulates only the bodies of the children of the selected one. In this way, if we select the pelvis node of the Skeletal Mesh, we will have the root bone still attached to the capsule and not simulating:

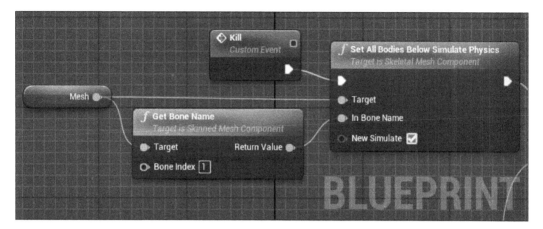

Now that the mesh is a ragdoll, we can continue by disabling the inputs from the player, start a timer for our Respawn function, and set the Boolean **Is Dead** as true:

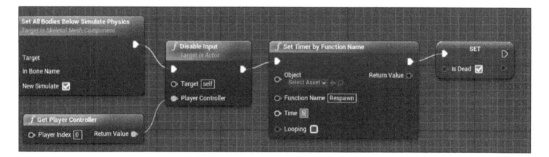

The **Respawn** event has a few more aspects to take care of. First, just reverse the simulation and restore the inputs:

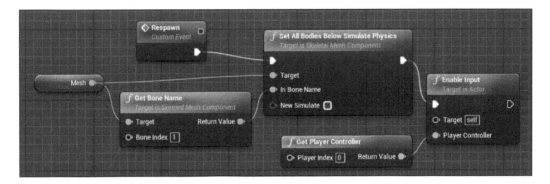

Now, the mesh needs to be reattached to the capsule. To achieve this, we use an **AttachTo** node. This node takes an object and attaches it to a **Target** input. You can specify a socket to attach it and **Attach Type** if you want to specify which transform will be parented:

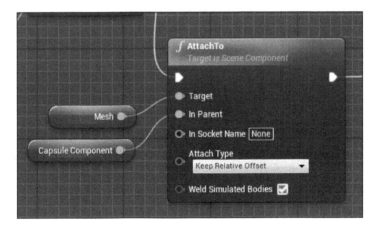

Lastly, we can reset the position and rotation of both of the objects by using the variables we stored and reset the **Is Dead** condition:

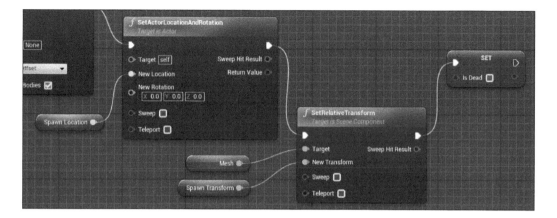

For the Actor, we set a manual rotation of (0,0,0). If your player is positioned with a different rotation, you could store it as we did for the location.

Now, let's solve the last issue. We use the **Is Dead** variable in the `Tick` function. When the player is dead, we can temporarily swap the focus of the camera to the mesh instead of the capsule:

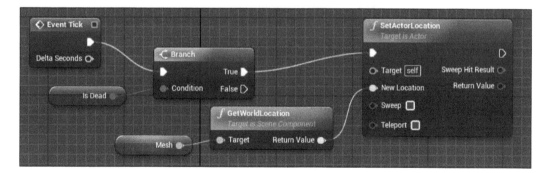

Create and use a function library

To create a function library, right-click on the **Content Browser** and go to **Blueprint | Blueprint Function Library**. From this Graph Editor, you can create as many functions as you need. The only restriction is that they must be static methods.

Name the file `Common_Functions` and add the first function to the graph that, when rised, will take care to call the Kill event we created before.

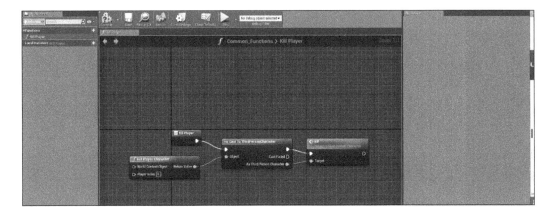

That's it. From anywhere in other Blueprint classes, if you want to kill the player, simply search for this function and add it on the desired node:

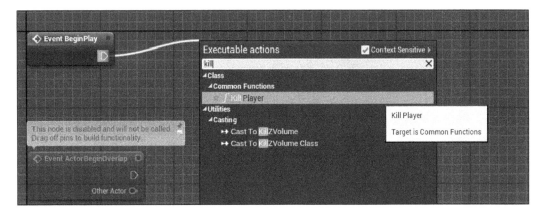

Door trigger volume

Another common element of a game are blocking objects such as doors that block the passage of the player until a condition (which can be a button press, solving a puzzle, or simply going near the player) is raised.

There are two ways to create a door Actor. The first one is using Matinee and Level Blueprint, and it is easier to create but the Actor cannot be replicated. Good if you have only a few doors in your level or if the door itself contains more than one element that needs to be animated.

If you expect to have several doors on your level and their movement is a simple translation, you could create them within a Blueprint class and a timeline.

Let's see both of these methods. There is no right one: it depends on your project and the environment required.

Doors within Matinee

Inside your level, using box meshes, create a wall with a hole and fit the hole with a door (in this case, another simple cube):

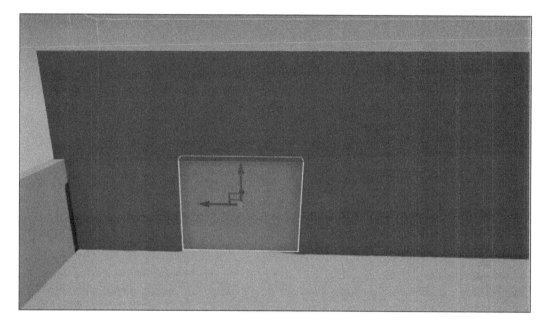

Create a Matinee exactly how we did earlier, with a single movement track on the *z* axis of the cube object:

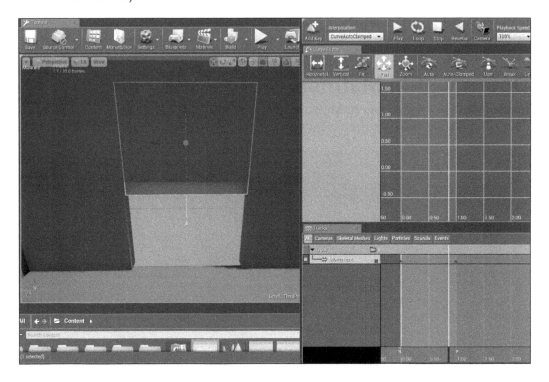

We want to open this door when the player is nearby and close it when they are far away. We can simply use a trigger box volume and the **OnBeginOverlap** and **OnEndOverlap** events. The code, because both Matinee and trigger box are within the scene, must be written inside the Level Blueprint.

So, first create a trigger box volume around the door and then open Level Blueprint. From there, browse the world outliner until you find the Matinee you created. Select it and from Level Blueprint, right-click and create a reference to it.

Do the same for the trigger box but instead of creating a reference, browse the events until you find the two we need, and add them:

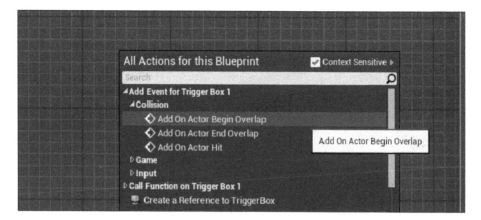

The last step is simple: play the Matinee on begin overlap and reverse the Matinee on end overlap:

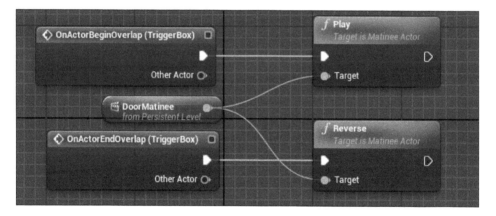

Doors within Blueprint

Create a new Blueprint class extending an Actor and call it Door_BP. As components, we need a trigger box and a cube with an arrow component to easily find the enter direction of the door.

Position them as shown in the following screenshot. Take particular attention to set the dimension of the trigger box. It must cover the whole door movement. If the door moves up (like in this case), the trigger must be as high as the final movement of the door:

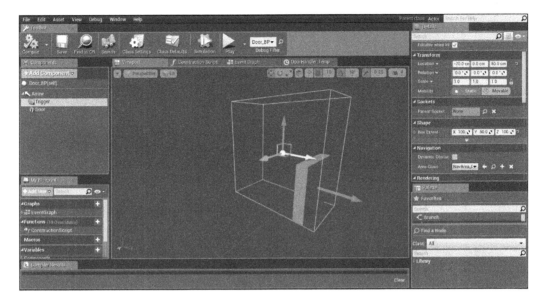

Instead of a Matinee, here we will use a **Lerp Vector** node and a timeline.

A lerp (or Linear Interpolation) function is a function that gives two inputs, and calculates a final value interpolated between those two inputs based on an alpha input. The alpha is a value between 0 and 1, and the result of this function is alpha =0 result=input 1, alpha=1 result=input 2.

For example, think of a straight line 10 meters long and it takes you 1 second to run across it. At time 0, you will be at 0 meters, you will reach 5 meters after half a second, and you reach the end of the line after the whole second.

If we combine this lerp function with the start and the end location of the door as input and a timer as alpha controller, we can create a smooth door movement.

Create two vector variables on the event graph. Set the first one at (0,0,0) and the second one at an higher location (0,0,100), and connect them on a **Lerp Vector** node:

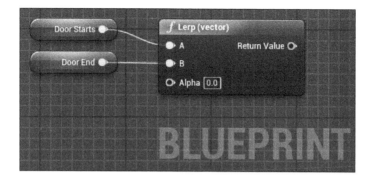

A timeline is a special node that allows for simple time-based animation to be quickly designed and played back based on in-game events. Timelines are somewhat like simple Matinee sequences in that they allow simple values to be animated and events to be fired off over time.

To create a timeline, simply add it as a normal node. A timeline can be edited directly inside the Blueprint editor by double clicking on the timeline in the graph tab, and its editor is similar to the Curve Editor of the Matinee:

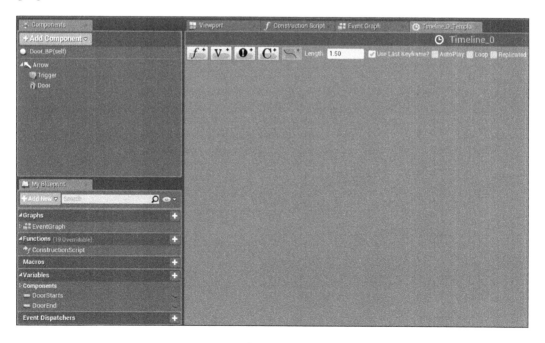

From the preceding window, you can add a desired track (float, vector, event, or color) by using the buttons on the top. The graph opened has the time (in seconds) on the x axis and the result value is on the y axis.

Add a float track and name it EndValue.

Like the Matinee, we can control the final value on this graph by adding keyframes. To add a keyframe, use *Shift* + left click on the red line (the final value curve).

Add two keyframes. The first one at time and value 0, and the second at time 1.5 and value 1. You will have a straight line. You can change the key interpolation to have a smoother movement by right clicking on a node and changing it with the desired one. Select user for our curve. The final result is a door that opens and closes slower than its middle movement:

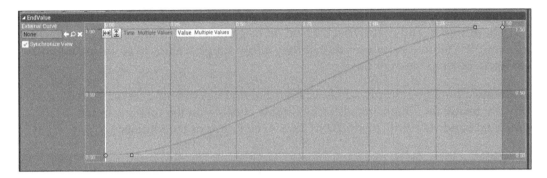

Now, connect the EndValue of the timeline to the **Alpha** value of the lerp one.

The output **Update** pin of the timeline can now be connected to a **SetRelativeLocation** node of **Door**, with the result of the lerp node as new location:

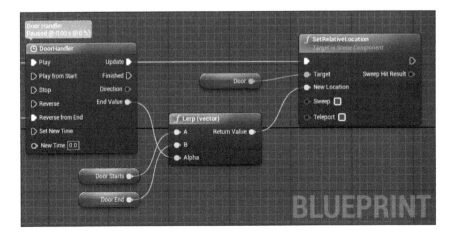

We call the **Play** timeline when a player overlaps the volume and reverse it when the player goes out of the volume:

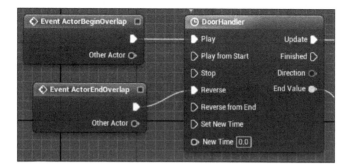

Killer objects

Let's add some dangerous objects for the player. The first one is an easier version of the KillZ volume. Create a new Blueprint extending an Actor and call it KillVolume. Add a box collision on the **Viewport** and extend its onActorBeginOverlap method with the KillPlayer function we created earlier as single node. You can understand the advantages of the function libraries now:

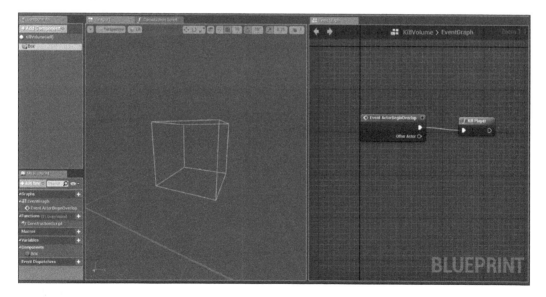

Duplicate this Blueprint and call it `RollingBall`. Change the collision box with a sphere and add a `Sphere` mesh with enabled physic. Those dangerous balls will be thrown down a hill ready to kill the player. Don't forget to choose **OverlapOnlyPawn** from the **Collision Presets** dropdown, unless you want that you player is killed by unwanted collisions:

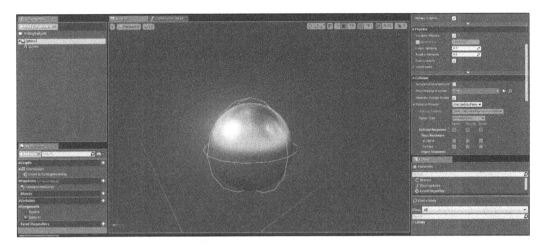

Duplicate this item and call it `Bullet`. Make it smaller, remove the physic simulation, and add a **Projectile** component. Use the same settings we used in the previous chapters: Autoactivate, **Initial Speed**, max force of 2000, and 0 gravity. On the Event Graph, set to destroy the project after a 5-second delay and when the projectile stops moving:

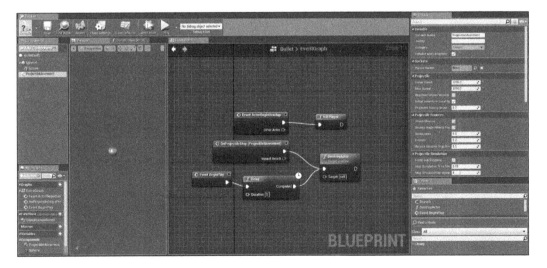

We have enough elements now to create a whole game.

The game

From the editor, create a new default map by going to **File | New level** and replacing the player start with our **ThirdPersonCharacter**.

The game will be divided into small section, each one with one or more elements of what we have learnt in this chapter.

Don't fall

In the first section, we use the kill volume. Here, the player must jump to some static platform without falling. Duplicate the original platform, set it lower than the original floor, add some cylinder shapes as a path and add the kill volume we created earlier between the platforms and the floor to recreate something similar to this:

Use your imagination to make the path you prefer and test it to find the more balanced way to do it (remember that a very easy game makes a gamer bored soon, but a very difficult game can be frustrating for even the most hardcore gamers).

Rolling stones

As second section, we use the killing balls: a long stair with lots of those balls rolling around. Search the stair BSP and position it after the first path. Enlarge it to be as wide as the corridor and add two blocking BSP on its size to prevent the balls from falling outside:

To control the behavior of this section, we use a trigger volume and some target points. The code for this and all the other sections will be written directly within the Level Blueprint. They are situational triggers and would be useless to create a dedicated Blueprint class only for one usage.

From the mods panel, add a trigger volume and modify its size to cover the stair. The idea is to activate the spawner when the player enter in the zone, and deactivate when it leaves.

 For laziness, we could activate everything within the maze without a flow control (like this trigger). However, be careful as each dynamic element uses memory and it is easy to consume all of it for useless behaviors.

On top of the stairs, insert five target points. They will be the spawn location for our spawner:

Open the Level Blueprint. The spawner mechanism is similar to the one we used in the previous chapter. A timer will call a spawn event that takes a random point from an array of elements and spawns there our rolling ball.

The first thing to do is to create the array of points. To populate it, we use the **BeginPlay** event and a **Make Array** node, which is connected to the five reference of the level. The **Make Array** node can have as many input pins we desire by clicking on its **Add pin** button:

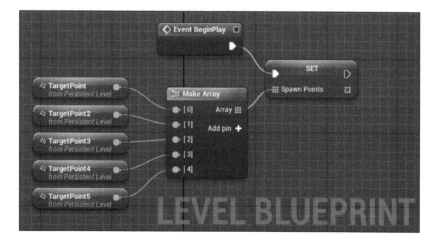

The spawn method is exactly the same of the other chapters:

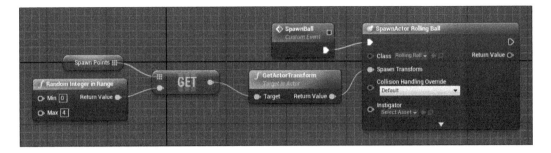

A trigger volume interacts with every object that touches it. To avoid interaction with the balls involved, cast **ThirdPersonCharacter** before creating the timer on the begin and end overlap methods of the trigger volume. To clear the timer, we use the same output pin of the set timer like this:

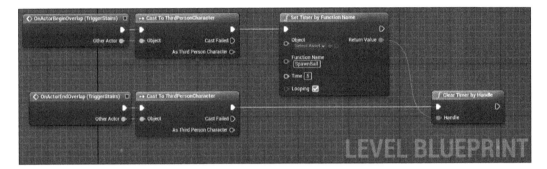

The falling path

Let's continue with the next section. For this, we use the fake platforms we created. We will put them into a dark corridor surrounded by walls, with two doors on its extremity.

Start by adding a series of Blueprint fake platform classes just after the end of the stairs:

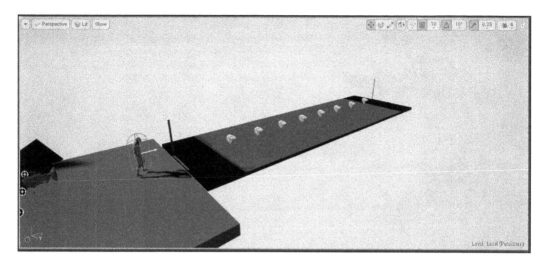

Now, using BPS box brushes, close this section and make two holes on it using the subtractive type of brush:

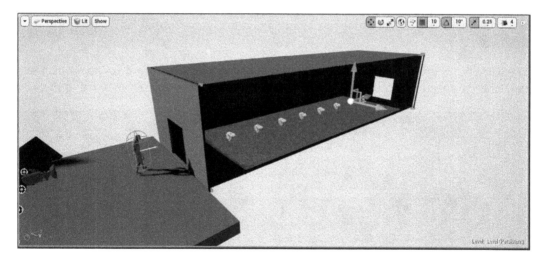

The inside is completely dark now. Use Blueprint ceiling lights from **Starter Content** to light it up. These are perfect elements to create a nice atmosphere within the tunnel:

To make this section more interesting, we could obligate the player to walk instead of run, so it must pay more attention to where they step along the tunnel. We put this code inside the Level Blueprint, using again a trigger volume as excitor for this event.

We want to modify **Max Walk Speed** of the **Charachter Movement** component. Use half of their speed when they enter the trigger, and restore it when they leave it:

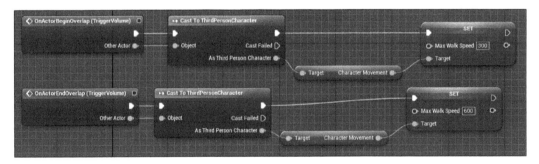

Finally, don't forget to put a kill volume on the bottom of this tunnel or the player will never die when falling.

Wrecking balls

As with the last section, let's implement the wrecking balls we created at beginning of the chapter. The idea of this section is to have a tight corridor, with moving wrecking balls ready to push you out of the corridor.

Because there is physic involved those balls don't move forever. We want to spawn them at a random starting angle and only when the player enters the zone. In this way, we should leave enough time for the player to run through the corridor without finding immobile balls along his way.

Create a corridor at the end of the previous section and add some target points on top of it. Those will be the spawning point of the balls so put them in a way that the ball component will swing on the player path. Use the object itself and the player pawn as reference, like on this picture:

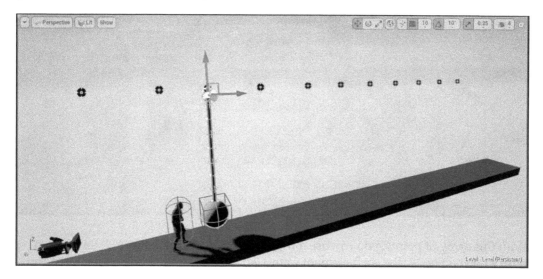

On the Level Blueprint, create an array of those target points just after the other array creation:

 You can create multiple references by selecting all the Actors that you want a reference for, and they are automatically added by clicking on **Create References of…** when you right-click on the Level Blueprint.

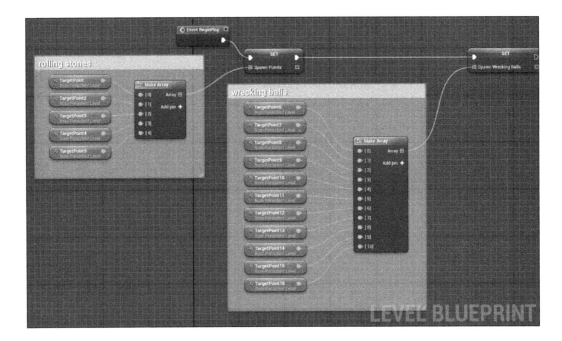

With this array of points, you can use a trigger volume to iterate through all of them with a for loop node. For each element found, spawn a wrecking ball on its transform.

To avoid spawning those elements multiple times, use a Boolean variable to store if they exist in the level before creating them like this:

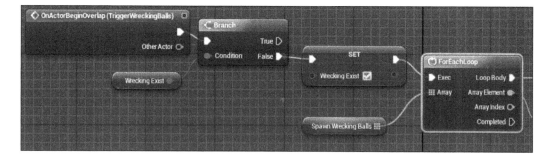

Now, if we simple spawn the elements on its transform like we did for the rolling stones, they won't move. This is because, as the ball simulate physic and as we built this object to be in a *relaxed position* it act as a real ball that, without stimulation, will sit there in its position. To solve this issue we can simply rotate the whole object (rope+ball) before spawning it on the level. This, combined with their physic simulation, will be enough to let them swing.

We need to modify the *X* value of the rotator of its transform. We need a few nodes to reach this value and, when set, another few of them to restore the transform variable needed to the spawn Actor node.

Find the Actor transform, break the transform, break the location, modify the *X* value, rewrite the location, rewrite the transform, and set that value to the final node:

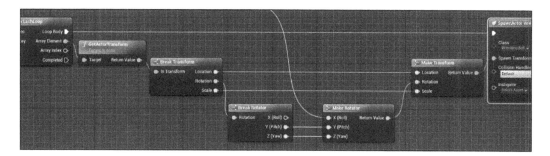

For the roll rotator, we use a math expression node. This special node allows us to write any math expression directly within the node name and the engine will take care to create the corresponding math nodes for you.

We want this value to be between 90 and 270 (so the upper side of the corridor). The math expression will be: *90+(rand()*180)* (*rand()* is a float value between *0* and *1*).

To create it, right-click on the **Graph Editor**, search for **Add Math Expression**, and write the expression directly to the node name:

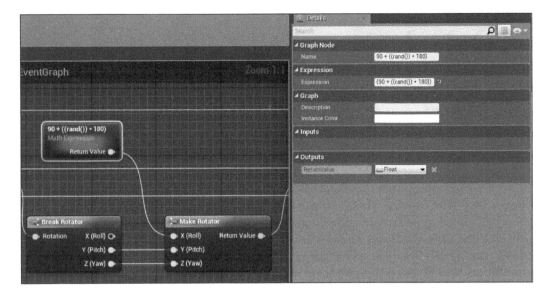

You can check the full expression by double clicking on the node itself. You can also add input pin value by adding the name of the variable within the expression.

Summary

In this chapter, you saw how easy is to create different elements for a puzzle game using just a few of and how it is possible to create potentially infinite game sections by tweaking their settings.

You know now how to manipulate the physic at your advantage, handle triggers in a dynamic environment, and create fun and reusable dynamic objects.

As usual, these are the possible extensions and tweaking for this game:

- We created bullets but we didn't implement in the game. Do it by creating a new section with shooting turrets around the path. To create them, check how we create the weapon on the previous chapter and use static meshes to create the shapes of the turret.

- Create a Matinee that shows the whole maze before the player starts it. Launch this Matinee on begin play of the Level Blueprint, use triggers within the level to avoid that matinee being launched multiple times. Swap the camera with the player one when it ends.

- Create moving platforms. Using Matinee and trigger volumes, try to create some moving platforms to transport your player between the zones.

In the next chapter, we will see how to create terrains and populate them using object pools and mod tools. We will also use everything we learned so far to create an open world framework with an inventory system, tied inside a dynamic user interface and with a basic crafting system.

7
An Open World Survival Game

Here we are, at the last chapter of this guide. In the previous chapters, we saw most of the aspects of UE4 and its Blueprint system, and we immediately used what we learned to create five interesting starting point for beautiful games. I used a simple approach in this book, why should we change now for this last chapter?

Here, we will look at the last few tools and aspects of a game and we will mix all the tools covered so far, improving our knowledge about them in order to create a more complex and variegate world for our games.

In this chapter, we will cover:

- Landscape manipulation
- Foliage
- Blueprint superclasses
- Light manipulation
- Inventory and crafting system

Landscapes

The main element of an open world is actually its landscape. UE4 offers a wonderful system that enables you to create any kind of terrain for your world (mountains, valleys, sloped grounds, caves, and holes for lakes or rivers) and easily modify both its shape and its appearance by using a range of tools.

The landscape tools are accessible by the **Modes** panel by clicking on its icon (it has an image of a mountain):

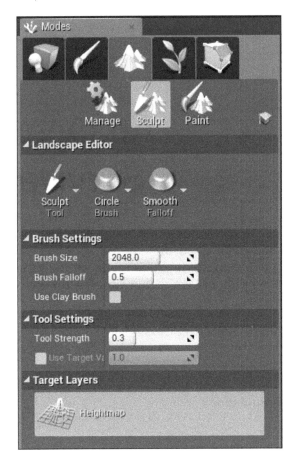

It is divided into three main modes:

- **Manage**: Enables you to create new Landscapes and modify Landscapes components. This is also where you work with Landscape Gizmos (a tool that allows you to manipulate volumes of layer data of your landscape to easily replicate or export).

- **Sculpt**: The main mode of the Landscape editor. It enables you to modify the shape of the Landscape by selecting and using specific tools.

- **Paint**: Enables you to modify the appearance of parts of your Landscape by painting textures on it, based on the layers defined in the Landscape's material.

Although there are external tools dedicated to the creation of heightmap Landscapes (such as World Machine or Terragen), the engine offers you all the basic tools to create them. As for the 3D models with the BSP brushes, those tools cannot completely replace a dedicated software but they are a great starting point.

Manage mode

To create a new Landscape, click on the **Manage** mode of the Landscape section:

You can immediately see a preview of the Landscape you are creating in your viewport, shown as a green grid divided in sections.

The properties that you can set are similar to any other Actor (after all, even if big, a Landscape is still an Actor), so let's check them:

- **Create New** or **Import from File**: You can choose whenever you want to create the Landscape with the engine tools or import a heightmap from an external file.

- **Material**: The material assigned to the whole Landscape. You can assign any kind of material you want at it. We will see soon the perfect type of material for a Landscape.

- **Location**, **Rotation** and **Scale**: Simply the location, rotation, and scale of the object within the world.

- **Section Size**: This property is used for Level Of Details and culling. Smaller section allows a higher definition of LOD but with and higher CPU cost.

- **Section Per Component**: Another property for the LOD. A component section 2 x 2 means that is possible that one component could be rendering four different LODs at once. Usually, higher LOD components are good for CPU calculation, but be careful because you can run into issues of rendering too many vertices at once.

- **Number of Components**: Along with section size, this sets the size of the Landscape.

- **Overall Resolution**: The number of vertices the Landscape is using.

- **Total Components**: The total number of components that will be created for the Landscape.

For our game, let's leave all the settings as the default ones, click on **Fill World**, and **Create**. A plane will be generated and the engine automatically brings you to the **Sculpt** mode:

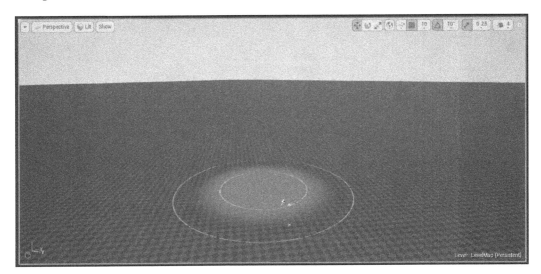

Sculpt mode

The process of sculpting a Landscape involves using one or more tools that modify the underlying heightmap. These tools range from the simple **Sculpt Tool** to other tools that use complex algorithms to apply interesting effects to create the desired terrain. Each tool has a set of properties that determine how they affect the Landscape. Each of these tools can be applied into the viewport by simply left-clicking and dragging the desired position to raise the heightmap, combined with shift to lower it:

At the very top of the Sculpt mode, you can set the aspect. Tool sets the kind of Sculpt algorithm to use with your brush, Brush sets the appearance and effect of the brush, and Falloff sets the type of falloff for your brush borders.

Let's take a look at the different tools available:

- **Sculpt tool**: Raises and lowers the Landscape uniformly within the brush's influence.

- **Smooth tool**: Smoothens the Landscape within the brush's influence by averaging the Z position of the Landscape vertices.

- **Flatten tool**: Raises and lowers the Landscape in its influence to be the same Z height as the location where you started using the tool.

- **Ramp tool**: Creates a ramp between two specified points, adding falloffs according to the settings.

- **Erosion tool**: This tool uses a thermal Erosion simulation to adjust the height of the heightmap. This simulates the transfer of soil from higher elevations to lower elevations. The larger the difference in elevation, the more Erosion will occur. This tool also applies a noise effect on top of the erosion.

- **Hydro Erosion tool**: Similar to the Erosion tool, this uses a hydraulic Erosion simulation to adjust the height of the heightmap. A noise filter is used to determine where the initial rain is distributed. Then the simulation is calculated to determine waterflow from that initial rains as well as dissolving, water transfer and evaporation.

- **Noise tool**: Applies a noise filter to the heightmap or layer weight. The strength determines the amount of noise.

- **Retopologize**: Similar to the smooth tool, this will push and pull triangles to smooth the transition of the terrain. However, it will attempt to keep the basic form of the terrain, minimizing change in the Z direction.

- **Visibility tool**: Combined with Hole Materials, this tool determines the visibility and collision of areas of your landscape.

- **Selection tool**: This tool permits you to lay down a mask on the landscape to control what you sculpt or paint on more accurately. This allows you to protect sections of the landscape from editing.

Play with these tools to create some cliffs and mountains around the player start. Try to avoid big differences of height and abuse with the Erosion tools. We are not searching to create a fully realistic world but a good starting point for future improvements:

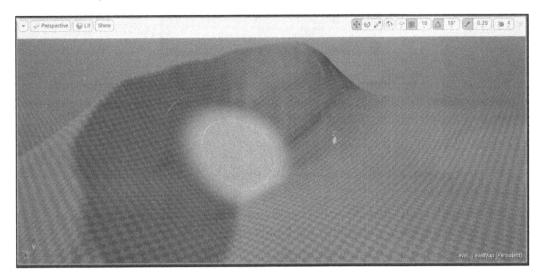

Create a terrain with a grid default material is not satisfying, so let's create a dedicated material for it.

Landscape material

Although any random material can be used with a Landscape Actor, the material system inside the engine does provide some special Landscape specific material nodes that can greatly help you to better texture the terrain.

Landscapes use weight blending rather than alpha blending, so the blend factors for all layers at any location will add up to 1.0. This has the advantage that there is no order dependence; you can paint any layer at any time and its weight is increased and the other existing layers are decreased. This allows you to have different aspects of a terrain (grass, sand, rocks, and so on) in one single material and the paint tool lets you blend between these layers freely.

We are now creating a blending material for our terrain, so we can paint the different materials wherever we prefer. In the future, you can create a weightmap to automatically blend the layers based on their weight of the component section of the landscape.

Create a new material and call it M_Terrain. From the material graph, search and add the **LandscapeLayerBlend** node:

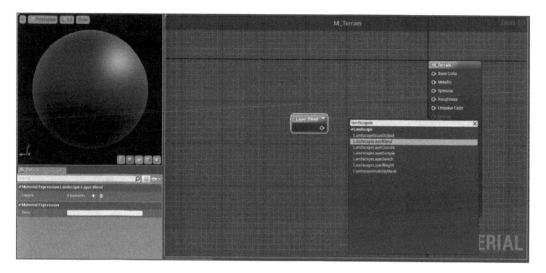

Using the **+** button from the **Details** panel of the **Layers** section, you can add new layers to the blend node. Add three of them and call them Rock, Sand, and Grass, respectively. Change the blend type of sand and grass to be **LB_Height Blend** and set **Blend Type** of rock as **LB_Alpha_Blend**.

When using multiple layers, it is possible that all the layers painted in a particular area will simultaneously have a 0 height value and the result is a black spot area because there is no implicit layer order. We use one of the layers (usually the most bottom one) to be Alpha blended to avoid this particular issue:

To map the layers of our terrain material, we use another specific node: search and add the LandscapeLayerCoords node. This node generates UV coordinates that will be used with the layer blend node to literally paint the different layers.

Now we need the textures for the layer. You can use your own textures but if you don't have one, **Starter Content** has good textures perfect for our needs—complete with their normal map. Add three **Texture Sample** nodes to the graph and search for T_Rock_Basalt_D, T_Rock_Sandstone_D and T_GroundGrass_D. Connect their **UVs** pin to the **LandscapeCoords** node and the output to the correspondent **Layer Blend** pin (the height, when needed, is the alpha channel of a texture) like this:

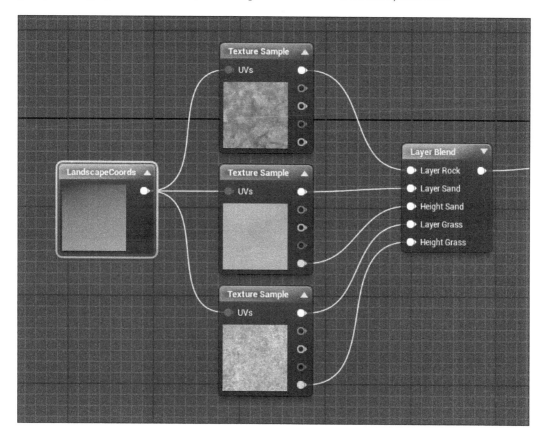

You can connect the output of the **Layer Blend** node to **Base Color** of our material. On the Landscape coordinate system, there is an important parameter that you can adjust to improve the overall performances of the calculation: **Mapping Scale**. A higher value results in a blurred and less detailed texture but will also result in much faster shading calculations:

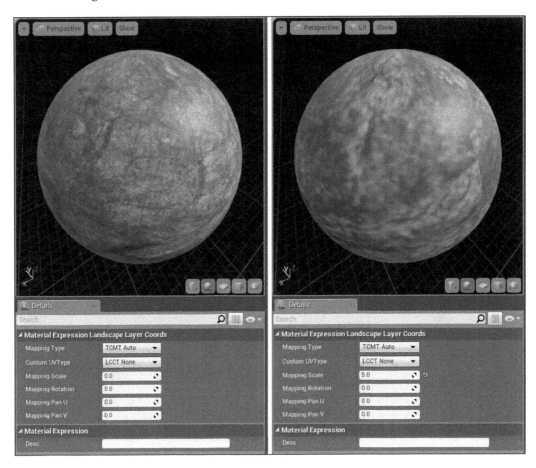

We can add depth to our material by using the normal map of those textures. Duplicate the whole nodes from the **LandscapeCoords** to **Layer Blend**. You can change only the textures to their respective normals (T_Rock_Basalt_N, T_Rock_Sandstone_N and T_GroundGrass_N) and connect the result to the **Normal** input pin. As final step, add a constant to the metallic and the roughness to set this material as less metallic and wet. A basic, multilayer terrain material is complete:

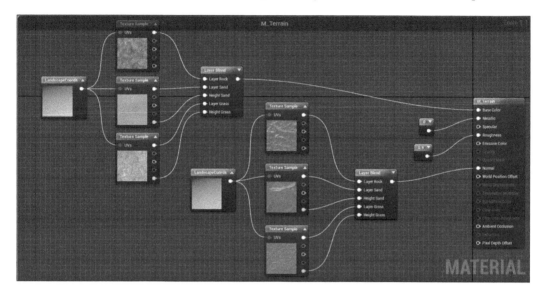

Now, let's go back to the viewport and apply this material to the Landscape. Do it by clicking on the **Landscape** from the **World Outliner** and going to the **Landscape** section of its **Details** panel. The result is a full rock terrain. Don't worry if you see your terrain divided into a squared grid; this is because the light needs to be recompiled. Just click on build to solve this issue.

Paint tool

We can now go to the **Paint** tool of the Landscape panel. You can see that on the **Layer** section, we have our three **Target Layers** labeled as we did on the material itself. Before you can use them, you need to create layer info for each of them.

Every Landscape layer must have a layer info assigned to it in order to be painted. We use a Weight-Blended info object. This layer, when applied, will decrease the weight of all other weight-blended layers. To create a layer info, simply click on the plus (**+**) button near them and select weight-blended layer (normal). The engine automatically sets a file and a location for it. Confirm without changing the name for each of them and this should be the result:

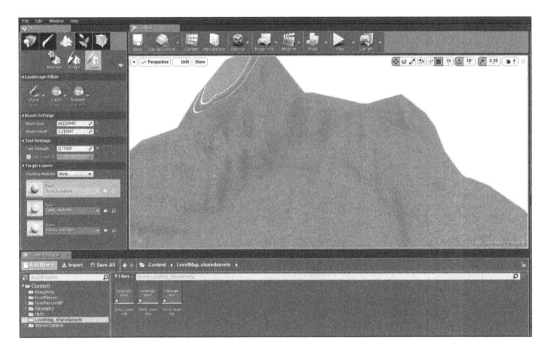

Now, exactly how we did with the Sculpt tools, select one of those layers and paint it on your terrain.

When you start to paint for the first time a layer, it could happen that the base material disappears or a whole section of your Landscape is converted into a single layer. This happens because there is no **Paint layer data** on the Landscape. To fix this issue, simply keep painting until you cover the whole area (by enlarging your brush size example). This issue should disappear and you are now able to paint correctly and see your modifications.

Foliage

Now that we have a Landscape with its hills and mountains, we should add some typical elements of an open space: trees and rocks. To do this, we could add the single Static Mesh one by one into the scene, but it is a tedious and long process. The engine gives you a perfect tool to help you on this process: the **Foliage Instanced Mesh** system.

This system allows you to quickly paint or erase sets of **Static Meshes** on **Landscape**, **BSP**, or other meshes. These meshes are automatically grouped together into batches that are rendered using hardware instancing, meaning that many instances can be rendered with only a single draw call (and also allows you to position a lot of them into the scene with only few steps). You can find this tool beside the Landscape tool (the icon is a seedling):

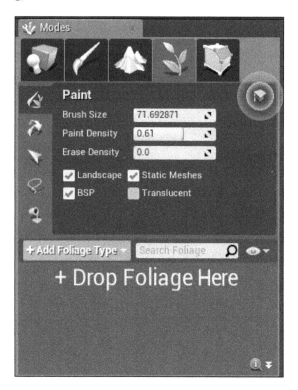

The interface is very similar to the Landscape tool; you can choose **Brush Size**, the density the meshes create, and where those meshes will be applied. A big **Drop Foliage Here** shows you where to drag and drop your meshes and when they are positioned there, you have access to other settings such as painting scale, offsets, random rotation, and so on.

For this project, I'm using the free example package from **SpeedTree** (a useful tool, used to be free on the previous version of the engine, which helps you to generate trees and natural elements for your game). It can be found at `http://www.speedtree.com/downloads/Free_SpeedTree_Samples_for_UE4.zip`.

Once you have chosen the mesh to use in your terrain and set the desired brush, simply **Paint** those elements in the Landscape. Any element can be added to your scene with this method, even collectables or enemies!:

You have the necessary knowledge to create a beautiful world for our game. It is now time to implement some logic to it.

Day-Night cycle

When talking about open world, one of the first things that pops in our mind is the necessity to simulate the real-world day and night cycle. UE4 is strong on this point. With just a few Blueprint nodes and a few changes at a default scene, you can create a perfect day cycle for your game.

Take a look at the default map of your game. In the world outliner you can find the two elements that, combined together, are the responsible of the lighting of our scene: the **Light Source** and the **Sky Sphere**.

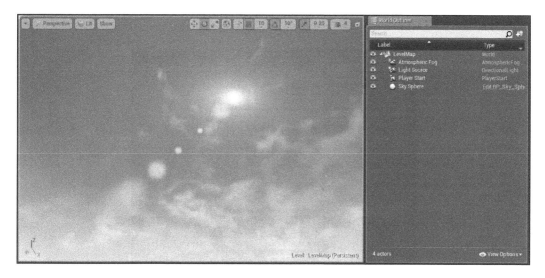

Light Source, as the name suggests, is responsible for the illumination of the entire world. It is a directional light. A directional light simulates light that is being emitted from a source that is infinitely far away. This means that all shadows cast by this light will be parallel, making this the ideal choice for simulating sunlight.

Sky Sphere is basically a huge Static Mesh and is the responsible for what the player sees in the background, including the sun planet. You can open the Blueprint Sky Sphere by clicking on **Edit BP_Sky_Sphere**. What you will see is a complex Blueprint class: on its Construction Script, all the nodes needed to populate the sphere with clouds and sky colors based on the light source rotation and within the functions, is one function called `UpdateSunDirection`. This class is perfect as is but remember that function, we will use it soon.

With this brief explanation, the next step is easy: rotate **Light Source** as you please and, thanks to the `UpdateSunDirection` function, change the whole background aspect of the game. Before doing so, there is something to change in the parameters of **Light Source**. By default, it is an unmovable object, so let's change it by clicking on **Movable** from its **Details** panel:

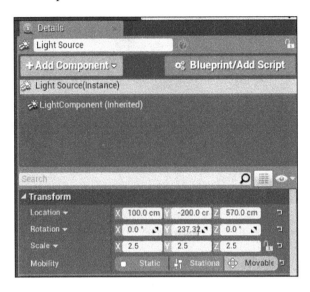

Because it was a static object, it has the property **Cast Static Shadows** set to true on its **Light** parameters. This allows the engine to bake the shadows of the static object before running the game. This is useful for performances, but not suitable for our purposes. Set it to false (if you don't find it, remember to extend the properties by clicking on the little arrow at the bottom of each section, or use the search tool on top of the panel):

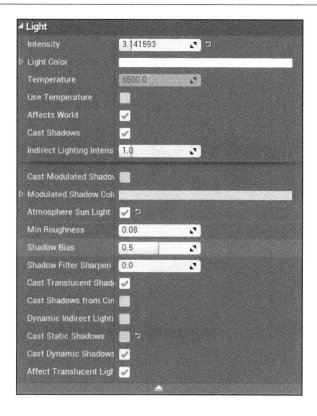

There are several ways to achieve our result and, as always, we are going to see the easiest and practice way: we will use a looped timeline inside the Blueprint level that dynamically changes **Light Source** and refreshes the sun direction on each update call.

Open the Level Blueprint and create a new timeline called **Day-Night Cycle**, double-click to open it, and add a single float track:

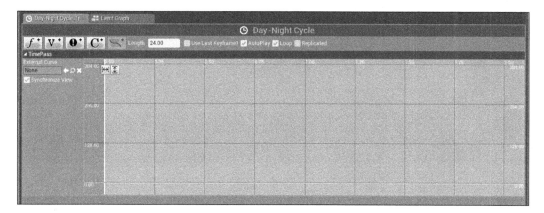

The idea is simple: use the length of the timeline as a whole day length (in seconds) and set a linear output value from 0 to 360 that will be used as angle for the light Actor.

Change the length to an acceptable value (300 seconds is suitable to test it) and create two keyframes by using *Shift* + left-click on the red line. The first key will have 0 for both time and value, and the second one will have the last keyframe (300) as time and the maximum rotation (360) as value:

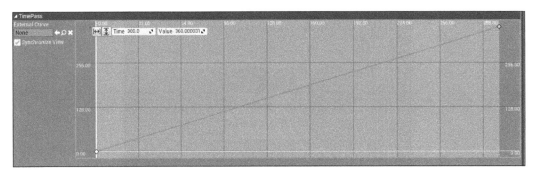

This linear setting will give you a cycle with 2.5 minutes of light and 2.5 minutes of darkness. You can play with the key interpolation of this curve to achieve a better result if you want, for example, more light during the day and a shorter night. As is, the day starts at 180 degrees, ends at 360, and has its apex at 270 degrees.

Let's close the timeline and implement it with the needed nodes. Drag a reference of both **Light Source** and **Sky Sphere** inside the Level Blueprint graph. On the update exec pin of the timeline, we want to call **Set Actor Rotation** with **Light Source** as **Target** and call UpdateSunDirection of the **Sky Sphere**. As Actor rotation, we use the MakeRotator node with its pitch modified as the calculated value from the timeline. This should be the final result:

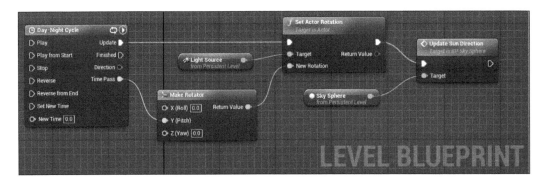

Nothing more is needed. Six simple nodes and, thanks to the engine, you have created a complete day-night cycle. Compile, save, and test it. Notice how the sun moves in the sky and how the whole atmosphere changes according to the time of the day (sun rise, blue sky, twilight, dark with stars).

Collectables and items

I know, we saw this element more than one time in this book but, hey, this is a very common element in a lot of games.

In a survival world, you must be able to interact with most of the elements around you. You want to collect stones, wood, grass, or fruits and be able to craft your tools, such as axes to cut the trees. You would also want weapons to hunt your food in order to survive in the hostile environment.

In this section, we will create an inventory system for the objects that can be collected in the world: we will use a new element (structure) that handles the properties of our items. We improve our knowledge of Blueprint wizard to populate a useful and dynamic user interface, and we will see how useful Blueprint Interfaces and superclasses are when talking about a vast number of different interactive objects and a crafting system.

Blueprint structures

A Blueprint structure is exactly like a structure of an object-oriented programming language: a special variable type that allows you to group different variables into one single name. Each element of a structure can have different types (not necessarily declared) and they can be used inside an Actor class like any other variable.

By creating a list of common information of an object (such as name, thumbnail, weight, or price), we will be able to track any information needed from anywhere in our project.

You can create a new structure by right-clicking in **Content Browser**, selecting Blueprint, and selecting **Structure**. Name it `ItemStructure` and open it.

The interface is poor but it doesn't need to be complicated. It has, on the left, a list of variables that compose the structureand, on the right, their default values.

The variables that we will need for our structure are as follows:

- ItemName (Text)
- ItemDescription (Text)
- Thumbnail (Texture 2D)
- Collectable (Boolean)
- Eatable (Boolean)
- Consumable (Boolean)

We will use the first information for the inventory UI, the collectable one, to distinguish which object can be collected (a player can interact with a tree, but surely he cannot collect it), and the last two Boolean will help us to create a contextualized menu when we interact with them. For the moment, no other variables are needed and don't worry if you forgot to add one of them. The structures are fully modifiable even if they are already implemented into the game logic:

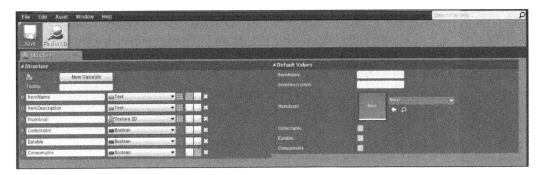

Superclasses

To get the best from our structure, we should use it with a dedicated superclass. This class will contain the structure and the first common component and logic of any object into the game. First, let's create a Blueprint class extending Actor and call it Super_Item.

We are sure that any item will have a **Collision** component for the interaction with the player and a Static Mesh to display it in the world. Add a collision sphere as root of the object (a radius of 200 will be enough to contain most of our objects), and an empty Static Mesh as its child. Now, add a variable and under structure you should find our **ItemStruct**. Remember to set it to public (by opening its eye near the name); otherwise we won't be able to access it from the UI:

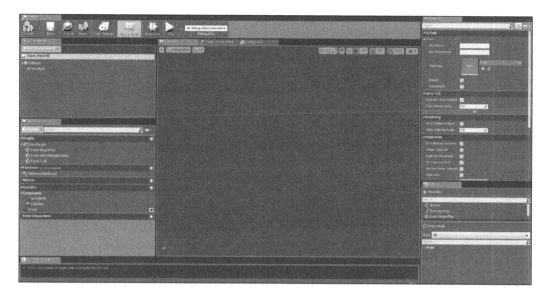

Notice how the struct default values are now available at the very beginning of the **Details** panel. Switch to the Event Graph and add the common logic of our items: the collision sphere will determine if a player is nearby the item and, consequently, if it can be collected when the user interacts with it.

Add a Boolean variable and call it `CanBeCollected`. This value will be used by the player class to check if that object can be actually collected. We will toggle this boolean using the `ActorBeginOverlap` and `ActorEndsOverlap`, checking if is the player object that interact with the collectable and toggling the `CanBeCollected` value only if the object IS actually a collectable (read from the Struct values).

To access the variable of a structure, you can use the **Break** node (like we did for vectors or transforms). In this way, you are able to access the single variable contained in it. This should be the final result:

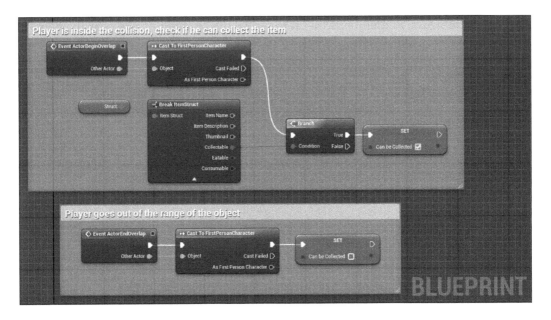

In order to interact with an item, the player will use an action key. In order to know exactly which object a player is interacting with (instead of the call a *player has fired an action* to all the objects in the world and checking which one is nearby), we will use a handy and powerful Blueprint Interface. We already saw it in the previous chapters and for this project it will be basically the same: an interface with an empty function named InteractionWithPlayer. This will be used to send and receive messages between the player and the desired object:

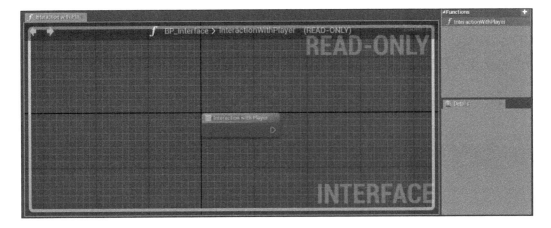

I'm not going to explain again the process of creating it, but be sure to create it correctly and to implement it in our superclass from its class settings.

Extending the superclass

Using our superclass is super easy. Right-click on the `Super_Item` Blueprint class and select **Create Child Blueprint Class...**. Notice how we have the same components inherited from the parent, our structure inherited form the parent, and a function pointing the superclass construction on **Constructor Script**:

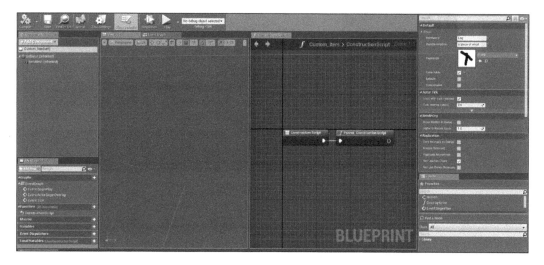

We can create as many objects as we want and all of them will have the same basic properties. We will now create a few common objects of the nature environment.

As meshes, I'm using primitive figures. It would be better to use realistic figures, but we are now focusing on the logic of the game. You will be able to change those meshes whenever you want.

About the thumbnail of the object, a PNG image of 128 x 128 is enough. The easiest way to create these images is to take the actual thumbnail from the editor. It's possible to create a custom thumbnail for an actor by placing it inside the viewport and when focused by the camera, right-click on it and go to **Asset Actions** | **Capture Thumbnail**:

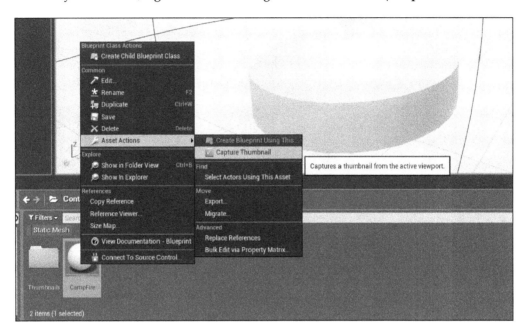

You can simply use a screenshot of the object. You can find the PNGs I'm using for them at (www.nicolavalcasara.it/packt).

These are the objects that we will use in our project. Create six children of the superclass according to these parameters:

Children	Parameters
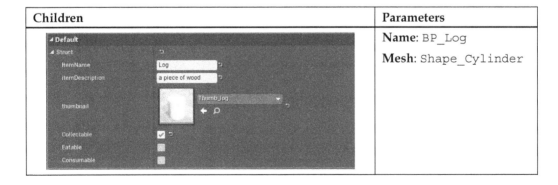	**Name**: BP_Log **Mesh**: Shape_Cylinder

Children	Parameters
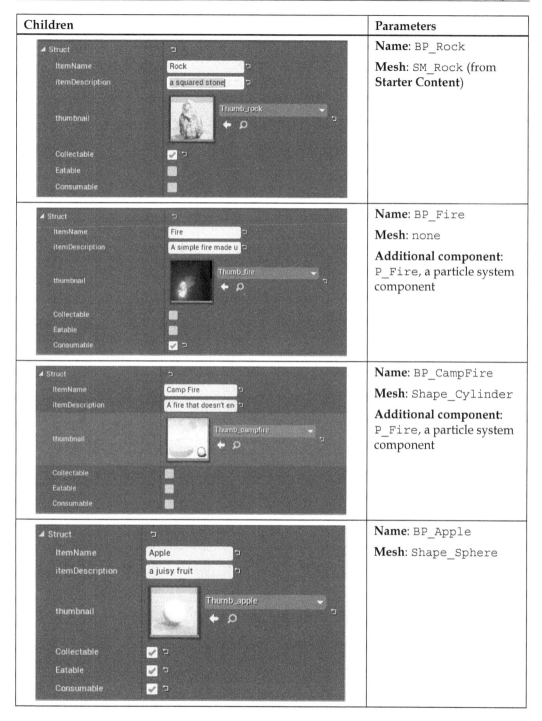	**Name**: BP_Rock **Mesh**: SM_Rock (from **Starter Content**)
	Name: BP_Fire **Mesh**: none **Additional component**: P_Fire, a particle system component
	Name: BP_CampFire **Mesh**: Shape_Cylinder **Additional component**: P_Fire, a particle system component
	Name: BP_Apple **Mesh**: Shape_Sphere

Children	Parameters
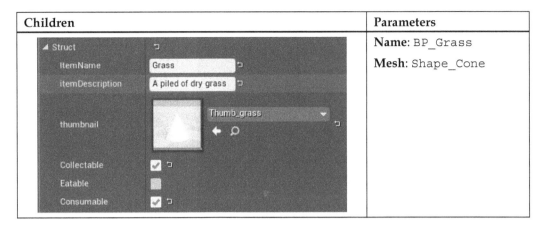	**Name:** BP_Grass **Mesh:** Shape_Cone

Crafting handler

To handle the possibility of crafting an item, we can add a new variable inside the item structure. This variable will be an array of super items. It must be populated before the game starts and each craftable item will contain the super_class needed for it.

The following screenshot is an example of its usage (the campfire will need a rock, a log, and a grass item to be crafted):

Implementing the Blueprint Interface

Now that we have some items, it is time to implement the player character logic to interact with them. Open the **FirstPersonCharacter** Blueprint class and get rid of all the useless pieces of code and components: On the viewport, remove the weapon mesh. On the Construction Script, remove the code that attached the weapon to the mesh socket. On the event graph, remove completely the whole section about the firing logic.

Now, handle the input keyboard buttons by adding two new **Action Mappings** from the project settings: **Interact** and **ToggleInventory**:

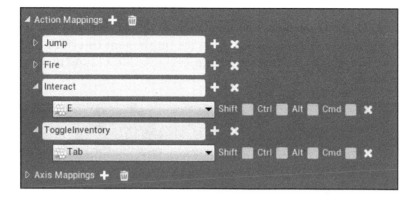

The logic behind the interaction of the player is the following: whenever a player presses the **Interact** button, we want to check what they are pointing at and if it's a collectable object, send a message to it.

To check what the player is pointing at, we use a **LineTraceByChannel** node (we already saw this node in the *Chapter 4, UFO Run - Play with the Environment Effects*). To get the points of the line trace, we use **CameraManager**. This node will return the camera object that the player is actually using. With this object, we can generate a ray from its location that goes forward by a number of units.

Add a **LineTraceByChannel** to the **InputActionInteract** event. Connect the **GetActorLocation** of the camera manager as starting point. As end point, connect the sum of the **ActorLocation** with the calculated multiplication of a **ForwardVector** of the **ActorRotation** by a Float value of 5,000 units:

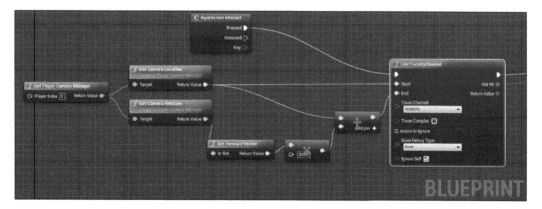

You can test it with set the **Draw Debut Type** and press the interact key around the level. You should see a red line going from you toward the middle cross point, with a red square to indicate whenever the ray hit something.

We can now break the **OutHit** result to find which Actor is hit, and use it to check if it implements our interface by using the **Does Implement Interface** node. Lastly, if the result is **True**, means we can send it a message to let it know that we are interacting with it:

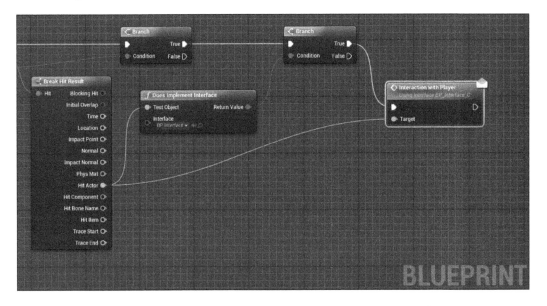

This is surely the easiest and fastest way to interact with different objects. It saves a lot of calculations (we are checking one single element at time) and time on developing new items.

Super item interaction

The last piece of code to add to our super item is the logic that handles what to do when the player interacts with it. Our struct contains a variable called `Collectable`; we can use it to determine if this item can be transferred to the inventory.

Implementing a Blueprint Interface inside your Event Graph is like adding any other event. Search for our custom function **Interaction With Player** and add it to the graph:

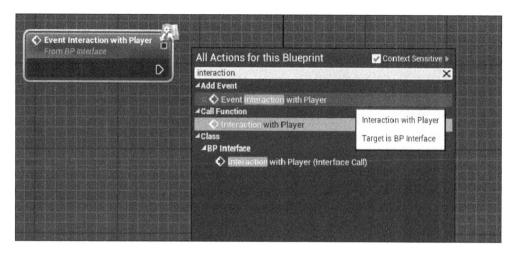

Now, we can connect this node to **Branch** with as input our **Collectable** variable. To access at a single variable, you can use the **Break ItemStruct** node. With this node, we can access any single variable contained inside the structure:

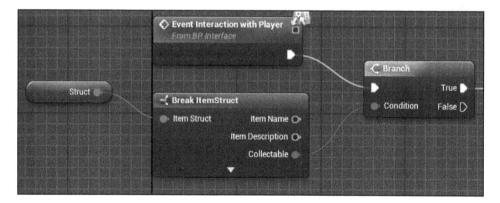

If the object is a **Collectable**, we must say to the player controller the class of the object we are collecting and lastly, destroy the Actor inside the level.

We use the class instead of the reference of the Blueprint Actor because the inventory we will use is based on classes and because of the crafting system we can't use references to items that don't exist in the scene.

To find a class of an object, we can use the **GetClass** node connected with **Self reference**. First, create a custom event inside the player character that has an input node of type **Super_Item** class:

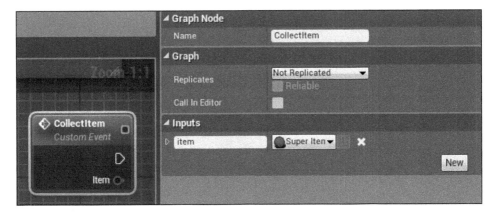

Now, you can complete the function of the super item by calling the **Collect Item** event of the player character on the **True** pin of **Branch** like this:

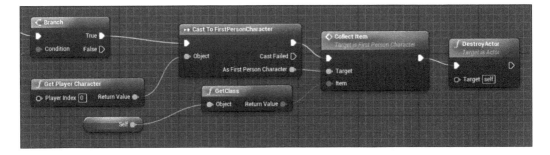

Inventory system

Let's now use some Blueprint Widget to create the user interface and the inventory system. We will need three classes: a main GameUI, Inventory Button, and Inventory Craft Button.

The main GameUI is what the player will see. It will contain a grid of objects (the actual inventory), a panel that shows the information of the selected item, and a cookbook that contains all the items that are available to be crafted.

The Inventory Button is the single button of our inventory and will be just a single squared button with an image over it.

The Inventory Craft Button is similar to the other button, but it also contains the name of the item that will be crafted and the items needed to the player to craft it.

The inventory button

Create a Blueprint Widget and call it `InventoryButton`. This object (and all the Widget that will be added into **Canvas Panel** dynamically) doesn't need a main canvas. The aspect (size, anchor, position, and so on) will be determined directly within the panel where this Widget will be added.

So, remove the original **Canvas Panel** from this Widget and from **Palette** add **Button** and **Image** as child of it:

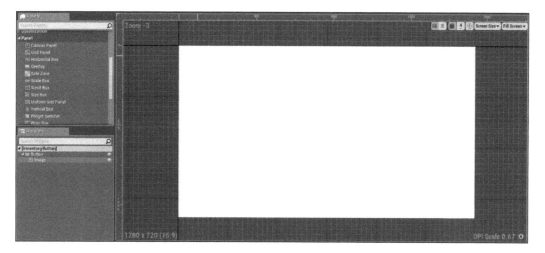

Notice how the options for the position and the anchor setting are disabled. About the code of this item, we only need to **Bind** the **Brush** of the **Button** and **Image** into our **Thumbnail** whenever an item is added into the inventory.

We need to add two variables inside this Widget: an inventory slot of type integer to identify which slot this button will occupy and a reference to our main UI panel (we will add this later).

The inventory craft button

Like the other button, this Widget doesn't need **Canvas Panel**, as will be added dynamically into the main panel.

As container for our needs we use **Grid Panel**, a Widget that can be found inside the **Panel** section of **Palette**. This Widget accepts a number of rows and columns and automatically fits the items within the grid according to their settings.

Add a grid as root Widget. From the **Details** panel, locate the **Fill Rules** section. From there, we can set how many rows and columns we want. From the single element float value, we can choose a percentage (between 0 and 1) of filling for each section of the grid.

The aspect of this Widget will have a **thumbnail** button of the item on its left. On the right-hand side column, we will have the name of the item, followed by the items needed to create it. Set the fill rules as follows:

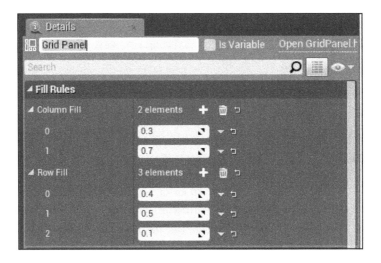

As children of **Grid Panel**, we use a button (with a child image), text, and a spacer.

If not specified, all the children of **Grid Panel** are set to be the on the first row and column. You can specify where those elements will be under the **Slot** properties of each element. Set their position as described before, use the **Span** property to set the button Widget to occupy two rows), and put the spacer at the very bottom of the grid:

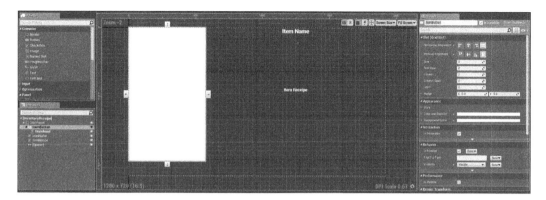

This should be the final result. About the variables required, let's add a variable of type **Super_Item** (class) and make it public. This will be the item held by this Widget. As opposed to the other button Widget, the cookbook will have static objects inside its list so we can use a class to store its information.

Main user interface

On **Main UI**, we want to insert all the possible information that a player might need. An ordinated grid to represent the inventory of the items collected by the user, a section that shows all the possible combinations of objects for crafting, and a section that shows the details of any single element. Lastly, all of this information must be handled in a smart manner without interfering too much with the gameplay of the player.

First, let's create a new Blueprint Widget and call it Game_UI. This Widget must be always available within the game and must be initialized as soon as the game starts. The best place to put the handler code for it is within the PlayerCharacter class: we already have the code that handle the interaction with the items around the level. This Widget is focused on them and the inventory logically belongs to the single character.

Main setup and visibility

Open the `PlayerCharacter` class. On **Event BeginPlay**, create the Widget based on **Game UI**, add it to the viewport, and set a reference to it directly within the character class:

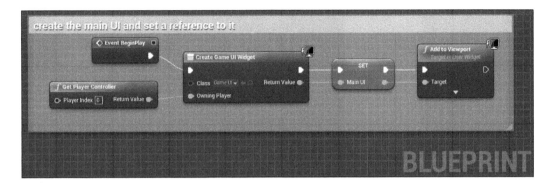

Now we want to be able to toggle the view of this Widget somehow. We can use the key we created earlier to handle it and a Boolean variable that stores whenever a player is inside the detailed inventory.

By doing this, we must consider the following: we must disable the player movements and enable the mouse cursor when a player needs to interact with the UI. At this moment, by default, you don't see the mouse cursor and you use the mouse to look around inside the level, with a red cross showing where the player is looking. The easiest way to handle this is to add a flow control for each of the elements that can be affected by this process: movement, look view, mouse, and cross point.

The first three logic codes are contained within the character itself:

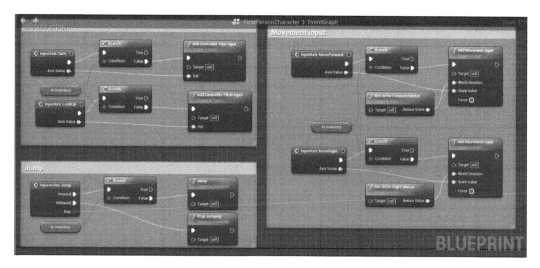

The cross point is instead contained within the `FirstPersonHUD` class. Within this class, there is an event called `ReceiveDrawHUD`. This event is called each frame the HUD is drawn and it simply finds the middle point of the panel and draws a cross there.

Add a flow control as we did for the other pieces of code by casting the **In Inventory** variable of the `ThirdPersonCharacter`:

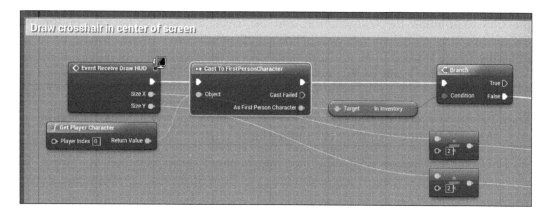

Now, for the main flow of the inventory the idea is that whenever a player hits the **ToggleInventory** key, invert the value of the **In Inventory** variable and toggle the cursor's view based on that result. Thanks to the flow control we added, a couple of nodes are enough to handle everything:

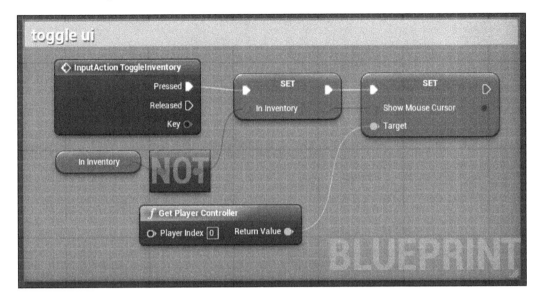

Design the UI

It is time to populate the Widget. First, add `UniformGridPanel` at the very bottom of the canvas. This Widget automatically takes all its child elements and resizes them to fill the whole Widget in an uniform manner. We use this as our inventory. It is the only element of the Main UI that will be always visible by the player, so set its size to be a small bar that sits on the bottom of the player view.

From **Palette** now you should find the **User Created** section available at its bottom and, inside it, our two inventory custom buttons.

Add 10 **Inventory Button** Widgets at the uniform panel, set each of them at a single univocal column, and assign the same value to its **Item Slot** value (available just above the **Slot** property of it). Notice the position and its property in the top-right corner:

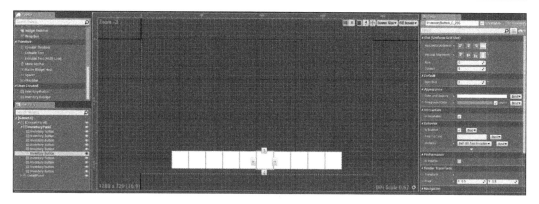

Now add a second panel inside the main one and call it `DetailPanel`. Here the cookbook and item information will go, and this is the panel that is toggled by the character, thanks to our **In Inventory** event.

Inside this panel, add a couple of caption text to explain what the player is looking at (**Item Details** on the left and **CookBook** on the right) and populate it with the following elements:

- **Image**: The thumbnail of the selected item.
- **Text**: The description of the selected item.
- **Vertical box**: The container of the interaction buttons:
  - A button called **Eat**
  - A button called **Use**
  - A button called **Drop**
- **Scroll box**: The container of the cookbook. It automatically adds a slider whenever the child number exceeds the dimensions.

The positions should be like this:

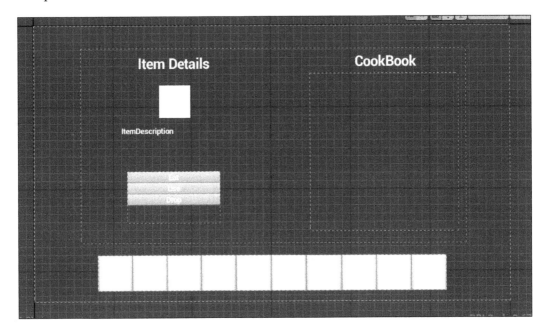

Prepare the cookbook

First, let's handle the cookbook: we must have somewhere an array of craftable items in order to populate the scrollbox. Go to the player character and create a variable of type Super_Item, set it to be an Array, and make it public. After compiling, add all the items that can be crafted (at this moment only the fire and the campfire) in the default section of the details property.

In this way, we can know all the craftable items before starting the game. Thanks to its public set, we can access it from anywhere and we are able to add new recipes later on the gameplay if, for example, the player finds them around the world.

Let's go back to the **GameUI** graph. Extend **Event Construct**, store a reference to the player character, and populate the scrollbox.

To achieve this, we use a **ForEachLoop** array for each of the elements in the cookbook variable. For each of them, we create a Widget of type **Inventory Receipe** and we add it as child of the scrollbox. Because the Widget doesn't know automatically, we set its **Item Class** variable as the looped **superItem** element:

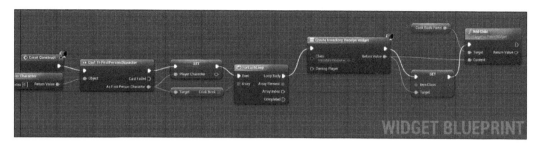

Receipe button bindings

Now that we have the **Inventory Receipe** button populated, we can proceed to create the proper logic and bindings.

We first need a reference to the **Main UI** Widget on **Event Construct** of it. This process should be familiar to you at this point:

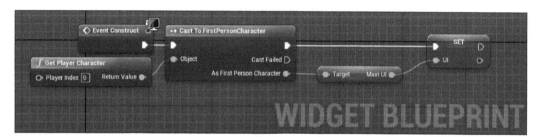

Now, we can bind the button image, the item name text, and the item receipe text. From the designer panel, click on their **Bind** button near the desired property and click on create binding.

The process for the thumbnail and the name is exactly the same. Get the defaults of the **Item Class** variable, break its struct, and take the desired property:

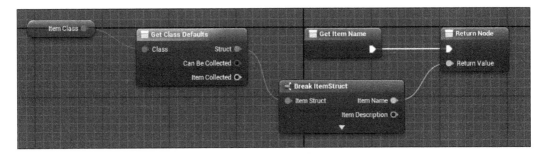

The receipe text is a little bit more complicated. We actually need to iterate through all the single items of the receipe variable and create a text that contains their names.

Create a local variable (these types of variables start and end their life cycle inside the selected function) of type text and call it **Text Receipe**. We use it as a temp variable for the final string.

Clear this text at beginning of the getter for the binding function and connect the return node at the **Completed** pin of an **ForEachLoop** node:

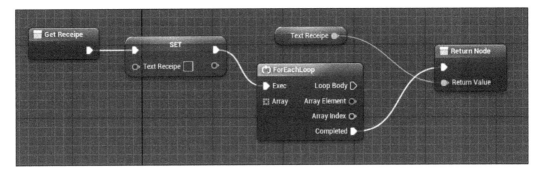

This will prevent undesired text inside the temp variable before the execution of the creation loop and return the created text only when the loop ends.

As input of this loop, we use the receipe of **Item Class** (as always, break the struct to access it). On **Loop Body**, we use a **Format** string node with the name of **Array Element** as first element and the temp string as the second element:

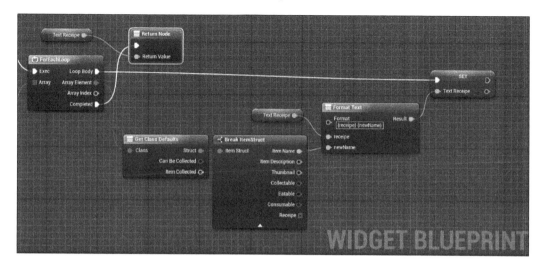

Add objects to the inventory

We created earlier the super item interaction handler but if you look at that function, we actually have no possibility to know whenever an item is added on the inventory or if it fails (because there is no space in the inventory or the player can't collect it).

To solve this problem, we can modify that function by adding an output Boolean value that will contain the outcome of the process.

Instead of calling the event CollectItem within the character class (that actually doesn't know the state of the inventory), we can call it directly within the GameUI thanks to its reference and add the output we need.

On the game UI, create a function and call it AddToInventory. Add one input pin of type Super_Item and one output of type Boolean. It is time to create the actual inventory variable: an array of Super_Item classes.

The idea of this function is simple. Check the length of the array and if doesn't exceed the maximum number of slots, add the input class to the inventory. Finally, call the return node with the Boolean result:

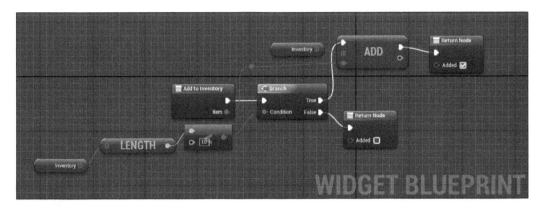

Now, let's go back to the Super_Item Blueprint class. We can replace the existing call at the CollectItem event to this new function and destroy the Actor only if the Boolean value is **True**:

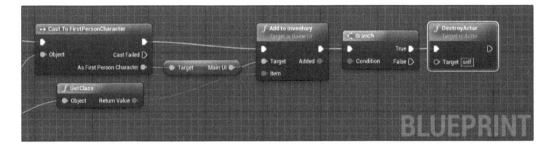

Remove and use items

After collecting items, we must be able also to remove them from the inventory. There are different ways to remove an object: by using it, by crafting it, or by dropping it. For this reason, we will use two different functions: The first one is simply to remove the desired item from the inventory. The second one calls a custom event inside the player character. That event will take care of dropping (spawning an Actor) the selected item based on its class.

The RemoveItem function is simple. It uses the **REMOVE INDEX** node. As an index, we use a variable called SelectedItem of type integer that will be used to store **Slot Selected** within the **Inventory**:

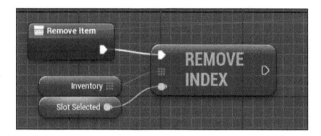

The drop function, when needed, is called before removing the item from the inventory. It takes the **Slot Selected** item from the array and calls a CustomFunction within **Player Character**:

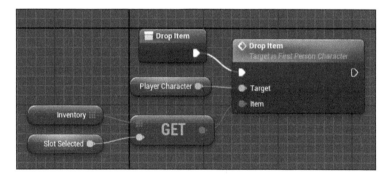

Drop item – character side

The drop function from the player character function will take that SuperItem class and use it to spawn an Actor within the level. As transform position, we use an Arrow component added expressly as a placeholder for the position and it is shown in the following screenshot on the ground level in front of the player:

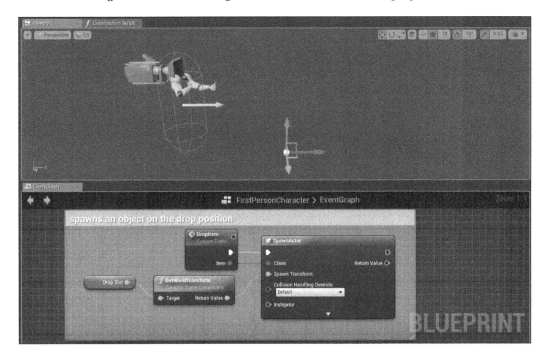

Craft items logic

To be able to craft an item, the player must have inside its inventory all the needed items. We can bind this check within the IsEnabled variable of the button of our recipe. This will gray out the noncraftable items and unlock them as soon as the needed items are collected.

To achieve this, we use a Boolean local variable and the idea is the following: an item is, by default, always **Craftable**. Before returning the IsEnable value, we use a **ForEachLoop** node within the inventory array. Whenever an item of the recipe is not contained inside the inventory, we change the **Craftable** value to **False**. In this way, when the loop ends, we are certain whether the player has all the elements to craft an item:

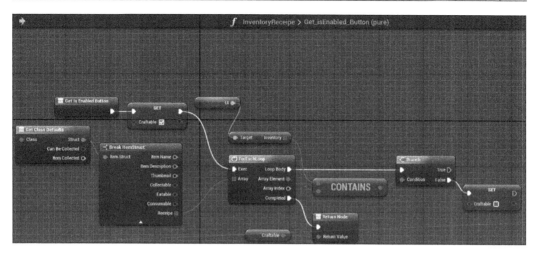

The next step is to actually handle the crafting of an object. If an **InventoryReceipe** button is enabled, it means that the object is **Craftable** and we can call a custom function within the main **UI**, and ensure that we have the needed elements inside the inventory:

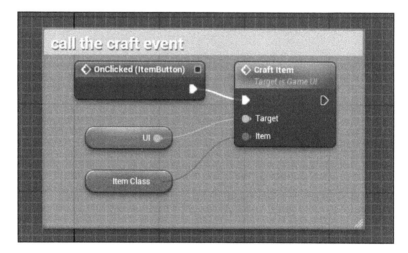

The **Craft Item** event loops through the receipe array and the **Inventory** array and, whenever it finds two equal objects, it removes it from the inventory (we don't want to be able to craft infinite objects, we must delete the object used).

Lastly, it calls the `DropItem` function we created earlier within the player character (the unseen part on the left is the get **default class** | **break struct** part to get the receipe):

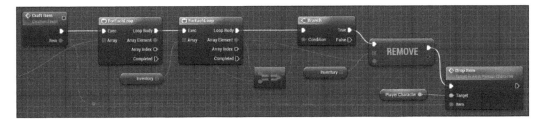

Inventory button logic

We can now complete the logic of the **Inventory** button by adding the binding of its thumbnail and the click handler.

The image should be easy for you now; it is exactly the same as the other thumbnail code we wrote before. The only exception is that we accede to it by the inventory variable and the **Item Slot** index instead of using a direct reference:

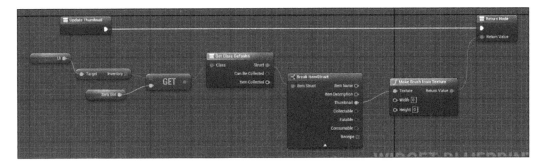

The click handler is even easier. We want to set the **Slot Selected** variable of the main **UI** to be the same as its **Item Slot** value. So, we will show the details of the item in the **Details** panel based on this value:

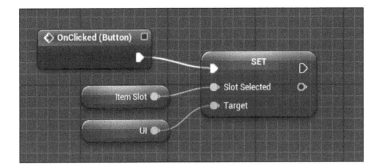

Item details and buttons

The last section to handle is the details section of the UI. Its image and description is like we did before but we must add a flow control on the SlotSelected variable before accessing the inventory index. We want to be able to show details only if there is actually a real existing item. We can set the selected slot to be any negative value when deselected and update the item detail only whenever its value is greater than 0:

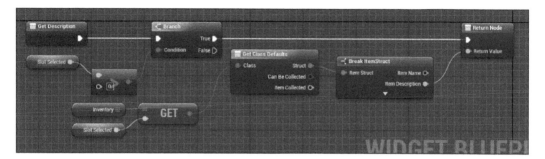

It is the same situation for the three buttons of the **Details** panel. Bind their **IsEnabled** property to be **True** only if the SlotSelected is greater than 0 and if, from its structure, its property is **True**:

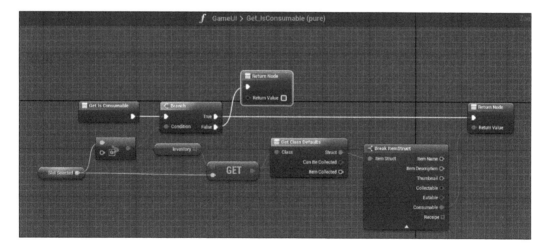

The **Drop** button is even easier; any object in your inventory should be droppable so we can ignore the getter of the inventory and set its return value only based on the first branch.

Implementing the last three buttons' click behavior and with the setup that we have, it is just a matter of calling the right function. The drop-click will simply call the Drop function followed by the Remove function:

The other two buttons will depend on what you want them to do in your game, but by now you should be able to work without my help. You could create custom event inside your player character to handle the eating of a fruit (by creating, for example, a life bar with a system that will increase by eating a fruit), or send a message to all the objects around the player whenever they use an object.

Summary

In this last chapter, we saw how to create a realistic environment with the tools that UE4 offers. We saw how to manipulate the terrains and how to use different types of brushes to build any kind of you world have in mind. Thanks to the materials and the light tools, we saw how to give our world the desired atmosphere.

We also built a strong starting point for the inventory of your player, an essential part for this and many others types of games.

We are at the end of our journey and it's time for me to say goodbye. I guided you in the first steps of the difficult process of game creation. I hope you enjoyed reading this guide as much as I enjoyed writing it. I'm sure you now have a better understanding than before and are willing to continue exploring the vastness of UE4 to explore all its secrets. Everything is in your hands now; use your imagination to create beautiful environments, use your knowledge to populate it with gameplay and logics, and use my suggestions to combine the elements together.

Good luck, my friend!

Index

About Packt Publishing

Packt, pronounced 'packed', published its first book, *Mastering phpMyAdmin for Effective MySQL Management*, in April 2004, and subsequently continued to specialize in publishing highly focused books on specific technologies and solutions.

Our books and publications share the experiences of your fellow IT professionals in adapting and customizing today's systems, applications, and frameworks. Our solution-based books give you the knowledge and power to customize the software and technologies you're using to get the job done. Packt books are more specific and less general than the IT books you have seen in the past. Our unique business model allows us to bring you more focused information, giving you more of what you need to know, and less of what you don't.

Packt is a modern yet unique publishing company that focuses on producing quality, cutting-edge books for communities of developers, administrators, and newbies alike. For more information, please visit our website at www.packtpub.com.

Writing for Packt

We welcome all inquiries from people who are interested in authoring. Book proposals should be sent to author@packtpub.com. If your book idea is still at an early stage and you would like to discuss it first before writing a formal book proposal, then please contact us; one of our commissioning editors will get in touch with you.

We're not just looking for published authors; if you have strong technical skills but no writing experience, our experienced editors can help you develop a writing career, or simply get some additional reward for your expertise.

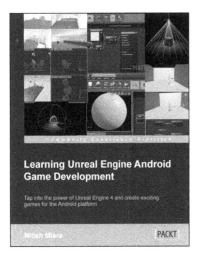

Learning Unreal Engine Android Game Development

ISBN: 978-1-78439-436-3   Paperback: 300 pages

Tap into the power of Unreal Engine 4 and create exciting games for the Android platform

1. Dive straight into making fully functional Android games with this hands-on guide.

2. Learn about the entire Android pipeline, from game creation to game submission.

3. Use Unreal Engine 4 to create a first-person puzzle game.

Blueprints Visual Scripting for Unreal Engine

ISBN: 978-1-78528-601-8   Paperback: 188 pages

Build professional 3D games with Unreal Engine 4's Visual Scripting system

1. Take your game designs from inspiration to a fully playable game that you can share with the world, without writing a single line of code.

2. Learn to use visual scripting to develop gameplay mechanics, UI, visual effects, artificial intelligence, and more.

3. Build a first person shooter from scratch with step-by-step tutorials.

Please check **www.PacktPub.com** for information on our titles

UnrealScript Game Programming Cookbook

ISBN: 978-1-84969-556-5   Paperback: 272 pages

Discover how you can augment your game development with the power of UnrealScript

1. Create a truly unique experience within UDK using a series of powerful recipes to augment your content.

2. Discover how you can utilize the advanced functionality offered by the Unreal Engine with UnrealScript.

3. Learn how to harness the built-in AI in UDK to its full potential.

Unreal Engine Physics Essentials

ISBN: 978-1-78439-490-5   Paperback: 216 pages

Gain practical knowledge of mathematical and physics concepts in order to design and develop an awesome game world using Unreal Engine 4

1. Use the Physics Asset Tool within Unreal Engine 4 to develop game physics objects for your game world.

2. Explore the Collision mechanics within Unreal Engine 4 to create advanced, real-world physics.

3. A step-by-step guide to implementing the Physics concepts involved in Unreal Engine 4 to create a working Vehicle Blueprint.

Please check **www.PacktPub.com** for information on our titles